# BLUNDERING TO GLORY

## NAPOLEON'S MILITARY CAMPAIGNS

# Napoleon in Italy, 1797

After a sketch by David                                          Connie Olson

# BLUNDERING TO GLORY

## NAPOLEON'S MILITARY CAMPAIGNS

*Owen Connelly*

A Scholarly Resources Imprint
WILMINGTON, DELAWARE

The paper used in this publication meets the minimum requirements of the American National Standard for permanence of paper for printed library materials, Z39.48, 1984.

Scholarly Resources Inc.
104 Greenhill Avenue
Wilmington, DE 19805-1897

**Library of Congress Cataloging-in-Publication Data**

Connelly, Owen.
  Blundering to glory.

  Bibliography: p.
  Includes index.
  1. Napoleon I, Emperor of the French, 1769–1821—
Military leadership.  2. Napoleonic Wars, 1800–1814—
Campaigns.  3. France. Armée—History—Napoleonic
Wars, 1800–1815.  4. Military art and science—
France—History—18th century.  5. Military art and
science—France—History—19th century.  I. Title.
DC203.9.C647    1987      940.2'7      87-9507
ISBN 0-8420-2231-7 (alk. paper)
ISBN 0-8420-2375-5 (pbk.: alk. paper)

# CONTENTS

# ACKNOWLEDGMENTS

It is a pleasure to begin by thanking my friends who were kind enough to read and critique all or part of the first draft of this book. Their helpfulness reconfirmed for me that the history profession still boasts scholars and natural gentlemen, the more because the list includes some of the world's most renowned experts on military history and theory, Napoleon, and Napoleonic warfare.

My readers were: Colonel John R. Elting, USA (ret.), of the United States Military Academy; Gunther Rothenberg, of Purdue University; Samuel F. Scott, of Wayne State University, Detroit; Steven T. Ross, of the U.S. Naval War College, Newport; John Gallaher, of Southern Illinois University, Evansville; Robert B. Holtman, of Louisiana State University, Baton Rouge; Donald D. Horward, of Florida State University, and 1986–87 visiting professor at the United States Military Academy; Peter Paret, of the Institute for Advanced Study, Princeton; Harold T. Parker, Professor Emeritus, Duke University; and my most constant advisers, Dr. Jack A. Meyer and Dr. George P. Winton (Col., USA, ret.), both of the University of South Carolina.

I am indebted as well to David Chandler, Esq., director of War Studies at the Royal Military Academy, Sandhurst, England, a jovial intellectual giant who gave me good ideas, encouragement, and tips on Napoleon's sense of humor.

And I must not forget Herbert Rowen of Rutgers, a historian of the Netherlands and the only American member of the Royal Dutch Academy, who has an astounding knowledge of history in general and European languages. No one can spot flawed syntax, purple prose, mistranslations, and factual errors quicker than this genial genius. It was my good fortune that he was academic editor of my first book, *Napoleon's Satellite Kingdoms* (Free Press Macmillan, 1965), and has been my friend and counsellor ever since.

This synthesis owes much to the books of the men mentioned above. The best extended general histories of the campaigns are: John Elting and Vincent J. Esposito, *A Military History and Atlas of the Napoleonic Wars* (1964), and David Chandler, *The Campaigns of Napoleon* (1966). Elting also has recently published *The Superstrategists* (1982) and *The Grande Armée of Napoleon* (1987). Chandler has written the very useful *Dictionary of the Napoleonic Wars* (1979), *Waterloo* (1980), and much else. Gunther Rothenberg is the authority on Napoleon's enemies; among his many books are *The Art of Warfare in the Age of Napoleon* (1978) and *The Archduke Charles*

(1982); I am particularly grateful for his insights on the Campaign of 1809 and Battle of Wagram. Sam Scott knows the armies of the Old Regime and early Republic; his best-known work is *The Response of the Royal Army to the French Revolution* (1978). Steven Ross wrote the lucid *European Diplomatic History, 1789–1815: France Against Europe* (1969), and the specialized *Quest for Victory: French Military Strategy, 1792–1799* (1973), and *From Flintlock to Rifle Infantry: Tactics, 1740–1866* (1979). John Gallaher's *chef d'oeuvre* is *The Iron Marshal: A Biography of Louis N. Davout* (1976). Robert Holtman is widely known for his *Napoleonic Propaganda* (1950) and *Napoleonic Revolution* (1969). Don Horward is recognized even in Spain and Portugal for his books on the Peninsular War, ranging from *The Battle of Bussaco* (1965) to *Napoleon and Iberia: The Twin Sieges of Ciudad Rodrigo and Almeida, 1810* (1984). Peter Paret, master nonpareil of military theory, wrote the chapter on Napoleon in *The Makers of Modern Strategy* (1986), which he edited with Gordon Craig and Felix Gilbert. He is also the author of such genre models as *Yorck and the Era of Prussian Reform* (1966), *Clausewitz and the State* (1976 and 1985), and the translator, with Howard, of Clausewitz's *On War* (1976 and 1986). Harold Parker, in recent years, has published on Napoleon's personality, his work habits, the imperial administration, and much else, but he is known among military historians for the classic *Three Napoleonic Battles* (1944; new edition, 1983), a pioneer military "history from below," written from the accounts of men of all ranks. Jack Meyer's *Bibliography of the Napoleonic Era* (1987) promises to be a standard.

In addition to the secondary works mentioned above and a larger number in the Bibliography, I found the following printed primary sources signally useful: Napoléon I, *L'Oeuvre et l'histoire*, 13 vols. (Paris, 1969); the *Mémoires* of Lazare Carnot and of Marshals Marmont, Ney, Masséna, Soult, and Grouchy; the *Souvenirs* of Marshal Macdonald, the *Correspondance* of Marshal Davout, and the *Lettres et documents* of Marshal Murat; the *Mémoires* of Bourrienne, Savary, and Caulaincourt; the *Souvenirs* of Mathieu Dumas; the *Journal* of P. L. Roederer; the *Dispatches* of Wellington; the *Mémorial de Sainte-Hélène* of Las Cases; the *Mémoires* of the valets Marchand and Constant; the *Histoire et mémoires* of Philippe de Ségur; and the *Souvenirs* and *Russian Campaign* of the Duke de Fézensac. And, of course, the 32-volume *Correspondance de Napoléon Ier*, with additions listed in the Bibliography.

In closing, if I may, I also would like to express my gratitude to the knowledgeable, industrious, and helpful people at Scholarly Resources, *viz,* Philip G. Johnson, managing editor; Richard M. Hopper, acquisitions editor; and Ann M. Aydelotte, my project editor.

O. C.

# LIST OF MAPS

# INTRODUCTION

> The essential quality of a general-
> in-chief . . . is the determination
> to win at all costs.
> —Napoleon to Montholon
> at St. Helena

Napoleon, during his early campaigns, was so successful with the strategical-tactical "broken play," followed by a scrambling recovery, that he presented the system again and again, in different words, as the "art of war." As he put it to Montholon at St. Helena:

> You engage, and then you wait and see.
> [*On s'engage, et alors on voit.*]

Of course, Bonaparte was speaking of a battle—a tactical situation—but the maxim applies equally well to his strategic maneuvers. He did careful planning, paying particular attention to movement and maximizing his numbers. But that done, he simply charged toward his enemy's presumed location, often with only a vague idea of where he was. His only rule on the march was to keep his corps close together so that they could be consolidated quickly. He planned to reach every battlefield with superior numbers, but he often decided that the "moment" was more important and fought with fewer men than the enemy. He had an uncanny instinct for the right moves, both strategic and tactical, and his mind went into high gear when the action began.

    Napoleon was a military genius, which, by his own definition, required more than superior intelligence. (Carl von Clausewitz later took the same stand in his famous chapter on leadership in *Vom Krieg*.) Brilliance was only one factor in Bonaparte's ability to triumph in situations which would have finished other commanders. His other crucial advantages were his awesome energy; his ability to scramble, to make his men follow him, to hit again and again; and his inability to accept defeat. Nevertheless, he also owed much to the ineptitude of his enemies and to luck (although he denied it; war, he said, was "nothing but accidents," and luck the ability to exploit them). Finally, he had superb subordinates, among whom Generals (later Marshals) Masséna

*1*

and Davout stand out. In the early campaigns Masséna literally won many battles for him. In the later ones, Davout very often ensured victory by incredible marches and personal initiative: for example, at Austerlitz (1805); at Jena-Auerstädt (1806), where his corps won at Auerstädt unaided; at Eylau (1807); and at Wagram (1809).

Napoleon began almost every campaign with a strategic blunder—almost deliberately, as in 1805, when he overshot Mack at Ulm and had to double back to defeat him. Mistakes did not bother him. They were part of his system. "One mixes it up" [*On se mêle*], he told Las Cases, then goes on from there. He began many battles with a tactical error; he was often caught off guard. But he never abandoned his system; he always charged ahead and rewrote his plans as he went, although in mid-career he acquired superior numbers which covered his blunders and ensured his victories.

No two Napoleonic battles are alike. Some early ones he won by sheer bullheadedness (Arcola, for example); in others he had to pull together his forces, often while fending off the enemy, judge his adversary's weakness, and attack. As emperor, however, Napoleon usually engaged first, while holding back a large reserve. He waited for the enemy to make a mistake or reveal a weak spot in the line and then threw in enough of his reserve to finish the battle.

Late in Napoleon's career, his enemies gained the advantage of greater mass. Earlier, partly because of their bad planning, he had fought the great powers' armies one at a time. In 1813, they were finally all united, and he was doomed by the weight of the Allied armies. Although he still scrambled spectacularly, the factors which had given him early victories—especially good subordinates—were missing, and he was beaten.

The glory remained to Napoleon, however.

### Legacy of the Old Regime and Revolution

Napoleon was a battlefield genius, not a theorist, purveyor of new doctrine or organization, or sponsor of new ordnance. If there was a Napoleonic military revolution, he was it. From his point of view, as he said at St. Helena:

> The art of war is a simple art and all in execution; there is nothing vague about it; it is all common sense; nothing about it is theoretical.

His forte was execution: fighting to perfection with the men and weapons available. As Chapter 1 will emphasize, he was educated in the best military schools in France—or Europe, for that matter. Generally, he used the schools' doctrines, although he knew when to violate them. He brought no new weapons into play, and throughout his career he used the basic organization, strategy, and tactics of France's Old Regime, all as adapted to the use of the armies of the French Revolution. His one major reform was to make the corps, rather than the division, the standard unit-of-all-arms, in order to better organize and use the greater numbers of troops produced by conscription, which had been introduced during the Revolution.

Bonaparte, remembered as the quintessential artilleryman, cannot even be credited with using more artillery or greater concentrations than eighteenth-century commanders. Frederick the Great of Prussia had the first massive artillery reserve, mostly of 12- and 18-pounders (referring to the weight of the shot). And Frederick also, in the Seven Years' War, had six guns per 1000 men, whereas Napoleon seldom had over three per 1000, and often fewer.[1] Napoleon's genius lay in using everything better than anyone had before.

Such revolution as had occurred in warfare had taken place during the Wars of the French Revolution. Napoleon liked to refer to himself as a "child of the Revolution." And so he was, in that it gave him a chance to command armies. The military legacy he had inherited, however, was chiefly from the Old Regime, modified by the experience of the Wars of the Revolution.

As might be expected, Napoleon tended to downplay his legacy, military education, and experience as well. "I assure you I have fought sixty battles, *eh bien*! I learned nothing at the last that I did not know at the first," he said to Gourgaud at St. Helena.

## *Weapons*

The Gribeauval artillery pieces on which Napoleon was trained, and which he used throughout his wars, represented no radically new designs but were the culmination of the development of the muzzle-loading cannon. In the eighteenth century, Frederick had pioneered in the use of massed artillery, primarily with 12-pounders. Frederick's triumphs over the Austrians in the 1740s directly inspired them to improve their field guns. By the time of the Seven Years' War (1756–63), all the powers were using 12-pounders; the Prussians had 12s, 6s, 3s, and some 18s; the Austrians, 12s, 6s, and 3s; the British, 12s, 9s, 6s, 3s, and some one-pounders; the French, 12s, 10s, 8s, 6s, 4s, and some 2s, but all very heavy.

The Gribeauval guns, developed between 1765 and 1774, were 12-, 8-, 6-, and 4-pounders, plus 6- and 8-inch howitzers. They were lighter by one-third than the cannon of any other country. For example, the barrel of the British 12-pounder weighed 3150 pounds, and the gun with carriage and limber about 6500 pounds. The Gribeauval 12-pounder's barrel weighed 2174

---

[1]For example, at Wagram (1809), where Napoleon commanded the greatest number of men in a single battle, he had 190,000 troops and 488 guns, or 2.5 + per 1000. At Borodino (1812), he had 4.5 per 1000, but only because he had decimated his infantry by forced march in pursuit of the Russians.

pounds (986 kg), and the gun with carriage and limber 4367 pounds (1981 kg).

As with the artillery, old designs were perfected for other weapons. The French ended with the 1777 Charleville musket for the infantry and carried it throughout the French Revolutionary and Napoleonic Wars. It was five feet long and muzzle-loading, by specification .69 caliber (17.5 mm), but often .70 or .71. The cavalry, engineers, and others carried the .69 musketoon or carbine; this was the same weapon, but ten inches shorter. The standard sidearm was the .69 muzzle-loading pistol. A cartridge had been developed for these weapons, but they had to be primed at the breech and fired with a flintlock. The rifle was known, but not used by the French except for a few skirmishers. Though more accurate, rifles still were muzzle-loading (except for expensive, handmade hunting models), and the balls were more difficult to ram home, which could mean the death of the soldier. The Prussians, however, had one regiment of *Jäger* (light infantry) equipped with rifles before the death of Frederick in 1786, but formed no more. After the Wars of the French Revolution began in 1792, the British formed a regiment, the 95th Rifles, and gradually issued rifles as well to three battalions of the 60th Infantry and some companies of the King's German Legion (KGL). The 95th and KGL would play a key role at Waterloo.

Except that they were made of better steel, cavalry sabers changed only in decoration. Typically, the light cavalry carried the slightly curved saber with a 33-inch blade; the heavy cavalry saber had a straight, 38-inch blade. Length and appearance varied with the regiment.

### *Officers*

In Europe in the eighteenth century, warfare had been conducted by aristocrats on both sides. The few nonnoble officers, mostly in the engineers and artillery, never were given command of armies. Generals of ancient title and entrenched wealth did not scratch and claw for reputations. Instead, they tended to avoid useless battles and unnecessary bloodshed and settled for putting their opponents in check, as in a chess game, and then letting them march away.

During the Revolution, however, the French officer corps of the Old Regime was decimated by the emigration of nobles and gave way to an amalgam comprising bourgeois and working-class officers, many of the latter ex-sergeants, and nobles (of whom Napoleon was one), who elected to serve the Republic. The officer corps of other major countries remained noble, or mostly so; Britain had the greatest percentage of commoners, but not at the top.

The French officer corps was reshaped under the Terror, with the emphasis on youth, by Lazare Carnot, who made generals of Napoleon and many other young officers. These new leaders abandoned what was left of the amenities and gentlemen's understandings of eighteenth-century warfare; they were out to win, and they fought with no holds barred.

Napoleon is the archetypical example. Nevertheless, some fine moments came when he reverted to his noble code and extended courtesies to valiant opponents (always after they were beaten), as when he returned Field Marshal Wurmser's sword after the old soldier surrendered Mantua in 1797.

## *Armies*

Eighteenth-century armies were small; France's standing army of 200,000 was considered huge. Field armies of 100,000 were unusual, and battlefield armies were likely to be about 30,000 on each side. However, they grew bigger with successive wars, and in the Seven Years' War, the Austro-Russians massed 90,000 against Frederick several times, although he normally had half their numbers. Fighting was serious when it occurred, and casualties high, but battles were fewer.

The division was the largest unit of maneuver in all major armies. Though not intended for independent combat, it had been introduced into the French army by the Marshal de Broglie in 1759 and had become standard in 1780. It was not of uniform size and tended to grow. Initially, the division was made up of one or two infantry regiments (1000 to 1500 men each), with an artillery battery attached, for a maximum of 3200 men. By 1796, an infantry regiment of the French Republic had 3000 men, and sometimes more. Some divisions had 15,000 to 20,000 men, comprising several infantry brigades (each of one or two regiments), with artillery, cavalry, and engineers assigned. There were also divisions of 3000 to 5000 men without even artillery. Much later, Napoleon would subordinate the division to the corps, which was capable of independent combat. (For his organization of the *Grande Armée* of 1805, see Chapter 4.)

Troops were both regulars and mercenaries. The latter comprised half of the French army and perhaps 70 percent of the Prussian, since the kings preferred to have their peasants at home, cultivating the fields and paying taxes. Wars were dynastic, fought to settle the Polish, Austrian, and Spanish successions or over disputed territories, usually quite small until Frederick went after Silesia (which a Texan would consider small). Civilians were uninterested and normally uninvolved, except for being taxed. No major country had conscription; all countries had militias but usually did not use them in foreign wars. France, for example, sent militia to man fortresses and perform other garrison duties at home in order to free regular troops for battle. Civilian life in war zones was only minimally disrupted.

## The Revolution and Warfare

During the Wars of the Revolution (1792–1800), in which Napoleon initially made his reputation, France decreed the first mass draft of manpower (*levée en masse*) in history and expanded its armies. Moreover, whereas the armies of the Old Regime carried supplies, those of the Revolution (and Napoleon) lived off the land. "The war must feed the war," as Napoleon put it. French armies devastated the areas through which they marched, whether of friend or foe.

In 1794, the French army, on paper, reached a strength of nearly 1,000,000 men, five times larger than that of the old monarchy, already the largest in Europe. French field armies did not grow proportionally, but they grew. In 1796, when Napoleon took command of the 38,000-man Army of Italy (see Chapter 2), the largest French armies, in Germany, numbered 78,000 under Jourdan and 80,000 under Moreau. Napoleon increased the size of French field armies, but not hugely until after the Russian Campaign of 1812, when the *Grande Armée* was two-thirds foreign. Most of his climactic battles were fought with fewer than 100,000 men. His army of 190,000 at Wagram in 1809 was the largest he ever commanded. Nevertheless, his enemies had to respond with even larger ones. The scale of war increased.

The French Revolution did more than increase the scale of war, however. On the French side, it produced ambitious, cutthroat officers, propaganda, and massive civilian involvement in wars—physically, through the *levée en masse*, and emotionally, through propaganda which glorified any task which contributed to the war effort and taught people to hate the enemy and love *la patrie* (the nation).

War, as a result, became more vicious and bloody. As Commandant H. Lachouque, the historian of the Imperial Guard, put it:

> A battle of this period was a fearsome spectacle. No longer a contest of honor, as in the 17th and 18th centuries, with its rules of elegance and its somber beauty, this was a struggle to the death, often without quarter, a veritable hell.

It was into such battles that Napoleon Bonaparte was thrown at an early age, and from which he emerged a hero. What sort of man was he? We must address this question before taking up his wars.

# 1

## YOUNG BONAPARTE
### Character, Education, and Early Triumphs

### The Bonaparte Character

Madame Germaine de Staël, who at first worshipped Napoleon but later came to hate him, set down a dead-right description of his personality:

> I was struck with his superiority: [but] it bore no resemblance to that of [other prominent] men . . . his conversation [was] . . . like that of the hunter in pursuit of his prey. His spirit seemed a cold, clean, sword-blade, that freezes while it wounds. I felt a profound irony in his mind. . . . *With him, everything was means to ends; the involuntary, whether for good or evil, was entirely absent.*[1]

Napoleon was unique: an incomparable lawgiver and ruler as well as a match-less general. But he was nothing like the public image he cultivated; he was neither the man of destiny whose star assured his triumphs, nor the casual genius who disdained preparation, nor a psychic who read his enemies' minds.

The real Napoleon was a loner and a workaholic: hard, cynical, cal-culating, tireless, and bent on success at any cost. "My element is work," he told Emmanuel de Las Cases at St. Helena in 1816. "I was born and made for work. I knew the limits of my legs . . . my eyes, but never of my ability to work." During his years of victory, he hardly slept on campaign, or let any of his officers rest, either. As emperor, when in Paris, he retired at 10:00 PM, rose at 2:00 AM and worked until 5:00, went back to bed, rose again at 7:00 and began a day which allowed for 15- to 20-minute meals. He bolted his food, sometimes eating while standing up. He had no friends, only useful favorites. (For a time he dined often with François-Joseph Talma, the actor, hoping to learn ways to improve his public appearances.) His only true pleasure was work; he could not bear to leave it for long. Even his dalliances

---

[1] Author's emphasis.

with women were scheduled. Constant, his valet, tells stories of young actresses, singers, ladies of the court, and others waiting interminably for an hour in bed with him. He liked simple dishes, workers' wine, hard candy, and cheap snuff. All this indicated a certain insecurity, but more on that later.

Bonaparte had almost no sense of humor. When he went to the theater or opera, he demanded tragedy. He did not understand comedy. Even the hilarious great rabbit attack of 1807 only made him angry. Marshal Alexandre Berthier had arranged a hunt and bought domestic rabbits to ensure high kills, but the scheme backfired. When Napoleon got out of his carriage, hundreds of rabbits charged him, mistaking him for a keeper bringing food. While his grooms flailed at the horde with whips, the emperor stalked to his carriage and departed, flinging furry beasts from the windows as he went. He never laughed about the incident but blamed later hunting fiascos on Berthier, whose embarrassment he found funny.

Napoleon had an almost paranoid sensitivity to everything around him, a trait very useful in judging people and reading battlefields. Perforce, he was high-strung but kept his feelings under tight control. His calmness, in battle or at court, became legendary, but when it broke, he often went into fits of rage, spewing verbal abuse and sometimes becoming violent. At various times, he lashed servants, soldiers, and officers with his riding crop. He once kicked a cabinet minister in the stomach and, when he fell to the floor in pain, curtly ordered him carried out of his sight. In 1808, he called in General Mathieu Dumas, who was leaving for Spain where the French had suffered setbacks, grabbed him by his coat lapels and shook him, shouting: "This coat must be washed in blood!" Some of his outbursts were staged, of course, for specific effects.

Ambition, Napoleon said, was "like the blood that flows in my veins, the air that I breathe." He had a lust for power and a mania for winning, a modern disease. "Power is my mistress," he admitted to Pierre Roederer (1804), and later (1809), "I love power, I do; but it is like an artist that I love it, . . . I love it like a musician loves his violin, . . . I love to draw out the sounds, . . . the harmony." In 1807 he wrote to his wife Josephine, "All my life, I have sacrificed everything, tranquility, happiness, to my destiny." In reality it was to success he sacrificed.

Finally, Napoleon won wars as much—perhaps more—because of his capacity for constant work as his military genius, although we grant him that. He labored continually on strategic plans ("I have the habit of thinking about what I ought to do four or five months in advance") and, in the field, turned his energies to driving his army ahead, with perpetual vigilance and modification to the infinite of all plans, both strategic and tactical.

Napoleon never let the work show, however. He wanted his troops to see him as the man of destiny. He was simultaneously the personification of French grandeur and glory and the Little Corporal, unafraid to get dirty feeding the cannon himself. His carefully staged appearances left unforgettable images which fed men's pride and were the stuff of tales of veterans and their descendants for generations. As emperor, he would enter the scene on horseback, surrounded by the magnificent cavalry of the Imperial Guard in uniforms of blazing color with gold or silver epaulets and plumed shakos, sabers gleaming and scabbards rattling, every man mounted on matching tall horses. Napoleon stood out, by contrast, in his grey greatcoat or faded green jacket (a touch that appealed to the troops), astride a little grey Arabian mare.

He also knew how to lead. He regularly visited the campfires of his troops the night before battle. In his younger days he had led charges in person; at no time did he lack the courage to show himself at points of extreme danger and rally the men. His orders were positive; he never showed doubt of success; he never showed fear. In his leadership he was cynical (or realistic) about primary motivation, however. "There are two levers which move men: fear and self-interest," he once told his secretary, Louis-Antoine de Bourrienne. Fear and self-interest: he knew how to use both.

## Growing Up in Corsica

Napoleon's basic traits may have been totally formed during his boyhood in occupied Corsica. When he was born, on 15 August 1769, the island had been French for about a year; it was garrisoned by French troops and governed by a French general, Count Louis-Charles de Marbeuf. To keep the British navy from creating bases there, Louis XV in 1768 had bought Corsica from Genoa, its longtime ruler, which had lost control of it to the independence fighters of Pasquale Paoli. The king's troops crushed Paoli's little army.

Napoleon's father, Carlo (Charles) Buonaparte, had fought against the French, but after Paoli's defeat in May 1769, he took the amnesty offered by Louis XV in return for an oath of allegiance. Still young (twenty-three years old), he returned to the family home in Ajaccio, the capital, with his wife, Letizia Ramolino Buonaparte, and their infant son, Giuseppe (Joseph). Their second son, Napoleone (Napoleon) was born three months later.

The Buonapartes were of Italian descent and members of the largely Corsican-Italian establishment. As a boy, young Napoleon tried to be both Corsican and French. When he entered school in France in 1778, he was quickly and brutally reminded that he was "foreign" by his classmates, and for a time he was belligerently Corsican. However, he changed his first name to *Napoleon* when he entered school, and he began signing his surname *Bonaparte* en route to take command of the Army of Italy in 1796. In the end, he became as French as possible, and in his will he asked to be buried "on the banks of the Seine, among the French people, whom I have loved so much." But he never forgot that he had been born a foreigner and never lost the compulsion to prove himself better than any native-born Frenchman.

Napoleon's father was handsome, gregarious, and always impeccably groomed; his clothes were tailored in Italy. ("Go hungry if you must," Carlo told his sons, "but never be without a good suit.") He had a law degree from Pisa, a Florentine patent of nobility, a beautiful young wife, and an eye for opportunity. Carlo quickly ingratiated himself with Governor Marbeuf and soon became his right-hand man and intermediary with the Corsican establishment. As a result, in time he became secretary of the Estates of Corsica and royal prosecutor and entered the French aristocracy as the Count de Buonaparte, by virtue of his Florentine pedigree. His connections gave the family status and enabled Carlo to obtain scholarships for his children to French schools,[2] but the most eminent "new Frenchman" in Corsica had encountered some problems. The Buonapartes found themselves treated with suspicion, envy, and sometimes hostility by Corsicans, while the French did not accept them fully.

Most Corsicans nursed a spirit of rebellion. The majority, who lived in the mountainous interior, avoided taxes, generally ignored French authority, and settled their grievances by vendetta. However, in Ajaccio and other coastal cities the people could not do likewise, and especially not the members of the propertied class, who were largely of Italian descent. Most of them became model Francophiles, at least outwardly. Their hypocrisy honed their resentment against real pro-French families such as the Buonapartes. As Napoleon grew up, he heard slurs against his father and even gossip about his mother, who some said was Marbeuf's mistress. This must have made him somewhat insecure, and he reacted by becoming taciturn and belligerent.

Napoleon grew up in the country; Ajaccio was a "city" of 2000. The Buonapartes had a house in town but subsisted from their nearby farm, largely managed by Letizia. Eventually, the Buonapartes had eight children (five others died in infancy): Joseph, Napoleon, Lucien, Elisa, Louis, Caroline, Pauline, and Jerome, the last three born after Napoleon left for school in France.[3] The family's food was simple; the children wore homespun; they had few toys and no luxuries. Letizia was a loving mother, but she knew how to use a birch whip. On clear days, the children were always outdoors, running, playing, and exploring the maquis and mountains. Napoleon's later legendary stamina and Spartan tastes stemmed from this childhood conditioning at home and on the farm.

The young Napoleon was quiet and obsessively competitive at everything from mathematics to climbing trees. His family environment compounded these traits, because he felt unloved. His brother Joseph was his

---

[2] For Joseph and later Lucien, Carlo obtained scholarships from the French Church to the College of Autun, and for his eldest daughter Elisa a place at the most exclusive girls' school in France, Saint-Cyr, where Napoleon later would place the French military academy. Joseph and Napoleon had to provide for the other children, since Carlo died prematurely at age thirty-nine, probably of stomach cancer.

[3] The children's original Italian names were Lucciano, Luigi, Girolamo, Maria Anna, Maria Paola, and Maria Annunziata.

parents' favorite as the first surviving child (two had died at birth before him) and, understandably, was spoiled. He was the image of his father, everyone said, which made Napoleon feel ugly. Joseph, indeed, was handsome, intelligent, and had a talent for pleasing his elders. His parents thought he would be perfect for the priesthood and surely one day would become bishop of Corsica. Joseph delighted them by frequent visits to his Uncle Lucciano, senior canon of the cathedral of Ajaccio, whose protégé he became.

From the time Napoleon could stand, he fought for attention, attacking his older brother and breaking his toys. As the two grew up, he challenged Joseph at play, in sports, and in school. There, Napoleon was a good student, but he often disrupted classes and was a terror on the playground. He was very bright, but belligerent and difficult. It was because Napoleon was a "little wolf"—not the favored son—that Carlo secured a scholarship for him to the Royal Military School at Brienne. No Buonaparte had ever been a professional officer, although there had been volunteers, such as Carlo himself. For centuries, the family had produced lawyers, judges, administrators, and clergymen.

In 1778, therefore, when Napoleon left Corsica for school in France, he was a physically strong, quiet, generally unsmiling, and self-sufficient nine year old, who hid his insecurities under a chip on his shoulder. As would be baldly obvious in time, he was infected with his father's opportunism, but he also had acquired much of Carlo's sense of elegance and style, and belief in making a good impression. Napoleon also had drawn a large measure of his father's charm, although it was forced, short-lived, and turned on for a purpose. He later would convert Carlo's gifts into an unexampled ability to dramatize himself and an almost hypnotic ability to persuade. From his mother he had learned self-discipline, industry, and loyalty. He was more like her. Montholon quotes him at St. Helena: "All that I am, all that I have been, I owe to the work habits I got in childhood, and to the excellent principles given me by my excellent mother." Work habits: those words are the key to his personality.

## School at Brienne, Paris, and Auxonne

In December 1778, Carlo escorted Joseph and Napoleon to France and deposited them at the College of Autun—Joseph to study for the clergy, Napoleon for a crash course in French, since their native tongue was a dialect of Italian. In just three months Napoleon was pronounced fluent, perhaps because his teachers were anxious to be rid of him, and sent on to the Royal Military School at Brienne. Bourrienne, who arrived at Brienne at the same time, records that Napoleon spoke only Corsican and had to be tutored in French.

There is no doubt that he sounded foreign. He also looked foreign, with a Mediterranean tan and strangely cut clothes. His schoolmates were all nobles, a requirement for admission, and many were not a little haughty, which gave an edge to the natural cruelty of children. They taunted him unmercifully, but he could not fight them all; until they tired of the game, he pretended not to hear and so kept to himself. The boy who had arrived a loner became even more of one.

Napoleon was gradually accepted, however, with one reason being that he did not rat to the principal. Even when he was a senior student and cadet officer, he remained staunchly loyal to his former persecutors, and several times he was punished for overlooking their misconduct. He was a lone wolf, nevertheless, who shunned the company of his fellows for the library, where he read history, especially Roman history (his favorites were Polybius and Plutarch) and some works of the Enlightenment. "At the age of puberty," Napoleon said much later, "[I] became morose, somber, [and] reading became [for me] a passion pushed to the edge of rage."

He clearly excelled only in mathematics, but he was classified a superior student by the king's inspector and in 1784 was sent to the elite Ecole Militaire in Paris for his final year. The vice principal was not pleased; his evaluation called Napoleon "domineering, imperious, and obstinate." Doubtless he remembered Napoleon's tirades against French tyranny over Corsica, or the snowball war which had quickly ended when Bonaparte's side put rocks in their snowballs and caused blood to be shed.

The Ecole Militaire reformed Napoleon. The king's allowance was princely and allowed him to live like his schoolmates, almost all of the highest nobility. His French was nearly perfect. Finally, and probably most important, he was impressed by the faculty. For the first time, he began to accept French culture as decidedly superior and to become as French as possible.

In September 1785, he graduated, was commissioned a second lieutenant (*sous-lieutenant*) of artillery, and embarked on a career in the Royal Army. It was a gentleman's profession, but otherwise a poor career. Pay was low; he started at 100 francs per month (a ditchdigger made 25 francs). He was unlikely ever to be a general, since he was a foreign noble and an officer of artillery, which in that day was a technical arm whose officers were not expected to ever command armies.[4] Had it not been for the conditions created by the French Revolution, he probably would have retired as a captain or major.

Following his graduation, Napoleon was posted to the Régiment de la Fère at Valence, in the south of France. It was probably the best artillery unit in the army, so that the experience he gained there must have been very

---

[4]Another reason for his assignment to the artillery was his height. Although average among male Frenchmen, he was short for an officer; the infantry and cavalry required commanding figures. After his death at St. Helena, his body was measured by his valet, Louis-Joseph Marchand, at *cinq pieds, deux pouces* (five feet, two inches). On the assumption that his corpse was measured with a French yardstick, which is longer than the British (the French foot = 33 cm., the British = 30.47 cm.), Felix Markham and others say Napoleon was 5'6" tall, converting 5'2" French to 5'6" English. Since the French had been on the metric system since 1793, however, and since Napoleon had used all means to make the French convert to it, it is doubtful that his entourage carried a yardstick from the Old Regime. Thus it is almost certain that he was measured with an English yardstick.

useful. He remained the loner when off duty, partly because he could not afford a social life, and he spent his spare time reading, but to no particular end.

Three years later, during 1788–89, he was posted to the artillery school at Auxonne, where both his military and self-education were notably advanced. Bonaparte became the favorite of the commandant, General Jean-Pierre du Teil. He studied the text written by his commandant's brother, Chevalier Jean de Beaumont du Teil, *L'Usage de l'artillerie nouvelle dans la guerre de campagne* (1778), which stressed the massing of guns at decisive junctures of battle. In addition, the commandant favored beginning battles with artillery fire and rapid movement of guns along the line.

Napoleon also absorbed the strategic and tactical doctrines of Count Jacques-Antoine-Hippolyte de Guibert, embodied in the *Essai général de tactique* (1772) and *Défense du système de guerre moderne* (1778), which emphasized the importance of speed, recommended the abandonment of much of the army train, and said "the war must feed the war"—the army must live off the land—often attributed to Napoleon himself. He was introduced as well to Pierre Bourcet's *Principes de la guerre des montagnes* (1780), which, expanding on Guibert, recommended the separation of divisions for movement and their concentration for battle, keeping a maximum of two-days march apart at all times. Both Guibert and Bourcet had served Marshal Victor-François de Broglie, who had adopted the division as the standard unit of maneuver in 1759, after many years of experimentation. It became standard in the French army in 1780 and persisted through the French Revolutionary era.

The tactics Napoleon learned came from the books of Guibert and from eighteenth-century manuals based on them. Guibert believed in defense in line (three ranks deep) or square, with the artillery initially in front of the infantry. For the attack, he recommended the *ordre mixte*, or attack with some battalions in column (50- to 60-man front) and others in line (three ranks), with some battalions moving from column to line for greater firepower, as they closed with the enemy. For the latter maneuver, he had the first three ranks move ahead while those behind moved up on their left and right flanks. The French Revolutionary armies favored the column, which served better to keep green volunteers and later conscripts together. However, as the army of the Republic became more professional, generals began to use both line and column, or returned to the *ordre mixte*.

At Auxonne, Napoleon became expert in using the artillery designed for Louis XV and Louis XVI by Count J.-B. Vacquette de Gribeauval. His special interest was in the mobile field guns: 12-, 8-, 6-, and 4-pounders, and 6-inch howitzers, whose effective range was 1000 yards or less; thus they were used in direct support of infantry.

Despite the rigorous training at Auxonne, Bonaparte still found time to read books which merely interested him. Among these were John Barrow's *History of England*, on which he took over one hundred pages of notes; a history of the Arabs and their conquests; a memoir of service in the Middle East by the Baron de Tott; and Laveaux's biography of Frederick the Great of Prussia. Curiously, his notes on Frederick show less interest in the man than in how he raised and financed his army.

### Corsica and the National Guard

In 1790, Paoli returned to Corsica as royal governor by edict of Louis XVI, prompted by the revolutionary National Assembly. Second Lieutenant Bonaparte got leave and was among those who welcomed him. Napoleon gained nothing, however, although Paoli promoted Joseph to the ruling council of the island and made Lucien his secretary. The old patriot did not like "that little lieutenant." Napoleon was reassigned to Valence and promoted to first lieutenant—after six years' service. That was not unusually long in normal times, but the French Revolution had begun—in 1789. The Revolutionary government had created a National Guard of citizen-soldiers under elected officers; thus an experienced lieutenant might become a colonel overnight without losing his rank in the regular service.

In 1791, Napoleon returned to Corsica when elections were scheduled for its two National Guard battalions at Ajaccio and Bastia. Paoli refused to support him, but Napoleon was elected lieutenant-colonel of the Ajaccio battalion anyway. His first assignment was nearly impossible for citizen-soldiers: keeping order at Eastertime, 1792, in Ajaccio, where the people were angry over Revolutionary restrictions on worship. Bonaparte had to withdraw the Guard in favor of French regulars.

In what proved to be a stroke of good luck, Paoli dispatched him to France. In Paris, he found that his name had been struck from the regular army list, but conditions were in his favor. Since 20 April 1792, France had been at war with Austria and Prussia, and it was losing. This was partly because officers were scarce; the Revolution had sent the majority, almost all nobles, flying into exile. Bonaparte not only had his commission restored, but he also was promoted to captain.

Unassigned, Napoleon was in Paris on 10 August when the mobs stormed the Tuileries Palace, massacred Louis XVI's Swiss Guards, and ended the monarchy in France. The king was imprisoned and a National Convention elected, which proclaimed a Republic in September and shortly tried Louis XVI for treason. Napoleon was contemptuous of the king, who, he wrote Joseph, could have saved his throne if he had "mounted his horse" and taken command of the Swiss. Without turning a hair, Bonaparte joined the winners. The officer by the grace of Louis XVI renounced his sovereign and became a republican and a Jacobin.

He returned to Corsica and commanded a National Guard battalion in an expedition to capture Sardinia, then allied with Austria. It failed miserably.

Napoleon's guardsmen were sent home, and he was left without assignment. Napoleon and Lucien, a romantic of eighteen drunk with the spirit of the French Revolution, immersed themselves in recruiting members for Jacobin clubs in Ajaccio and Bastia.

In France, meanwhile, Louis XVI was convicted, and on 21 January 1793 he was sent to the guillotine. Paoli was shocked at the news. "The barbarians!" he shouted, "They have killed their king, the best of men." Lucien, who was still his secretary, was present and listened while Paoli considered calling on the British to protect Corsica. Overcome with revolutionary zeal, Lucien took ship to France, where he denounced Paoli for treason before the Jacobin clubs of Marseilles and Toulon. Corsicans' opinions that the Buonapartes were dangerous Francophiles were fully confirmed.

In June, they were outlawed and had their property confiscated by a Corsican National Assembly called by Paoli. The Assembly also declared Corsica independent and approved Paoli's call for aid from the British fleet. Napoleon and Joseph somehow found a ship. Letizia, by then a widow, led the younger children through the maquis and swamp, and, after some days and nights of adventure, the family was united and sailed safely to Toulon. Probably, they were allowed to escape; Paoli, after all, would not have wanted the stigma of imprisoning Letizia and the children. Once on French soil, Joseph took the family to safety near Marseilles, while Napoleon returned to the army as a captain.

## Toulon

Shortly after the Bonapartes arrived in France, the Government of Terror took control of the country. It was a war government, headed by Maximilien Robespierre's Committee of Public Safety, which disciplined the French by the threat or use of the guillotine, dropping the bloody heads of traitors into baskets at an unprecedented rate. Its mission was to unite the people and save the Republic, which was now at war with all the powers of Europe (save Russia) plus Britain. It had to contend with civil war as well: a revolt by peasants in the Vendée on the Atlantic coast and a revolt of the Federal Cities—Lyons, Bordeaux, Marseilles, and Toulon—which followed the moderate Girondins (republicans expelled from the Convention by the Jacobins) and some royalists.

Royalists dominated in Toulon, which had the largest French naval base on the Mediterranean. The city asked for help from Admiral Sir Samuel Hood, commanding the British Mediterranean fleet. Hood responded, and when his ships appeared, the French fleet at Toulon ran up the lily banner of the Bourbon dynasty. Hood supplied not only naval artillery fire for the defense, but also 2000 British, 7000 Neapolitan, and 8000 Spanish troops, which almost doubled the number of defenders. The Terrorists, with religious zeal, were bent on reducing the Federal Cities; the life of the Republic depended on it. Toulon, held by aristocrats and British invaders, seemed wholly vile and especially dangerous.

Fate, luck, and some conniving brought Napoleon to Toulon, where his climb to glory began. He was assigned to the French Army of Italy on the Italian border, but he learned as he passed near Toulon that the artillery commander of the besieging Republican army, General Auguste de Dommartin, was wounded and out of action. At the same time, he heard that one of Robespierre's representatives on mission at Toulon was an old friend of the family, Antoine-Christophe Saliceti, a Corsican Jacobin. Such civilian commissars had life-or-death authority, wherever sent, over both generals and civil officials.

Napoleon flew to Saliceti's door and begged for the artillery command. It was hardly approved behavior for a mere captain, but in character for Napoleon, and conditions were hardly normal. Saliceti knew his military qualifications, and Napoleon took pains to certify his political reliability, citing his Jacobin activities and writings, such as the *Souper de Beaucaire*, which defended Robespierre's policies. Saliceti, in turn, easily persuaded the other civilian commissars, Paul Barras and Augustin Robespierre (Maximilien's brother), that Bonaparte was the man for the job. The commanding general, Jean-François Carteaux, accepted Bonaparte in good grace; he had no other choice. He made Napoleon a temporary major (*chef-de-battalion*) to bolster his authority.

But Carteaux soon felt plagued by Napoleon. Bonaparte appeared repeatedly to argue that a large part of the army should be concentrated to seize Fort Eguillette, on a high cliff between the inner and outer harbors. There, he said, he could emplace artillery which could fire down on the fleet of Admiral Hood and force him to withdraw, taking his land forces with him. Carteaux agreed that the plan might work but was in no mood for end runs; he believed that the risk of concentrating forces on Eguillette was too great. He had perhaps 35,000 troops; the defenders numbered about the same, but they could operate on interior lines behind strong forts which circled the city. Hood's troops, especially, might mount an offensive or even envelop the French if they were concentrated to attack. The general thought that time was on his side. The other Federal Cities had fallen; he would soon have reinforcements. He was content to keep pounding slowly on Toulon from all sides until he had a victory.

Moreover, Carteaux knew all too well that generals who lost battles were likely to be accused of treason and end up on the guillotine. This "small problem" he would not discuss with a junior officer. Napoleon was aware of it, all the same, but gave not a damn. To him, risk was the name of the game, and he despised Carteaux, who had been a court painter before the Revolution. Bonaparte went over everybody's head to present his plan to Lazare Carnot, the "Organizer of Victory," the military authority on the Committee of Public

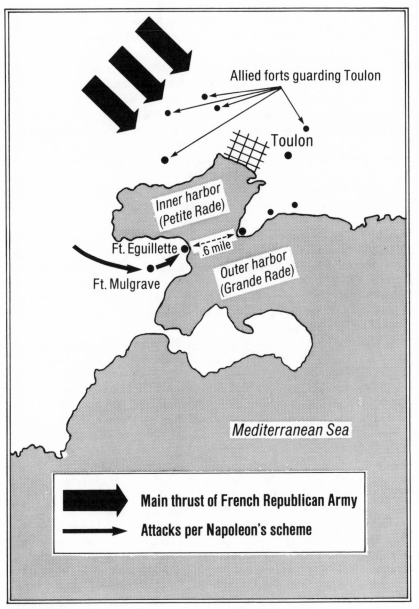

**Map 1. Siege of Toulon, September-December 1793**

Safety. He also made bold to recommend the dismissal of Carteaux. Carnot approved the plan and had already dispatched a new commander. Before Carnot's answer on the plan arrived, Napoleon had sold it to his new general, Jacques Dugommier, a professional soldier and veteran of the Seven Years' War.

The attack on Fort Eguillette (and Fort Mulgrave, which protected it) began on 14 December 1793, with Bonaparte in the forefront, directing first the siege guns and then going in with the infantry. He sustained one of only two wounds of his entire career—both minor—this one by a bayonet in the leg. The fort fell on the 17th, and Napoleon had his artillery emplaced and began bombarding the British fleet. Hood embarked his troops and sailed out of the harbor on 18 December. Four days later Captain Bonaparte was promoted to brigadier general. He was twenty-four.

At this stage, Bonaparte was just another of Carnot's fledgling generals. The Organizer of Victory promoted scores of young officers during the Terror; he made generals of eight of Napoleon's future marshals, out of a total of only twenty-six. Some were raised to higher rank than Napoleon, e.g., Jean-Baptiste Jourdan; some brigadiers were even younger than Napoleon, e.g., Louis-Nicolas Davout. Bonaparte knew that he had to continue to prove himself. Carnot believed in "careers open to talent," a policy continued by Napoleon, who made the phrase. Careers could close, however, as quickly as they opened, and during the Revolution, the closings could be abrupt and violent. No sooner had Napoleon finished with Toulon, therefore, than he began looking for a new field of glory. He found none, but Augustin Robespierre made him chief operations planner for the Army of Italy in the spring of 1794, and he did well.

Suddenly, in July 1794, the Government of Terror was brought down, Maximilien Robespierre was sent to the guillotine, and Jacobins became hunted beasts. Napoleon was seized and flung into prison in the south of France, but he was released after two weeks when the authorities accepted his argument that he had only been a soldier serving France, and not truly a Jacobin. Saliceti also seems to have helped. That wily politician still had influence, since he had foreseen the demise of Robespierre and actually helped bring him down. Again Bonaparte was posted to the staff of the Army of Italy, and in early 1795 sailed with an expedition to recapture Corsica, but it was stopped cold by the British navy.

In the spring of 1795, Bonaparte was transferred to Paris and offered a brigade in the Vendée. He refused the command. There was no glory, he thought, in chasing French peasant rebels. For that insubordination, he lost his commission. Barras and Saliceti intervened and had him assigned to the Topographic Bureau (general staff) in Paris, where he again took up planning for the Army of Italy. Life was dull, and his future seemed grim. But then whimsical Lady Luck smiled on him again. "Luck means nothing," he later wrote Joseph. That was hardly so in his early career, although it must be admitted that he helped luck along.

## The "Whiff of Grapeshot"

In October 1795, the National Convention, sitting in the Tuileries Palace, came under threat of attack by the Paris mobs, irresistible since 1789. The Convention had written a new constitution creating the Directory, a moderate republican government. The Parisians were miserable. They blamed their plight on the Government of Thermidor, formed after the death of Robespierre and named for the month of Thermidor in the Revolutionary Calendar, and they expected the new government to be no different. They still suffered from high unemployment, shortages of bread and fuel, and starvation and exposure. Thousands were ready to march under the improbable leadership of royalists, who promised to take care of the people, and a few wealthy bourgeois who feared a return of the Terror.

Barras was appointed to defend the Tuileries. He had once been an officer in the Royal Army, but for twenty years conquests of the boudoir and politics had occupied his time. He summoned Bonaparte to take actual command. He knew Napoleon from Toulon; he knew that he was ambitious and would ruthlessly use all his weapons. He also realized that if Bonaparte shocked the establishment, he was expendable; he was a foreigner and a loner, resented for his success in the officer corps.

Bonaparte found that artillery was his major need. He had 5000 regular troops, some volunteers (the "Patriots of '89"), and a few gunners, but no cannon. He was certain that the infantry alone could not stand before 80,000 Parisians, an average mob when the people were aroused. Out of the swarm of officers in the foyer of the palace, Bonaparte therefore picked a tall Gascon cavalry major, Joachim Murat—a man he barely knew but who radiated force like his pawing stallion outside—and ordered him to take a troop of horsemen to Sablons, in the suburbs, and seize the cannon of the National Guard. As night fell, Murat led his men at a wild gallop through the narrow streets of Paris, scattering people, vehicles, and animals as he went. At Sablons, he spurred his horse through the gate with a final burst of speed, leaving guards standing agape; his men followed. Back through the streets he came in the early hours of the morning, bringing forty cannon, some pulled by artillery horses, others dragged by his cavalry with ropes.

By dawn on 5 October, Napoleon had the guns emplaced to cover all approaches to the Tuileries, principally at the Rue de la Convention, which ran south from the Rue Saint-Honoré, then the "main street" of Paris, directly to the palace gardens. He had the guns charged with extra powder and loaded

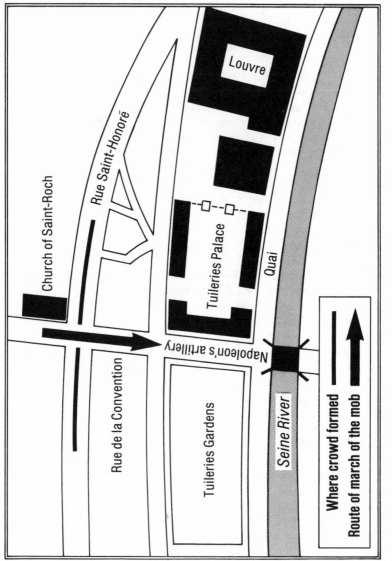

**Map 2. Locale of the "Whiff of Grapeshot," 5 October 1795**

with canister (grapeshot) and, to make more shrapnel, nails, links of chain, and scrap metal.

All day the people gathered in increasing thousands along the Rue Saint-Honoré. They were hidden by densely packed buildings from the defenders of the Tuileries, who could only gauge the size of the crowd by the noise, which became ever louder. The people were building up their courage with the aid of free beer and wine furnished by their middle-class backers; their leaders were waiting for their numbers to become "irresistible."

At 4:00 PM the people could be seen forming ranks at the head of the Rue de la Convention. At 4:45 they came on, shouting the *Marseillaise*, with pikes high, red liberty caps bobbing, in full confidence of victory. Napoleon's gunners, their cannon trained on the street, stood, torches lit, waiting for his command. They grew edgy as the mob moved in, first to 100 yards, then to 50 yards, and finally to point-blank range.

FIRE! The cannon cut bloody swaths through the crowd, and the people fled, leaving their dead and wounded among pools of blood on the cobblestones. The same scene, on a smaller scale, was enacted on the east side of the palace. It was all over. A few diehards held out in the church of Saint-Roch, but they were blasted out in short order. Napoleon disarmed the city.

The Convention was saved. By grace of Bonaparte, the Directory became the government of the Republic. Four years later, by grace of the same general, it would fall and be replaced with a government of his own. At this point, however, his thoughts were far removed from being head of state. He sought promotion by pandering to Barras, the man who was de facto head of state and the only one of the five directors destined to serve for the whole life of the Directory. Accordingly, Napoleon's report credited General Barras with everything which had made victory possible, beginning with ordering the cannon brought from Sablons. Murat was not mentioned at all. (Not that Napoleon forgot him; he was later to be a marshal, the "First Horseman of Europe," husband of Napoleon's sister Caroline, Grand Duke of Berg, and King of Naples.) The report emphasized that the action had been defensive and called the attackers royalists, one and all. It made no mention of casualties but pointed out that among the dead were many émigré nobles, reactionary priests, and rebel guerrillas from the Vendée. Privately, Napoleon wrote Joseph that his gunners had killed "*beaucoup de monde*"—uncounted numbers of the attackers.

Apparently he was afraid he might be accused of excessive brutality, but he need not have worried. As he wrote Joseph on 11 October: "We were victorious, and all is forgotten." Parisians were quiet, if hardly in love with Bonaparte. The republican establishment was jubilant; the officer corps accepted the politicians' opinion. Napoleon was promoted to major general and given command of the Army of the Interior. In March 1796 he was made general-in-chief of the Army of Italy, which he soon led to victories that made him world famous.

## Josephine

Meanwhile, for the first time in his life, Napoleon found himself to be a social lion. He was sought after by the most celebrated hostesses in Paris, all of whom wanted to meet the shocking little master of cannon. At the salon of the outrageous and beautiful Madame Thérésa Tallien, "Our Lady of Thermidor," he met Josephine de Beauharnais, the widow of General Viscount Alexandre de Beauharnais, guillotined during the Terror. She was thirty-two, six years older than Napoleon, and had two children, Eugene, fourteen, and Hortense, twelve. Nonetheless, Rose, as her fast-living friends called Josephine, was charming, slim, lovely, chic, and perfectly endowed for the fashions of the day, which revealed the breasts, usually behind the thinnest gauze. And, by marriage, she was of the high aristocracy of the Old Regime, of which Napoleon stood in awe, although he would never admit it.

Napoleon, apparently indifferent to Josephine's reputation for giving sexual favors as suited her whim, soon proposed marriage. In fact, she had been the mistress of several powerful men, most recently of Barras. She found the little general amusing and became his mistress, but she refused to marry him. When he was appointed commander of the Army of Italy, however, she agreed, and they were wed on 9 March 1796. He left for Nice to take up his new command two days later.

The ugly rumor went with him that his post was a reward from Barras for making Josephine an honest woman. We shall never know if there was any truth to it. It is patently clear, however, that if Barras paid, he paid unnecessarily. Napoleon's letters to Josephine are those of a man totally in love: "I do not pass an hour without loving you; I do not drink a cup of tea without damning the glory and ambition that made me separate me from my soul and my life. . . . My soul is sad; my heart is enslaved." He lived with fantasies of their physical lovemaking. A typical closing to one of his letters ran: "A kiss on the heart, and then a little lower, much, much lower." And he called her letters cold and questioned if she loved him. It is doubtful; she had a lover (or a homosexual friend who passed for one), a perfumed lieutenant named Hippolyte Charles, and was back among her old friends in Paris.

# 2

# THE SCRAMBLER EMERGES
## The First Italian Campaign, 1796–97

### The Army of Italy

In 1795, Prussia and Spain had made peace with France, and the United Provinces of the Netherlands had been conquered and turned into the Batavian Republic. Britain was limiting itself to war on the high seas. Thus in 1796 France was faced only by Austria and its minor Italian and German allies. The mission of Napoleon and the Army of Italy was to defeat the Austrian and allied armies in Italy. The Directory's expectation, however, was that Bonaparte would merely tie up enemy troops in Italy, possibly assisted by the Army of the Alps under François Kellermann. The war was to be won by French armies in Germany, commanded by Generals Jourdan and Jean-Victor Moreau.

In mid-March 1796, as Napoleon traveled to Nice, his thoughts were on how he would take control and set the army in motion. He knew he had disabilities and tried to downplay one—his foreign origin—by signing his name *Bonaparte*, which was as neatly French as *Buonaparte* was Italian. A more serious problem was that in the eyes of front-line generals, including his immediate subordinates, he was no combat commander. What had he done? Commanded guns in the siege of Toulon, true. But he was famous for shooting down unarmed civilians in Paris; a necessary evil, perhaps, but hardly noble combat. He knew that many considered that politics, not merit, had gained him the command. He had become accustomed to being resented for his intelligence and ambition, however, and hardly gave it any thought.

Napoleon also had advantages. He knew the Army of Italy, the enemy forces, and the terrain better than any man alive. He had served on the Italian frontier in 1794 and 1795; he had specialized in planning for the Army of Italy while in the Topographic Bureau in 1795. He had taken a part in making the current plans of the Directory, spelled out in the orders he carried. He also knew the generals whom he would face at Nice and had calculated his approach to each one of them. Bonaparte thus assumed the air of a high-wire walker who has prepared a lifetime for his act and bounds onto the wire with total confidence, because he knows he will not fall.

Napoleon actually took command of the Army of Italy at Nice on 27 March 1796. Most accounts emphasize the miracle of leadership by which the twenty-six-year-old prodigy took control of his subordinate generals, all hardened combat veterans and older than he, and set the army moving within days of his arrival. There is no doubt that Bonaparte had leadership ability, charisma, and presence, although it would be foolish to assume that in 1796 he was the electrifying figure he became as a myth of invincibility grew about him. The fact is that he was accepted by his generals largely because they had no other choice. To oppose him was politically dangerous: he was the protégé of Barras and Carnot, the two most powerful members of the five-man Directory.

Napoleon's connections in Paris also helped him gain acceptance with his men. He had demanded and gotten the transfer of two fresh regiments of cavalry from Kellermann's Army of the Alps and brought with him, as it were, provisions for three infantry divisions. In addition, Carnot had insured a 3,500,000-franc loan in Genoa for Saliceti, chief supplier of the Army of Italy, which allowed him to buy clothing, shoes, and food desperately needed by the soldiers. (British woolens, ironically, were among the items purchased; Genoa was technically neutral.) Purchasing was also facilitated by the French consul in Genoa—Joseph Bonaparte.

On paper, the Army of Italy numbered 96,000 men. However, 22,000 were in garrisons along the coast, 36,000 in hospital, on leave, or prisoners of war, which left the field army with 38,000. This army had been neglected in favor of those on the Rhine. The men were demoralized from lack of action and were short of food, clothing (many had no shoes), arms, ammunition, horses, everything. Napoleon had begun repairing these deficiencies before he left Paris. His next problem was to gain control of his generals, restore discipline, and get the campaign under way.

The key generals were four: André Masséna, Pierre Augereau, Jean Sérurier, and Alexandre Berthier, all superb soldiers. They were there because of Carnot's level-headed retention of loyal noble officers, even under the Terror, and his policy of "careers open to talent," applied to nobles and commoners alike. Carnot had saved the careers of Berthier and Sérurier, both noblemen, and promoted the other two, despite their humbler origins, to general.

Masséna, age thirty-eight, of medium height, burly, with the face of a boxer, had gone to sea as a mere boy and then enlisted in the French army, where he rose to the rank of sergeant major. He had left the service to become a smuggler of goods from the Orient and returned to the army under the Revolution by way of the National Guard. Napoleon knew him from Toulon; he was a hard, clever soldier, whose men feared and respected him. His weakness was avarice, which Napoleon would exploit. Masséna had been promoted to brigadier general in 1793 and major general in 1794, a year earlier than Napoleon.

Augereau, thirty-nine, was another tough ex-sergeant, "whose great height gave him a martial-enough air." He had enlisted in the French army at fourteen, where he was known as a brawler and swordsman, served in the Russian army against the Turks, and deserted from the Prussian army. He had reentered the French army as a volunteer under the Revolution. He intimidated his troops and expected to do the same to Bonaparte, whom he referred to behind his back as "the little bastard."

The other two were career officers of the Old Regime. Sérurier, fifty-four, handsome and gentlemanly, was one of the older generals retained in the Army of the Republic. Finally, Napoleon had brought with him, to be chief of staff, Berthier. At forty-two, he was small and swarthy, known throughout the army as a wizard with maps and paperwork. Bonaparte had used influence to get him transferred from the Army of the Alps. He would be Napoleon's right hand on this campaign, and on all his others through 1814.

## Taking Charge

"I have been well received by the army, which has displayed great confidence in me," General Bonaparte wrote to Carnot on 28 March. That was not true, but Napoleon meant to make it true.

Masséna appeared at first not to take him seriously and surely had some resentment at having Bonaparte, who had less time in grade than he, placed over him. Augereau greeted him with barely suppressed surliness. Napoleon handled the two by striking a fearless pose, embarrassing them with questions they could not answer, and name dropping: Barras and Carnot were behind him, they were reminded. He demanded a full accounting of their divisions, the rounding up of deserters, the clearing from the hospitals of malingerers. He harassed them and their brigade and regimental commanders day and night, literally. He was, he said later, *un homme terrible* with the officers. However, he let them know that if they fought well for him they would be richly rewarded from the booty to be taken in Italy. That was talk the generals, especially Masséna, understood well.

With the men, his approach was familiar and pragmatic. He went among them, listening to their complaints and promising them better food, clothing, shoes, arms, and ammunition—and delivering. At the same time, he told them that they could loot Italy of fabulous wealth. The proclamation beginning "Soldiers, you are naked, you are starving," dates from St. Helena, but Napoleon surely told the troops something similar, and more than once: "Rich provinces, great cities will be in your power; you will find there honor, glory, and riches." It seems significant that he made scant mention of the vaunted

Revolutionary mission of the liberation of oppressed peoples from aristocratic regimes; instead, he appealed to the baser instincts of the men, like an Italian *condottiere* of old.

The plan approved by the Directory was for Bonaparte to separate the armies of Piedmont-Sardinia and Austria, force Piedmont to make terms, and concentrate on the Austrians. (Napoleon had helped formulate the plan, of course.) The Piedmontese army, some 70,000 strong, under the Austrian General Baron Michel von Colli, was deployed in and behind the Maritime Alps in Piedmont proper. The Austrian field army of 30,000, under General Baron Johann Beaulieu, was deployed behind the Ligurian Alps to the east. Beaulieu commanded both armies, in theory. He also had 50,000 troops in garrisons and forts strung across northern Italy.

To get between the armies, Napoleon had to move his forces east along the coast, then north across the Ligurian Alps. Two passes were possible attack routes: the Cadibona, above Savona, and the Bochetta, north of Genoa. Beaulieu had concentrated north of Savona. Bonaparte divided his force of 38,000 into three corps under Masséna (17,000), Augereau (11,500), and Sérurier (9,500), and set his army in motion along the coast toward Genoa.[1]

### Montenotte to Mondovi and Cherasco

For the first two months, Bonaparte gave little indication that he would behave differently from any other army commander. He stayed in the rear with Berthier and his staff, making decisions based on reports, maps, and occasional reconaissance forays. He let Masséna and Augereau do most of the fighting, and they did well. That his plans were so beautifully carried into action was a matter of some amazement to him, but his reports to the Directory never let this be known. He gained confidence rapidly and soon abandoned his command tent for the thick of action.

On 6 April 1796, Napoleon sent Masséna flying toward Genoa, or so it seemed to the enemy. Actually the cavalry and some light infantry made a noisy advance. Beaulieu, as Napoleon had hoped he would, sent half his army to the Bochetta. On 11 April, the same day the Austrians completed their redeployment, Masséna concentrated at Savona. In a swift night march he went over the Cadibona, and on the morning of 12 April emerged from the mists at Montenotte, caught the Austrians sleeping, and put them to rout. It was Masséna's victory. Napoleon himself was not at Montenotte, but at Carcara, five miles away, and he gave Masséna only a share of credit in his report to the Directory: "Today, the division of General Masséna and that of

---

[1]The term *corps* did not become standard in the French army until 1803, but we shall use it to refer to units of greater than division size.

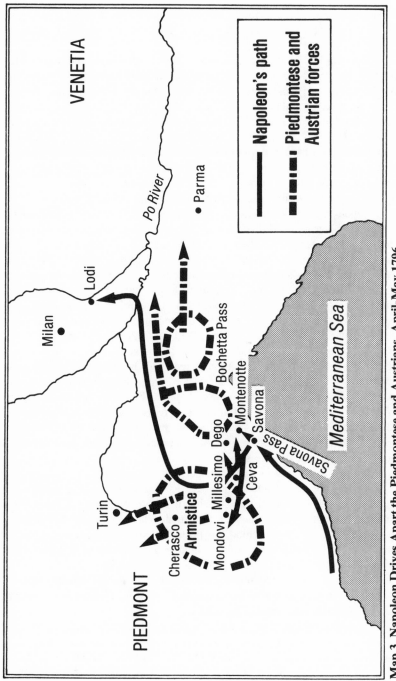

VENETIA

Po River

• Parma

Napoleon's path

Piedmontese and
Austrian forces

Lodi

Milan •

Bochetta Pass

Mediterranean Sea

Montenotte

Savona

Savona Pass

Dego

Turin •

Millesimo

Ceva

Cherasco •

Armistice

Mondovi

PIEDMONT

Map 3. Napoleon Drives Apart the Piedmontese and Austrians, April-May 1796

General Laharpe [who was under Masséna] attacked the Austrians . . . commanded in person by General Beaulieu . . . [at] Montenotte. The republicans completely defeated the Austrians."

Masséna had exploited Beaulieu's mistake of dividing his forces. The Austrians retreated eastward. Augereau joined with Masséna the same day and the two turned west to test Colli and the Piedmontese. On the 13th, at Millesimo (just ten miles away), they hit Colli, who had only 20,000 troops of 50,000 available and drove him toward Ceva. Masséna then turned eastward again to ensure that the Austrians did not have time to reorganize. He defeated them at Dego, on 14 April, and Beaulieu withdrew all the Austrians eastward toward Alessandria to regroup. Augereau and Masséna then recombined and attacked Colli at Ceva (18 April), forcing him to retreat westward and widening the gap between the Piedmontese and Austrian armies.

Napoleon consolidated all his corps—Masséna, Augereau, and Sérurier—and turned the army on Colli, whom he now had outnumbered. At Mondovi, on 21 April, he forced the Piedmontese into retreat by stages toward Turin. The corps commanders followed, without much direction from Napoleon, harassing the enemy's rear units. Colli hastened to Turin where, disheartened by the indifference and timidity of his troops, he accepted the judgment of King Victor Amadeus of Piedmont-Sardinia that further resistance was useless. On 26 April, at Cherasco, the king's plenipotentiaries signed an armistice with Bonaparte, which effectively put Piedmont out of the war.

Napoleon exacted an indemnity in gold and silver coin or bullion from the Piedmontese. With the first monies received, he paid the troops and let them know that they came first. Some men, and even generals, got the first hard cash they had received in years; they had been paid in Revolutionary script (*assignats* or *mandats*), if at all. This represented the practical side of Bonaparte's leadership. He always saw to pay, promotions, or trinkets of glory (medals). He also sent heavy contributions to the treasury of the Directory, which generated more goodwill in Paris.

In the Cherasco armistice, Bonaparte, to reassure the Piedmontese that his troops would depart quickly and that looting thus would be minimized, agreed to march directly for the Duchy of Milan, crossing the Po River at Valenza. Since the Austrians were informed by agents of all this, Beaulieu arrayed his men to fight behind the Po at Valenza. But Bonaparte had no intention of giving the enemy this advantage. In an end run, he struck south into Parma, a neutral state, and on 9 May crossed the Po at Piacenza, which put him south and in the rear of the Austrians. He had clearly violated international law, such as it was, but he could not have cared less. Winning took precedence over any such niceties.

Beaulieu retreated eastward, making for the Quadrilateral, the four forts—Peschiera, Verona, Legnago, and Mantua—which guarded the passes over the Alps to Austria. Napoleon put his army into forced march northeastward for Lodi, where he expected Beaulieu to cross the Adda River.

**Lodi: Glory on the Cheap**

About 11:00 AM on 10 May 1796, Napoleon's advance regiment, led by Colonel d'Allemagne, was stopped at Lodi by the Austrian rear guard of 9000 men under General Sebottendorf. The enemy had taken up positions on the far side of the Adda River at the end of a wooden bridge some 200 yards long, over swift and deep water. Napoleon was informed, rode forward, and began calling up all the artillery he could muster, supervising the emplacement himself, and giving the Austrians an ever heavier pounding. By 6:00 PM, he had 30 guns blasting the enemy at point-blank range from the banks alongside the west end of the bridge. (Remember that none of his guns had a range of over one-half mile.)

Napoleon was having himself a lovely, noisy little battle that he could scarcely lose. Dirty, sweaty, his face and uniform blotched with black powder, he was having a fine time aiming the artillery, a corporal's job. The troops, astounded, decided this was a general after their own hearts. After Lodi, they called him the Little Corporal.

All day at intervals, as more of the French army arrived, assaults across the bridge were made by Colonel d'Allemagne, Colonel Jean Lannes, Masséna, and even Berthier, the chief of staff. Masséna led the final charge which took the bridge and drove the Austrians into retreat. It was Masséna's victory as much as Napoleon's. Moreover, General Beaumont's cavalry, which had forded the Adda upstream, hit the Austrian flank just as Masséna charged across the bridge and may have been the decisive factor in the victory. To the troops, however, the glory of the day belonged to the Little Corporal, and it was useless to suggest otherwise.

Lodi was hardly an important battle. The Austrians were in full flight. If the French had waited until the next morning, they could have had the bridge without a fight. Sebottendorf would have been gone. Of course, even at this stage of his career, Napoleon's rule for victory was to destroy the enemy army, not occupy territory. At a price of 350 French killed and wounded, his army killed 153 Austrians and captured 1700, many wounded. Lodi was a spectacular little battle, however, and Bonaparte made the most of it to balloon his reputation. For starters he sent a report to the Directory which set the Austrian force at 18,000 men, double the number actually there, and estimated enemy casualties at 3000, a figure much too high. This sort of fiction would become habitual in his later bulletins.

Most importantly, the victory at Lodi solidified Napoleon's self-confidence. He had early become disdainful of the enemy commanders, then increasingly certain that he was better than most French generals. After Lodi he was convinced that he was the best of all generals of whatever nationality, surely of any alive. He confided to his aide, Colonel Auguste Marmont: "They haven't seen anything yet. . . . In our time, no one has the slightest conception of what is *great*. It is up to me to give them an example."

After the battle at Lodi, Bonaparte, with aides and a suitable escort, made for Milan. He was full of himself, irritated only that Josephine refused to join him. To that chronically unfaithful one, who had clung to her Paris haunts and deputized her daughter Hortense to write the "little general," Napoleon wrote pathetically, "I shall be frantic if I do not have a letter from you tonight." But if Josephine defied his understanding, nothing else did. In Milan, Napoleon plunged into politics, working with Italian republicans such as Francesco Melzi d'Eril, Ferdinando Marescalchi, and Giovanni Paradisi to form the core of what became the Cisalpine Republic, much later the Napoleonic Kingdom of Italy. He had already gained influence in France by sending gold, silver, and jewels to help the Directory's sagging finances— only a fraction of what he would dispatch later.

To distribute the news of his expected triumphs, Bonaparte bought two newspapers, *Courrier de l'Armée d'Italie* and *La France vue de l'Armée d'Italie*. No one questioned where he got the funds. They were to be used to make him famous, as it were. Although the news which they purveyed over the next year had a solid basis in victory, it was much embellished. Without these newssheets Napoleon might not have returned from Italy so overwhelmingly famous. He realized the value of propaganda early on.

## On to Mantua

The members of the Directory were not so impressed with Bonaparte, however, as to hesitate to give him orders, and those which reached him in Milan made him furious. They told him to give over Lombardy to the Army of the Alps, under General Kellermann, and lead his forces southward to secure central Italy and Naples. Bonaparte threatened resignation; he was determined to have the glory of defeating the Austrians, not the task of plundering helpless Italian states.

Kellermann was a good general, Napoleon wrote Carnot. That much was obligatory; Kellermann was the hero of Valmy (1792) and a very senior commander. However, Bonaparte continued, one general was enough; even one bad general was better than two good ones. Such tough talk might have ruined another man, but Napoleon believed, and rightly, that the directors would not recall the only general currently winning victories. He also reminded them of his usefulness by dispatching to Paris more money and art treasures, including priceless paintings by such masters as Correggio and Michelangelo. As a result, the directors let Bonaparte retain his command and even gave him 10,000 troops from Kellermann's army.

At the end of May 1796, Napoleon rejoined his army, which had been moving eastward. By early June it had taken Peschiera, Legnago, and Verona. Beaulieu retreated into the Tyrol, leaving a garrison of 14,000 men with some 500 guns in Mantua, the strongest of the Quadrilateral fortresses. Napoleon had the centuries-old fortress blockaded in June, and on 15 July had it fully invested. It lay in the course of the Mincio River, surrounded by rivulets and marshes, which made direct attack without unacceptable losses impossible. The best hope of the French was to starve out the defenders and the civilians of Mantua as well, which they set themselves to do, while probing for weak points in the defenses.

The war, for the next seven months—almost until the end, in effect—would involve Austrian attempts to take Mantua and the French responses to them. Before the Austrians could begin their first offensive, however, their army had to be totally reorganized, which required time. Bonaparte took advantage of the lull to send out forces to neutralize all the Italian states which he had not already overrun. Augereau successfully completed the most important assignments, arranging peace terms with the pope and the king of Naples. The Holy See gave over Bologna and Ferrara to France (ultimately to the Cisalpine Republic), paid 34,000,000 francs, and "donated" art works. Naples contributed 50,000,000 francs. The Directory in Paris was impressed.

Meanwhile, on the Austrian side, Beaulieu was replaced with Field Marshal Count Dagobert von Wurmser, whose army was reinforced to 50,000. In July 1796, he divided it into two wings—a crucial error, it would prove—and marched southward. With 35,000 men, he went down the eastern shore of Lake Garda, while General Quasdanovich, with 20,000 men, moved down the western shore. Of Wurmser's men 5000 were detached to besiege Peschiera, and another 5000, under Meszaros, to approach Mantua by way of Verona, thus reducing his forces to 25,000. And Quasdanovich's forces were not consolidated, either.[2]

When he became aware of the threat, Bonaparte alerted Masséna, whose corps was nearest Lake Garda, and ordered Augereau to move northward to reinforce him. Simultaneously, he took the dangerous step of pulling his siege forces (Sérurier's corps) off Mantua and concentrating this reserve 25 miles to the west. Thus the garrison in Mantua could have emerged to take the French in the rear when they engaged the Austrians at the foot of Lake Garda, or it could have combined with the Austrian division of Meszaros, which approached from the vicinity of Verona. Bonaparte was gambling, counting on the skill of his subordinates and the ineptitude of his enemies.

## Lonato and Castiglione

Napoleon's orders were not very precise, since the positions of the enemy were unknown, but it did not matter. Masséna drove his corps toward the nearest Austrians and fixed on the main force of Quasdanovich, which he

---

[2]The division of forces was purely strategic. There was no logistical reason to divide forces which were marching a maximum of 60 to 80 miles, measuring from Trent to Mantua, the objective. Moreover, the Austrian armies had not and never did adopt a system of living off the land. The troops carried rations, and heavy trains followed every regiment. These trains undoubtedly slowed Austrian operations in Italy.

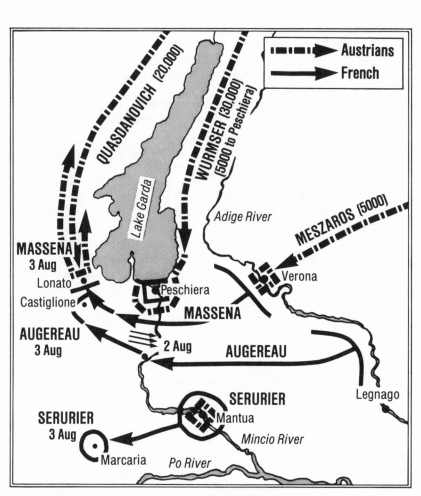

**Map 4. Wurmser's Approach and the Battle of Lonato,
28 July-3 August 1796**

drove northward, forcing a battle at Lonato on 3 August. This sent the enemy flying back north along the west shore of Lake Garda, depriving Wurmser of 20,000 men. Masséna then turned south to reinforce Augereau, who had fixed and slowed Wurmser's main force near Castiglione. On the next day, as Augereau and Masséna firmed their position against the Austrians, Bonaparte appeared, having ordered in elements of Sérurier's corps and two reduced divisions (Kilmaine and Despinoy). By grace of Masséna's victory at Lonato and Wurmser's detachment of 10,000 of his own troops, Napoleon had his enemy outnumbered, 30,000 to 24,000.

On 5 August, Napoleon opened the battle of Castiglione with some very dangerous maneuvers. He ordered first Masséna and then Augereau to advance and subsequently fall back. Two or more companies of their lead battalions were in line, moreover, and quite vulnerable, though followed by battalions in column. The "retreat" of the French brought Wurmser forward quickly and in force, and it appeared for a time that he would turn the planned withdrawals into a rout. The Austrian, however, was not content to drive straight ahead but tried to turn Napoleon's north flank, which spread out his men and made them vulnerable. At this juncture, at Napoleon's order, Masséna and Augereau turned their corps about and went into a coordinated frontal assault on Wurmser's lines.

The Austrians fell back and, as the momentum of the French attack slowly accelerated, General Beaumont, with the cavalry, protected by an infantry division from Sérurier's corps, hit the Austrian left (south) flank, throwing the enemy into confusion. Wurmser kept his force organized, personally leading cavalry charges, despite his seventy-two years, to take the pressure off his infantry. Nevertheless, he was probably saved by the appearance late in the day of 5000 men under Bejalich, detached earlier to besiege Peschiera. In any case, he retreated in good order up the Adige River.

Bonaparte thus had another major victory. Castiglione, however, if less clearly than the first battles of the campaign, was won by Masséna and Augereau. Less skilled commanders could not have taken their men forward, then back, then forward again. When troops turn their backs to the enemy, they tend to keep retreating. This is true even if, in the first stages, units follow orders with alacrity and cover each other's withdrawal. Moreover, few experienced generals would have given the orders Napoleon did. Whether he knew the risks at this stage of his career is doubtful. What is certain is that without Masséna and Augereau, he probably would have been destroyed. Besides, Bonaparte began the battle before the infantry sent by Sérurier were on the scene; he gambled that they would arrive, and they did, thanks to another good subordinate.

Bonaparte restored the siege lines at Mantua and replaced Sérurier, who was ill with malaria, with General Sahuguet. He posted Masséna to Rivoli and Augereau to Verona and left the Irish-born General Charles-E.-S. Jennings

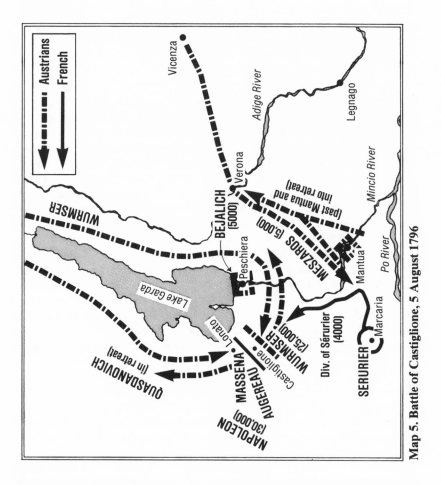

Map 5. Battle of Castiglione, 5 August 1796

de Kilmaine, with under 3000 men, mostly cavalry, to outpost the line of the Adige from Legnago to Verona as a precaution against attack from the east. General Charles-Henri Vaubois was ordered from Leghorn to command a new division formed from smaller units already present. He was directed to the north shore of Lake Garda. The French dispositions made Wurmser think that Bonaparte meant to march for southern Germany to reinforce Moreau for a push on Vienna. In fact, the Directory had given Napoleon such orders, and the enemy knew it; the Alps were very familiar to the Austrians, and they or their sympathizers waylaid many French messengers.

### Trent, Bassano, and Mantua

The Austrian commander decided to surprise him and strike for Mantua from the east, which meant marching east, then generally south via Vicenza, and finally southwest across the Adige. If successful, he would drive off the French besiegers and free the 15,000 men locked up in the fortress; he might then be able to attack Napoleon with superior numbers from the south. Wurmser left 20,000 men under Davidovich to defend Trent and the approaches to the Tyrol. On 1 September he took the road to Bassano with another 20,000 but made the mistake of dividing his force three ways: about 10,000 in the advance guard under Meszaros and 5000 each under Sebottendorf and Quasdanovich, marching some 15 to 20 miles apart. But for that, and his slow movement, he might have given Bonaparte a telling setback—perhaps enough of one to induce the jittery Directory to replace him.

On 1 September, Napoleon was still trying to draw his three marching corps together before Trent. On 3 September, still oblivious of Wurmser's march, he sent Masséna to blast a way through the approach passes and Vaubois to reinforce him on the next day. On 5 September he took Trent and only then learned that he was not fighting Wurmser. He put Vaubois in a blocking position north of Trent and ordered Masséna into pursuit of Wurmser, and then Augereau, who struck eastward from south of Trent. Each plunged ahead, hell bent for glory, confident that each commanded over 10,000 men. But they were on opposite sides of the Brenta River, which was not fordable.

On 8 September, totally out of Napoleon's control and still on opposite sides of the Brenta, Masséna and Augereau caught half of Wurmser's army (Sebottendorf and Quasdanovich) at Bassano. Somehow, they managed to capture the town bridge and unite to rout the Austrians. Quasdanovich, without orders, fled toward Trieste with 3000 men; the Austrians lost another 3000, killed and captured. Wurmser retreated with his headquarters to Vicenza, where he was joined by Sebottendorf, and kept going south. He recalled Meszaros, who had run into stiff French resistance at Verona. On 9 September Wurmser united the remaining Austrian forces at Villanuova.

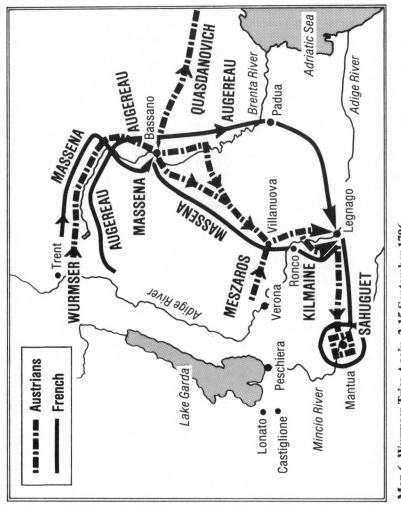

Map 6. Wurmser Tries Again, 2-15 September 1796

Wurmser, now reduced to less than 14,000, was still confident he could take Mantua. Since Bonaparte had followed him through Bassano with apparently (and in fact) the better part of the French army, he rated his chances even better than before. There was nothing to stop him except the besieging corps of Sahuguet (less than 6000 men) and a thin force on the Adige (Kilmaine), which had been hastily concentrated on Verona to stop Meszaros, abandoning Legnago to the south without destroying the bridge. Wurmser marched for Legnago. Napoleon, meanwhile, had ordered Masséna to pursue Wurmser and Augereau to seize Padua to the east, confident that the Austrian general would retreat toward Trieste. He expected Wurmser to be blocked by Augereau at Padua while Masséna took him in the rear. Actually, this only served to divide Napoleon's forces and gave Wurmser an even better shot at Mantua.

On 9 September, Bonaparte woke up to what Wurmser was doing and responded by adopting an almost suicidal plan. He ordered Masséna, already following the Austrian army, to cross the Adige at Ronco, race south along the west bank of the river, and block Wurmser as he emerged from Legnago. Augereau was ordered to march west from Padua, drive through Legnago, and take the Austrians in the rear. This put Napoleon's two major corps on opposite sides of the Adige, a major river, swift and deep. Masséna stood a chance of being annihilated before Augereau could reach him. Of course, Sahuguet or Kilmaine might assist Masséna, but then Wurmser could count on the Austrian garrison in Mantua of 15,000 men, of whom 8000 could be deployed. Numbers were on the Austrian side, as were concentration of forces and the initiative, since they were acting and the French reacting.

For six days the war went in Wurmser's favor. He reached Legnago on 10 September, installed a 2000-man garrison in the fortress, crossed the Adige, rested his troops for a day, and on 11 September marched for Mantua. On the same day, Masséna finally crossed the Adige and Augereau reached Legnago. On 12 September, thanks to the failure of Sahuguet to destroy all the bridges in his path, he entered Mantua with 10,000 men. The garrison brought his numbers to 20,000 effectives (25,000 total). On the next day, Wurmser came out of Mantua and drove Sahuguet northward in disarray, and on 14 September he mauled Masséna's corps, which approached from the east. On 15 September he emerged again, confident of victory, to bludgeon the French. Napoleon, however, by now had finally united all his forces. Augereau, though desperately ill, had stayed with his corps until he defeated the Austrian garrison at Legnago (13 September), then sent it toward Mantua under General Louis-André Bon. His men were with Bonaparte, as were the corps of Masséna and Sahuguet. Napoleon drove Wurmser into Mantua, where he was locked up until he was ready to surrender in February 1797. Again, Bonaparte's subordinates had made everything work out well.

Baron General Jozsef Alvinczy von Børberek was dispatched from Vienna to take command of the Austrian forces. A veteran Hungarian officer born in Transylvania, he had fought in the Seven Years' War and during 1792–1794 had served against the French in Belgium and the Rhineland. Since 1795, he had been with the *Hofkriegsrat* (Imperial War Council) until he was detached to meet the threat of Bonaparte. Like his predecessors, he had greater numbers of troops than Napoleon, about 50,000 effectives. But also like them, he seemed under a compulsion to divide his forces which, in the end, meant disaster for him. It did not come before he gave Bonaparte some hairy moments.

By late October, Napoleon had been reinforced. Most of the men were replacements for casualties, however, and there also was much illness in the army as winter approached. His forces numbered 47,000 on paper, but he had fewer than 30,000 effectives, including those besieging Mantua. There, Bonaparte had a division of 9000 men under General Kilmaine and 1600 cavalry nearby under General Jean Beaumont. The remainder were stationed to watch all the northern and eastern approaches to Mantua. Vaubois's division of 10,500 was near Trent, guarding the passes from the Tyrol. Masséna's 5200 was at Bassano, and Augereau's 13,000 was guarding the Adige line from Verona to Legnago. General François Macquard had another 6500 men northwest of Mantua. Napoleon was violating what he later made into an ironclad rule: "The art of placing troops is the great *art de guerre*. Always place your troops in such a way that, whatever the enemy does, they can be united within a few days."

The army could not have been massed in less than a week. His divisions and corps were very vulnerable, less because of the distances involved (40 to 75 miles from each other) than because of the extremely rugged terrain, muddy and rutted roads which worsened in almost continual rain, and troops affected by both the wet and near-freezing temperatures. If Alvinczy had struck with the entire Austrian army, he might have triumphed. Instead, he marched from Trieste in October with 30,000 men and sent Davidovich south from the Tyrol at the same time with about 18,000. As it turned out, Vaubois, taking advantage of the terrain and his enemy's lack of aggressiveness, was able to block Davidovich in the mountains, so that he never figured in the campaign to follow. Napoleon had to contend only with the 30,000 directly under Alvinczy's command, which the enemy commander accommodatingly subdivided further.

### Caldiero

At the end of October, Alvinczy moved slowly forward and encountered Masséna's forces near Bassano. The French withdrew in good order toward Vicenza and then to Verona, where Masséna was reinforced to 7000 and Augereau joined him with 4700 of his corps and 2000 cavalry. Macquard marched at all speed from the foot of Lake Garda to garrison the fortress of

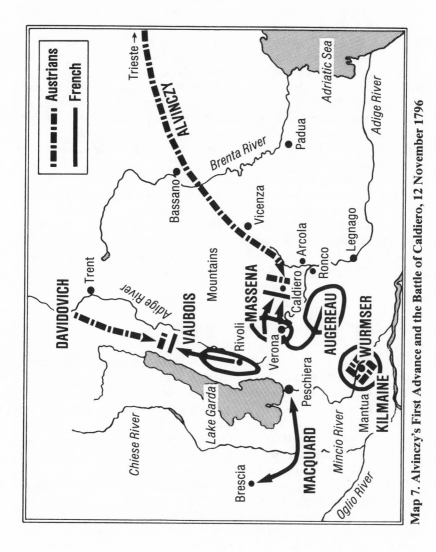

**Map 7. Alvinczy's First Advance and the Battle of Caldiero, 12 November 1796**

Verona with 2600 men. Napoleon marched east from Verona to meet Alvinczy with the corps of Masséna and Augereau, or fewer than 14,000 men, although he could fall back on the Verona garrison behind him if necessary. On 12 November 1796, hoping to surprise and destroy Alvinczy's advance guard of 8000 at Caldiero, Bonaparte went on the offensive. His maneuver failed.

Alvinczy brought 18,000 men onto the battlefield, which still gave him a small advantage. However, the attacks of Napoleon's two corps were not well coordinated. The Austrians were able to dislodge Masséna and then turn on Augereau. The French troops were tired and dispirited from days of marching and recently had heard news of defeats in Germany. Moreover, the rains came in torrents at midday, wetting cartridges and attenuating French fire as well as adding to the dismal mood of the troops. At dusk, Bonaparte retreated to Verona.

Had Alvinczy been able to strike with his whole force of 30,000, he might well have destroyed the French. But he had sent 3000 men on a flanking mission to the north and 3000 to carry out a demonstration to the south, near Ronco. Another 6000 were just lagging behind, some as far back as Bassano. Although Alvinczy won at Caldiero, he missed the chance to annihilate the French corps. Had he exploited the opportunities Napoleon gave him in the next few days, Bonaparte would have been finished.

**Arcola: The Scrambler in the Swamps**

At Verona, Napoleon conceived a bold plan: hold Verona with Macquard's 2600, who were to try to make it appear that the whole army was standing there; move south of the Adige to Ronco, cross the Alpone, and take Alvinczy in the rear at Villanuova or at San Bonifacio. He built his strike force to 19,000 by calling forces from the siege lines at Mantua and from Vaubois. Napoleon gambled that Davidovich would not move in force against Vaubois during the next week, and the gamble paid off. He also gambled that Wurmser was too weak to break out of Mantua, and again he was right.

On 13 November, engineers quietly journeyed to Ronco to make preparations for emplacing pontoon bridges. On the night of 14 November, the strike force, led as usual by the corps of Masséna and Augereau and accompanied by Guieu's brigade (from Vaubois), marched the 10 miles in rain and mud down the riverbank road to Ronco. Alvinczy, meanwhile, was massing before Verona, after detaching forces to the south to guard his flank and perhaps later to cross the Adige and flank Verona. The Austrian general considered the swamps north of the Adige in the Ronco-Arcola area to be impassable to a major attack force. Napoleon could not have known that, but he doubtless chose the area because it gave good odds for surprise for his flanking movement-envelopment. Otherwise, it makes no sense that he did

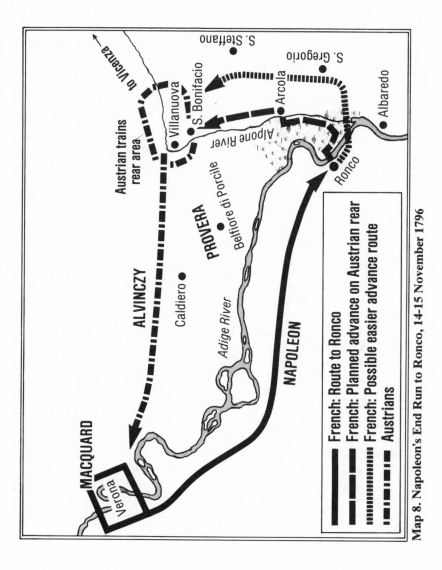

**Map 8. Napoleon's End Run to Ronco, 14-15 November 1796**

not choose to cross the Adige to the south, move a mere mile to the east, and attack Alvinczy's trains and rear over solid, hard ground.

On 15 November, Augereau and Masséna crossed the Adige from Ronco, again in the rain, into swamps where the men could move only along dikes about 35 feet wide and only a few feet above the marshes. Augereau made for the bridge at Arcola, from which he could strike for Villanuova, where the Austrian supply trains had stopped. Masséna headed for Belfiore, where at least one regiment of Provera's division had been reported. Marching confidently, Augereau was surprised by 3000 men under Divisio, who suddenly opened fire on him near Arcola. He rallied and attacked, trying to force the bridge again and again, but failed. Napoleon even came up and led a charge, which was thrown back, and in the confusion, he was thrown by his horse and rolled into a swamp. Masséna, meanwhile, drove the Austrians out of Belfiore but found his troops exhausted. At the same time, Guieu crossed the Adige on hastily floated pontoon bridges opposite Albaredo and marched on Arcola. But since Augereau had failed to cross the Alpone, he was without support, and his attack stalled.

At nightfall Bonaparte recalled them all to Ronco. Little had been gained except that Alvinczy had called off his attack on Verona, retreated toward Villanuova, and deployed more of his forces south and east to meet the threat on his flank. He knew where Bonaparte was but did not see his advantage. Apparently his only thought was to protect his communications and slow-moving trains. In short, Alvinczy considered himself in jeopardy and thought in terms of escaping, not attacking Bonaparte. Perhaps he could not believe that Napoleon was as vulnerable as he indeed was.

Defying logic, Napoleon ordered the same advances on 16 November, except that he kept Guieu's brigade in reserve. He could have taken advantage of Alvinczy's inactivity to throw a bridge across the Alpone, less wide and deep than the Adige, which Guieu had successfully crossed the day before. With the Alpone bridged, he could have thrown Guieu across, or a whole division, or his whole force. Once across the Alpone, he could have moved farther east—a mile or two, onto solid ground—and then attacked north, straight for the Verona-Vicenza-Trieste highway, bypassing the Austrians in the swamp at Arcola. But Bonaparte simply repeated his moves of the 15th. The result was much the same. Augereau was stopped at the Arcola bridge; Masséna drove Provera through Belfiore and toward Caldiero. At day's end, both were again ordered back to Ronco.

Alvinczy easily might have capitalized on Napoleon's situation. Once he discovered that most of the French army was in the swamp, he might have massed against Verona, or bypassed Verona and gone for Mantua. Mantua, after all, was his objective. That aside, the bulk of the Austrian army was 2 to 5 miles from Provera's division. He could have reinforced Provera, crushed Masséna, and then turned to what was left of the French army, either on the same day or the next. At all times, since Bonaparte divided his forces,

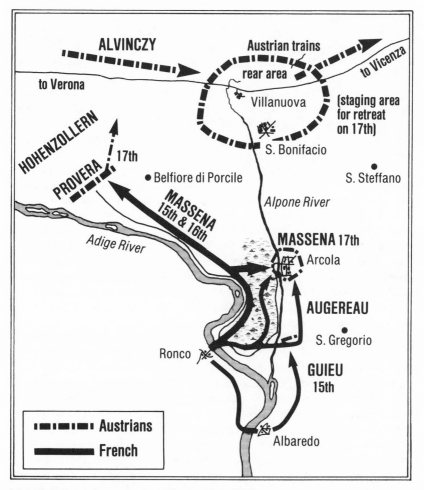

ALVINCZY

to Verona

Austrian trains

rear area

to Vicenza

Villanuova

(staging area
for retreat
on 17th)

S. Bonifacio

HOHENZOLLERN

PROVERA 17th

• Belfiore di Porcile

MASSENA
15th & 16th

Adige River

S. Steffano

Alpone River

MASSENA 17th

Arcola

AUGEREAU

S. Gregorio

Ronco

GUIEU
15th

Albaredo

Austrians

French

**Map 9. Battle of Arcola, 15-17 November 1796**

Alvinczy could have massed vastly superior numbers against either Masséna or Augereau. Instead, he ordered the bulk of his army toward Villanuova, and sent his supply trains toward Vicenza. He did reinforce his units at Arcola and along the Alpone to the south, but with numbers inferior to Napoleon's. In effect, they were to cover a retreat he had already begun. It is true that he had not heard from Davidovich, but this hardly excuses his timid behavior.

On the night of 16–17 November, Napoleon finally ordered a plan which might have ended the campaign days earlier. He had a bridge thrown across the Alpone. Augereau was to cross it on the morning of the 17th and drive for Arcola; Masséna would cross the Adige at Ronco, attack the bridge at Arcola, and detach a regiment to block Provera if he again approached from Belfiore. This plan worked.

On 17 November, Augereau's crossing went perfectly. Masséna's was delayed because Austrian forces from Arcola, displaying unusual initiative, blew one of the French pontoon bridges opposite Ronco early in the morning. It was soon repaired, however, and Masséna advanced on Arcola, reached the bridge, and then feigned being repulsed, with his battalions withdrawing according to a prearranged plan. The Austrians stormed across the bridge in triumph and some disorganization, only to be met by a sledgehammer counterattack. There was some confusion, during which Napoleon, according to Marmont, went forward with the troops, but stumbled, fell into a canal, and was dragged out by his aides. Masséna took the bridge and Arcola, and he and Augereau went into measured pursuit, pushing the Austrians before them.

At dawn the next day Alvinczy was apparently in full retreat on Trieste. Actually, he doubled back, but meanwhile Davidovich had been bloodied by Joubert (who took over Vaubois's division) with some help from Augereau, and retreated on Trent. On hearing of this Alvinczy withdrew to the east.

The battle of Arcola was touted as a great triumph, with many accounts giving Napoleon personal credit for leading the last attack on the bridge. Surely Jacques-Louis David's painting, "Bonaparte at the Bridge of Arcola," gives that impression. It was a triumph, no doubt. However, Alvinczy had handed it to Napoleon. If the Austrian commander had summoned the courage to throw all his forces against the "scrambler in the swamps," if he had had the imagination to cross the Adige and block Bonaparte's nightly withdrawals to Ronco, if he had thus trapped him in the swamps, the outcome surely would have been different. The victory at Arcola must be chalked up to the incompetence of Alvinczy—and to the stubbornness of Bonaparte.

Alvinczy then consolidated his forces east of Trent and again was reinforced to 50,000. In January 1797 he divided them, when he again marched to engage Bonaparte. With the main body of 28,000, he descended the Mincio toward Rivoli, leaving some 6500 to guard his rear. Bejalich, with 6000 men, marched via Bassano on Verona. To the south of him, Provera, with 9000, made for Legnago. As in his first attempt, if Alvinczy had attacked with his whole army, he might well have crushed Bonaparte, but he chose otherwise.

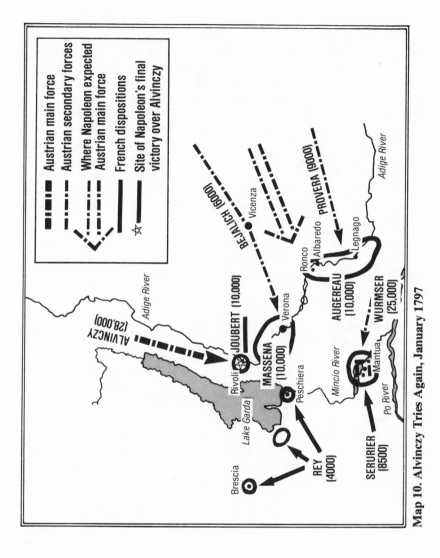

**Legend:**
- Austrian main force
- Austrian secondary forces
- Where Napoleon expected Austrian main force
- French dispositions
- Site of Napoleon's final victory over Alvinczy

ALVINCZY (28,000)

BEJALICH (6000)

Vicenza

PROVERA (9000)

Albaredo

Legnago

Adige River

Ronco

Adige River

JOUBERT (10,000)

Verona

AUGEREAU (10,000)

WURMSER (25,000)

Mincio River

Mantua

MASSENA (10,000)

Rivoli

Peschiera

Lake Garda

Adige River

Po River

SERURIER (8500)

REY (4000)

Brescia

**Map 10. Alvinczy Tries Again, January 1797**

Napoleon had fanned his forces out to guard the approaches to Mantua from north and east. Joubert (10,000) was north of Rivoli. Masséna (10,000) was at Verona. Augereau (10,000) was on the Adige between Ronco and Badia. Sérurier, replacing Kilmaine, commanded the Mantua siege lines with 8500 men. Rey, under Macquard, had 4000 in garrisons at Brescia, Peschiera, and elsewhere at the south end of Lake Garda. Again, the major formations were 40 to 70 miles apart. Moreover, Napoleon was not present initially to take command. When word of Alvinczy's advance reached him on 10 January, he was in Bologna, along with Lannes and 3000 men, engaged in intimidating the pope.

On 11 January, however, he was at Roverbella and received reports of contact with Austrian forces between Legnago and Badia. He jumped to the wrong conclusion, that Alvinczy's attack would be from the direction of Trieste again, whereas it was the advance guard of Provera's division which was skirmishing on Augereau's front. On 12 January Napoleon ordered Masséna and Augereau to prepare for an offensive from the east and ordered Rey, 75 miles to the west, to reinforce them, along with additional cavalry.

**Rivoli and Final Victory**

On 13 January, the truth dawned. Joubert reported that overwhelming enemy columns had forced him to retreat southward to the vicinity of Rivoli. Alvinczy was coming south, out of the Tyrol. Bonaparte quickly ordered Masséna to Rivoli and galloped ahead himself to join Joubert, arriving at 2:00 AM. He ordered Joubert to move at once to occupy the highest promontory just north of Rivoli, the hill of the Trombalora. It was secured in the predawn hours, and Joubert's 10,000 men were readied to give battle.

Napoleon attacked at dawn to keep the enemy off balance while he waited for Masséna to arrive. This could have been disastrous. However, Alvinczy's penchant for complicated maneuvers and detaching troops played into Napoleon's hands. The Austrian general faced Napoleon with only 12,000 men. He had sent Lusignon with 4500 far to the west, with orders to circle through the mountains and take the French in the rear. Quasdanovich (8000), on the near bank of the Mincio, had orders to march past the Trombalora and also attack the enemy in the rear. Vukassovich (3000) was in support of Quasdanovich, but on the far, or east, bank of the Mincio. Apparently, Alvinczy meant to surround and destroy the French.

Napoleon, however, attacked the three divisions in front of him (Liptay, 5000; Knoblos, 4000; Ocskay, 3000), exploiting gaping holes between them. At about 10:00 AM the old dependable, Masséna, came rolling through the winter mists with some 6000 men. The new infantry bolstered Joubert's men on the right, while Lasalle's cavalry, in mid-afternoon, broke the back of the enemy by crashing between Liptay and Knoblos and charging through the Austrian rear.

Meanwhile, the forces which Alvinczy had sent to attack the French rear also were defeated. Quasdanovich arrived south of Rivoli only to be set upon by Leclerc's cavalry (Masséna) and sent running back the way he had come. Observing Quasdanovich's withdrawal, Vukassovich retreated up the Mincio without ever engaging the French. The hapless Lusignon, arriving when the battle was already lost, was captured by Masséna's rear guard. The Austrians flooded northward. Murat, who had crossed Lake Garda with 600 cavalry in gunboats, galloped via the Mount Baldo road and reached the enemy's flank; he followed along, striking at will and running up the Austrian casualty and prisoner count by the hour. He continued the pursuit the next day, cooperating with Vaux's infantry brigade. Joubert's men, pushing the Austrians from the south, joined in.

In the south, Provera made a determined effort to drive through to Mantua but was stopped and surrounded by Augereau's corps (brigades of Lannes and Victor). Napoleon's division of forces, one could say, had paid off. Again, however, his victories at Rivoli and before Mantua were attributable in good part to Alvinczy's ineptitude.

After Rivoli, Alvinczy was replaced by the Archduke Charles, Austria's prize general. He was the brother of the emperor and young (twenty-seven), the same age as Napoleon, but he had justified his field marshal's baton against the French on the Rhine. He was to have 90,000 troops, evidence that the Austrians had finally recognized that, to win the war, Bonaparte had to be defeated. Italy became the main theater of war.

Meanwhile, on 2 February 1797, Wurmser surrendered Mantua to the French. He had held out valiantly for six months; his garrison had been reduced from 24,000 to 16,000 by disease and malnutrition. More soldiers were ill; 6000 civilians had died, and the death rate for both was increasing by the day. Wurmser had done his best. Napoleon refused to take his sword and paid tribute to his courage, a rare gesture for him. The old warrior was destined to die before the end of the year.

Wurmser's surrender freed Napoleon to fight Charles without the perpetual threat of the Mantua garrison in his rear. Moreover, when Charles took command in mid-February, he found only 44,000 troops, not 90,000, and his army was scattered and demoralized. The troops he had been promised from Austria and the armies in Germany had not arrived, and he had to fight with the remnants of Alvinczy's army. Napoleon gave him no chance to reorganize. He took the offensive in early March, moving in force over the Carnic Alps toward Vienna. His men covered 400 miles in 30 days, reaching Klagenfurt in Carinthia, where Charles made a last effort to stop him with only 10,000 men. The archduke's force was not wiped out, but he saw the hopelessness of the situation. On 7 April, Charles asked for an armistice, which was granted. Preliminaries of peace were signed at Leoben, in Styria, on 18 April. Although Austria did not make definitive peace until October, the war was over.

These victories made Napoleon a national hero in France and *stupor mundi*—the wonder of the world—elsewhere. In one year he had defeated five armies, each larger than his own. He had captured 160,000 prisoners. He had sent millions of francs in precious metals to Paris, together with priceless works of art. Since he had kept the Directory solvent and even had sent Augereau (September 1797) to support a coup d'état which preserved a moderate government, he had political clout as well as fame.[3]

If we look at his military errors, it is evident that Napoleon was not a seer who could divine the movements of the enemy from the start and plan his campaign flawlessly. He had no secret weapons, or even any new ones. He won because he never stopped going after the enemy. He did not brood over his mistakes and failures; he developed new plans to win or, as at Arcola, doggedly made a bad plan work. He never quit. He was a working general, studying his enemy and his maps through the night, visiting his units at all hours, and in some cases, as in Rivoli, moving them personally.

He also had exceptional subordinates, especially Masséna and Augereau, who were key men at all stages but early on gave Bonaparte the victories which built his faith in himself. With a candor which he lost in later years, he nicknamed Masséna "*L'Enfant chéri de la victoire.*" Indeed he was the man who sealed the victory in battle after battle, from Montenotte to Rivoli.

There was also, of course, the ineptitude of Napoleon's enemies. Beaulieu, Wurmser, and Alvinczy were all of the eighteenth century, trained in a more gentlemanly style of warfare. (The Archduke Charles had no chance.) They never understood Napoleon's overweening zeal to win, a zeal which made him fight night or day, on Sundays and holidays, in any weather, and never to ask for a truce. The Austrians were all nobles with social rank established by birth and military grade by birth and seniority. They lacked the sense of urgency of the scrambling soldier of the Revolution they faced. They commanded more nobles and careerists, though not professionals, since they regarded schooling as debasing; many of them were totally useless and even an impediment to operations.

Finally, whereas the Austrian soldier lacked motivation, Napoleon's men did not. The French soldier's zeal for "spreading liberty" was wearing thin but was more than compensated for by "careers open to talent": rapid promotions, increased pay, and the glory of serving Bonaparte, the all-time winner, in the bargain.

---

[3]The coup d'état of 18 Fructidor occurred because the elections of 1797 had returned a dangerous number of royalists to the legislature. Augereau took over command of troops in Paris and, with the help of Barras and two other sympathetic directors, expelled the royalists and sent the more prominent ones to prison or into exile. There were a few executions and suicides. The government was restored to its middle-of-the-road character, which it had preserved against Jacobins on the left and royalists on the right.

**Peace of Campo Formio**

Installed in the Palace of Mombello at Milan, Napoleon, surrounded by his family, therefore dictated peace to the diplomats of minor powers as if he were a king. He also controlled the negotiation of peace with Austria, signed at Campo Formio in October 1797. The Treaty of Campo Formio dealt Austria severe blows, which some historians (including Georges Lefebvre) think made it an irreconcilable enemy of France—one who would declare war every time it regained its strength. By this thesis, the stage was set for Napoleon's wars even before he became head of state, and his later settlements with Austria, always made after victorious campaigns, only made matters worse.

Austria recognized French possession of the Austrian Netherlands (Belgium) and the west bank of the Rhine, both conquered earlier by the armies of the French Republic. Austria also recognized the Batavian Republic (Holland, or properly the former United Provinces of the Netherlands), a "sister republic" of France created in 1795, and the newly established Cisalpine Republic, sponsored by Bonaparte in northern Italy. France was also to have a part in the remapping of Germany, made necessary to compensate princes who had lost territory on the west bank of the Rhine.

In return, Austria got Venetia, which had peacefully admitted Napoleon's troops, only to be conquered. However, the Ionian Islands, outposts of Venetian trade off the Greek coast, were given to France. The excuse was a need for naval bases in the Mediterranean. However, some historians (including Emile Bourgeois) have attributed this provision to Napoleon's fixation on the East, his desire to be a new Alexander the Great. Perhaps. His next exploit, promoted by Bonaparte himself, would indeed be in the Middle East.

But first, in December 1797, he returned to Paris. He was received as a conquering hero and elected to the Institut National, where he took his seat among France's leading writers, artists, scientists, and intellectuals. All this frightened the directors, who suspected he had political ambitions. (He did, but judged the time not ripe to act.) They offered him command of an army forming at Boulogne to invade England. He refused it. He asked instead to lead an invasion of Egypt, and the Directory shortly decided it was wise to let him do so, if only to get him away from Paris—far, far away.

# 3

# FLIRTING WITH OBLIVION
*Egypt, 1798–99*

## The Expedition

Bonaparte's campaign in Egypt involved no blundering to glory. The entire affair was a blunder, a waste, and accomplished nothing, militarily or in terms of the power balance. Of glory there was none. Even the victories were over enemies with weapons so primitive and organization so faulty as to be foredrawn. That is not to say that Bonaparte's men did not suffer and die; they did, in full measure. All the same, it was an unexampled romantic adventure in the public's eye. It put Paris agog over Egypt and things Egyptian. It produced reports of victories over enemies conceived as exotic and mysterious, and thus formidable. Of that Bonaparte made good use—so good that he emerged as the ruler of France.

Initially, of course, the Directory believed there was a convincing rationale for the expedition. Both the foreign minister, Charles-Maurice de Talleyrand-Périgord, and Bonaparte thought that the best way to strike at the British— the only power still at war with France—was to strike at Egypt. It was part of the Ottoman Empire but actually ruled by the Mamelukes, once the elite troops of the pasha and for over three hundred years the ruling caste. Talleyrand was to travel to Constantinople and convince the Porte that Bonaparte would restore the sultan's power in Egypt. With or without Turkish cooperation, if France held Egypt, its navy could better challenge British control of the Mediterranean and wreak havoc on Britain's trade with the Ottoman Empire, Persia, and, to a degree, India. (Some Indian goods were carried overland to Middle Eastern ports; there was as yet no Suez canal.) If the sultan cooperated, Bonaparte felt certain he could march to India, or to the shores of the Indian Ocean, where units of the French fleet could carry him to India.

Talleyrand and Napoleon presented this scheme to the Institut and the Directory, and it was approved. The directors believed they could risk a small army—35,000 men—on the off chance that Bonaparte would perform miracles again, as he had in Italy. Defeat would hardly ruin France and might even have the benefit of ridding the Directory of Napoleon, a valuable general but clearly a dangerous threat if he chose to enter politics.

Napoleon began organizing his expedition at Toulon in March 1798. He chose for commanders mostly younger generals (he preferred men on the make); some of them had served him in Italy, including Lannes and Murat; others were volunteers. He retained Berthier as chief of staff, but Masséna and Augereau were not available: Masséna had an army command in Switzerland; Augereau had the equivalent in Paris and was a national legislator in the Council of Five Hundred as well. He was given 35,000 good troops, and the army eventually was fairly well supplied and equipped, but not lavishly. There were some gross deficiencies. For example, it had only 1350 horses; of these, 700 were needed for the cavalry, and the remaining 650 were not adequate for the artillery and baggage trains.

Playing the role of soldier-intellectual and polishing his image to ensure that his deeds would be chronicled, Napoleon had Gaspard Monge and Claude Berthollet, a mathematician and a chemist, recruit a coterie of scientists, cartographers, writers, and artists. The London *Times*, which had its own spies at Toulon, was impressed both with the size of the force and the civilian contingent: "An immense number of infantry, with artillery, vast quantities of mortars, furnace bombs, grape and cannister shot, with ammunition and *men of letters* have been put on board."[1] The expedition sailed from Toulon on 19 May 1798. Almost four hundred transports carried the troops and supplies; they were escorted by 13 ships-of-the-line (50 guns or more) and 4 frigates. The naval commander was Admiral François-Paul Brueys d'Aigailliers, whose flagship, *L'Orient*, with 120 guns, was the most heavily armed ship in the world.

The British, well-informed about the expedition by numerous spies around Toulon, knew when it sailed. War Secretary Henry Dundas knew that Bonaparte was bound for Egypt, but he could not convince the whole ministry. Thus Admiral John Jervis, Earl of St. Vincent and commander of the British Mediterranean fleet, was told that his first priority was to protect Naples, but that the French expedition might instead go to Spain, Portugal, or Egypt. St. Vincent ordered Admiral Horatio Nelson, with a part of the fleet (14 ships-of-the-line, 7 frigates), to find and destroy Bonaparte's expedition at sea. Nelson himself elected to watch the coast of Egypt. He was there when the French would have arrived, in mid-June, had they made no stops.

Bonaparte, however, did stop. To please French commercial interests and the navy (which needed bases) and to secure his line of communication home, he captured and garrisoned Malta. It was easily taken from the show troops of the Knights of St. John, who had ruled it since the time of the Crusades. Organizing a military government delayed the expedition for a week. Meanwhile, Nelson had sailed to Sicily for supplies and was absent

---

[1]London *Times*, 5 June 1798.

when the French reached Alexandria. The Malta stop had been an insane move on an already insane expedition, considering British naval superiority in the Mediterranean.[2] But the Bonaparte luck held.

On 1 July, the expedition landed at Marabout, near Alexandria. The ships had to anchor several miles at sea, and the men were rowed ashore, some landing very seasick. There was no opposition. Napoleon immediately sent 5000 men against Alexandria and seized the city. Then, with 15,000 troops, he struck out for El Rahmaniya across the desert, where he and the soldiers suffered terribly. The men's clothing was too heavy, they had no canteens, and they had to slog along in deep sand under a blazing sun; those who discarded clothing, however, froze at night. Nevertheless, some 1000 men short, Napoleon reached his rendezvous at El Rahmaniya in ten days. General Louis Desaix, an enthusiastic volunteer of about Napoleon's age, brought the remaining 10,000 troops, covered by gunboats, up the Nile.

On 13 July, just north of El Rahmaniya at Shubra Khit, Napoleon found Murad Bey with 10,000 Mamelukes ready to give battle. (Murad and another Mameluke chief, Ibrahim Bey, ruled Egypt.) The Mamelukes, all cavalrymen, originally had been European boy-slaves, mostly from the Balkans or Greece, bought in the slave markets of the Middle East and raised as Moslems and fighters. They replenished their ranks the same way. Great horsemen and fierce fighters, they were hampered by the medieval style of their weapons— the scimitar, ball and chain, spiked mace, and dagger—plus a few antique firearms which they were reluctant to use, since they saw closing with the enemy and seeing his blood flow the honorable way of combat. Marmont recorded an anecdote about Murad Bey's reaction to the news of the French landing: "'Are they on horseback?' he asked. The reply was that they were on foot. 'Ha, good,' he said. 'My household alone will be enough to destroy them, and I will cut off their heads like watermelons in the fields.'"

### Battles of Shubra Khit and the Pyramids

Murad was innocent of the effects of modern firepower. Napoleon had devised formations to use it to the maximum. He positioned his five understrength divisions in squares, with cannon in the corners, initially outside, firing and retreating within the squares, to emerge and fire again as opportunity offered (when the enemy was not too close). The infantry was five or six ranks deep,

---

[2]British naval power was overwhelming, although Nelson had not yet demonstrated the fact. The British navy had almost 200 ships-of-the-line and 300 other warships, versus about 70 and 150 for the French. Thus the expedition's best chance of reaching Egypt was to run at top speed. Admiral Brueys had, in fact, about as many ships as Nelson, and more firepower, but he did not know that. Moreover, assuming that Brueys was capable of defeating Nelson, warship to warship, he probably would have lost many of his 400 virtually unarmed cargo and transport vessels, so that many, if not most, of the troops would have perished.

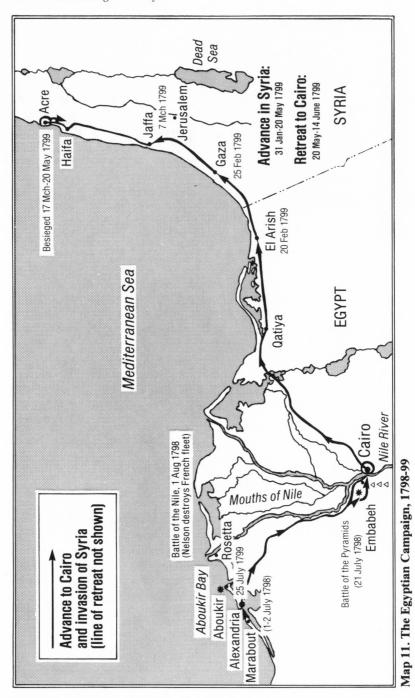

**Map 11. The Egyptian Campaign, 1798-99**

with the front rank kneeling, firing, and being replaced by the second, and so forth. The Mamelukes charged bravely but were decimated by French cannon and musketry and, after a few charges, they suddenly withdrew, in a great cloud of dust, as if by common signal. They had elected to find reinforcements and fight another day. Harder fighting took place in the Nile between French and Egyptian gunboats; that ended quickly, too, when Napoleon brought up field artillery to support his gunboats, and the French scored a lucky hit and blew up an enemy munitions ship. The French killed numbered 20, with some 50 wounded, while the Egyptians lost several hundred killed and wounded.

The French marched ahead toward Cairo. At Embabeh, on 21 July, they found the enemy awaiting them. On the west side of the river, directly facing Bonaparte's army, were 6,000 Mamelukes under Murad Bey, backed by 20,000 entrenched Egyptian infantry, strengthened by a few Turks. To their rear and barely involved, as it turned out, were some 14,000 Arab horsemen. Across the Nile, under Ibrahim Bey, were 6,000 Mamelukes and another 14,000 Egyptian infantry, bringing the total enemy force to 60,000 troops. Murad had 40,000 men; Ibrahim, 20,000; but Ibrahim already was preparing to retreat into Syria and gave Murad scant help. As the more cold-blooded pragmatist, Ibrahim meant to secure Turkish aid in Syria and return to become sole ruler.

There ensued the Battle of the Pyramids. "Soldiers, forty centuries look down upon you," went Napoleon's famous allocution. In fact, the Pyramids were not in sight, but it mattered little. Again, Napoleon put his army in five division squares and actually ordered them forward, off and on, in that formation. His plan was to push forward his two right-wing divisions, echeloned to the right, cave in the enemy left, and push the enemy into the Nile. Desaix, commanding the lead division, did move onto the enemy flank.

Unlike the action at Shubra Khit, this battle was bloody, especially for the Mamelukes, who charged repeatedly. When they rested, Napoleon shoved his divisions forward, and the Mamelukes—largely Murad's, reinforced sporadically by volunteers from Ibrahim's—charged again until they were bled beyond endurance. The Egyptian infantry barely moved; the Arabs made only disorganized attacks.[3] Throughout, regimental bands blared the *Marseillaise* and other march favorites from relatively safe positions within the squares. As the sun set, the French were again the winners. Some 2000 Mamelukes were killed (almost none were taken alive, wounded or not), and there were 3000 to 5000 Egyptian casualties. The French casualty count was 300.

The French, and not least Napoleon, were mightily impressed with the Mamelukes. They had broken into the squares often and, when their horses

---

[3]The Egyptian peasants were "rice soldiers," with no intention of dying unnecessarily for their alien Mameluke masters. The Arabs were nomads, personally brave and even bloodthirsty, but with strong loyalties only to their clans and a chronic inability to cooperate above that level. Moreover, they did not love the Mamelukes, either.

were shot from under them, had hit the ground fighting, and they had fought on to the death with scimitar, dagger, or whatever weapon available. It was as if they had to be killed over and over. They were motivated in part by the tenet of Islam that guaranteed immediate access to heaven for those killed in battle. (And it was not a heaven of clouds and harps but of harems of beautiful girls, attentive to the warrior's every wish.) Their colorful dress also impressed Bonaparte: turbans, silk shirts with blousing sleeves, embroidered vests. Napoleon's sense of showmanship demanded that he recruit some of them, an exotic element on parade, for his bodyguard and later for the Consular and Imperial Guard. There were never more than 100, however, since they were so savage and difficult to discipline. One of the best-known figures of the next fifteen years would be Napoleon's personal Mameluke, Roustan, a giant sinister figure always behind his master, on foot or on horseback, turbaned and scowling, scimitar at the ready.

After the engagement at Embabeh, Murad Bey retreated up the Nile. Napoleon sent Desaix in pursuit, and he eventually demolished Murad's force at Sadiman, then drove him into total disarray beyond Aswan. Ibrahim Bey retreated into Syria, where he joined forces with the Turkish governor. Napoleon occupied Cairo, but he had barely arrived when there was shocking news from the coast. On 1 August, Admiral Nelson had returned to the mouth of the Nile at Aboukir Bay, found Admiral Brueys's fleet, and blown it to pieces.

### Battle of the Nile

Nelson sailed in with 14 ships-of-the-line and a number of smaller vessels. Brueys had 13 ships-of-the-line, but greater firepower. On Nelson's approach, the French admiral anchored his fleet in the shallows along the coast, too close, he thought, for the British to get behind him. He hoped this maneuver would make them sail along his line, where he could blast them away, though firing from only one side of his ships. They would be broadside and vulnerable, and he had more guns. His flagship, *L'Orient*, for example, had 120 guns, 60 on each side; 60 was more than the total on most of the British ships. His logic seemed impeccable, but he had committed a fatal error.

The British swarmed in head-on, as Brueys had expected, but many of them shot the gaps between his vessels and penetrated his line. The French ships thus were fired on from both sides, with devastating results. Eleven ships-of-the-line were sunk or burned; only two escaped, along with two frigates, to Malta. *L'Orient* itself was sunk; Admiral Brueys was killed. Nelson did not lose a single ship. French seapower in the Mediterranean and worldwide was drastically reduced. Since France had only a total of about 70 ships-of-the-line in commission, Nelson had eliminated one-sixth of them in one day.

The British victory, combined with the declaration by the Ottoman sultan of a holy war against the French, sparked off a rebellion in Cairo. The French were caught unawares, since the Egyptians, inured by hundreds of years of servitude, had seemed totally beaten, submissive, and eager to serve the new conqueror. Suddenly the people rose up, killed Frenchmen in the streets and groups of them detached from their units, and attacked French hospitals, killing the sick and setting the buildings on fire.

Napoleon put his army on the streets. Assisted by some Mamelukes who had attached themselves to him, he quickly defeated and killed any Egyptians fighting in the open. Informers (for pay, of course) appeared in legion, as if by magic. With their help, the French ran down anyone with arms; they entered buildings and homes, searched out rebels, and usually shot them on the spot. Since the French had been attacked so barbarously, the troops showed little mercy, and their officers did little to deter them. The revolt died quickly, but Napoleon's expedition to Syria was delayed for some months until he was certain of his control of Egypt. Especially, he waited until Desaix signaled from Upper Egypt that Murad Bey was no longer a threat.

## The Campaign in Syria

On 10 February 1799, Bonaparte began the march into Syria with 13,000 men and 52 field guns. In preparation, he sent an ultimatum (and published it for the benefit of his own troops) to the military governor of Syria, Ahmed Pasha Djezzar, "the Butcher." He also sent a message to the only Indian prince who was fighting successfully against the British, Tippoo Sahib of Mysore, in which he said that he, General Bonaparte, would soon arrive to support Tippoo with an "invincible army." Before the message arrived, the future Duke of Wellington had defeated Tippoo and restored British control.

On 3 March, Bonaparte took Jaffa, after three days of fighting against the Turkish garrison. Although the population of Syria was predominantly Arab, the garrisons were manned by Turks, representing the Ottoman ruler. The French captured 2000 to 2500 Turks, and Napoleon was startled to discover that nearly half of them previously had been captured in Egypt at El Arish, in a lesser engagement, and freed on parole with the understanding that they would not fight against the French again.

Napoleon had fewer than 13,000 men at this point. Many of his troops had contracted the plague, and more were dying every day. He could not spare troops to guard prisoners, much less escort them back to Egypt. The Turks already had demonstrated that they could not be trusted on parole. If he freed them they would undoubtedly turn up to fight him at some place ahead or strike at his men as they marched. And considering the size of his force, 2500 enemies were not a negligible number. It almost came down to a choice between killing them and marching on, or calling off the expedition. Accordingly, Bonaparte had the prisoners shot, a decision made easier for him by the fact that the Turks had shown no mercy to French soldiers and in fact had usually tortured them to death. Naturally, British propagandists made the most of the incident, picturing Napoleon as consistently callous and cruel. In reality, he was adopting the morality of his enemy. He was never guilty of such behavior during his campaigns in Europe.

Napoleon visited the hospitals, exposing himself to the plague and stating repeatedly, with seeming conviction, that the disease would not strike anyone who did not fear it. Since he was not infected, he accomplished his purpose, to reduce his men's fear of the plague. This, in turn, reduced their fear of the desert and made them more willing to resume the campaign. Leaving a detachment to guard the sick, he marched on to Acre, 300 miles into Syria.

On 17 March, Bonaparte's army laid siege to Acre. He was at a disadvantage because he lacked siege artillery (44-, 24-, and 16-pounders and heavy mortars), which he had unwisely sent by sea. The guns had been captured by a British squadron commanded by Sir Sidney Smith. Moreover, Acre was an ancient fortress, antedating the Crusades, but held and strengthened by European Crusaders. Its stone walls were impervious to field artillery, and it was defended by 250 guns.

The defense was well commanded for the Turkish pasha by Colonel Antoine Le Picard de Phélypeaux, a French émigré who had been at the Ecole Militaire with Napoleon. With only field artillery and short of ammunition, Bonaparte was reduced to staging infantry assaults on the walls, which failed. His efforts were interrupted by the approach of the Turkish Army of Damascus, which he defeated in the Battle of Mount Tabor, but with losses of several hundred men and much time. Throughout, Smith's gunboats harassed the French along the coast. To add to Napoleon's troubles, his men were again dropping from the plague.

When in mid-May he heard that Smith was ferrying a Turkish army to Egypt, Napoleon had to break off the siege. He marched on 20 May, after giving orders (which were disobeyed) to administer lethal doses of drugs to the worst-off plague victims. He was certain that the Turks would torture them. Of his original 13,000 men, 2500 were dead (half of disease), and another 2500 were sick or wounded; half of these did not reach Egypt.

### Battle of Aboukir

Back in Egypt in early June, Bonaparte could assemble only 7,700 men and 17 guns to meet the Turks—20,000 men under Mustafa Pasha—who had already landed at Aboukir. Had the Turks been aggressive, they might have taken Cairo before Napoleon arrived and picked up local support and French hostages. However, they had dug in for a defensive battle; presumably, if they won, they would then move to recapture Egypt for the sultan. The Turks had come ashore on 10 July, occupied the fortress of Aboukir at the tip of a narrow peninsula, and formed two defensive lines, one behind the other. The first line, nearest the French, was about a mile and one-half before Fort Aboukir and was anchored on two fortified hills, with an undefended gap between. The second, about 600 yards from the fort, spanned the narrower part of the peninsula—about 1000 yards—and was a solid line of defenses. Some 5000 men were in Fort Aboukir, 7000 in the second line, and 8000 in the first. They were supported by 30 guns and gunboats along both shores of the peninsula.

On 25 July at dawn, Napoleon attacked, sending Lannes's division against the fort on the French right, Destaing's against the fort on the left. Murat, with the cavalry, waited for the infantry attacks to take hold, then swept through the gap between the forts, undermining the defenders on first one and then the other. The Turks fled; many were cut down or driven into the sea as they retreated, but most reached the second line. The French infantry advanced, but the heavily manned, short, second line held until Napoleon sent forward the artillery, which managed to bombard and force the enemy to abandon a 200-yard stretch at the western end of the line. Murat and his cavalry swept through the gap, turned the Turkish position, and drove the enemy into the sea, cutting and slashing "until the waves frothed with blood." Fort Aboukir held out until 2 August, but the Turks were really beaten in one day. The final count showed they had lost 2000 killed in action and 11,000 drowned; 5000 were prisoners of war, and 2000 more were missing and unaccounted for.

Smith negotiated for the withdrawal of the prisoners, who included Mustafa Pasha. During the talks, as a matter of courtesy (one gentleman to another, and all that), Smith passed to Napoleon copies of the London *Times*. Perhaps Smith also wanted Bonaparte to know that French arms were not doing well everywhere. At any rate, Napoleon learned from the newspapers that France was being hit hard by a new coalition of Britain, Austria, Russia, Turkey, and lesser powers. All Italy had been lost to Austrian forces; the last French outpost was at Genoa. An Anglo-Russian force had invaded the Netherlands, and Russian forces were in Switzerland.

## Return to Paris

Bonaparte decided that he must return to France. His ego was such that he thought only he could save the nation—and that it was time, finally, for him to enter politics. He had no orders,[4] but he was willing to risk a court-martial.

---

[4]The Directory had sent orders, which Napoleon had not received, to return with his army, an impossibility. For most of his first sojourn in Egypt, Napoleon and his army were, in

He was determined to go. No glory was to be won in Egypt; the expedition had been a dragging disaster, lightened by a few ego-boosting victories. No foreign policy goal had been gained, nothing but loss of men and money. The scholars traveling with the expedition had established the science of Egyptology—it was seen in retrospect—but that was about all.

Napoleon had two ships prepared and alerted the key officers he wanted to take with him, along with some of the scientists. On 24 August he sailed with Berthier, Lannes, Murat, and others for France. He left sealed orders for General Jean-Baptiste Kléber to take command of the army.[5] It was a harrowing journey. The ships, becalmed and easy prey for the British navy, hung off Egypt for almost two weeks. The Bonaparte luck held, however, and they finally were away. After a stop in Corsica, they landed at Fréjus, near Cannes, on 9 October. Naturally, the news of the Battle of Aboukir arrived simultaneously and was presented as a triumph in the best Bonaparte style. Napoleon was cheered as a conquering hero in every village and town en route to Paris, where he arrived on 15 October. The Directory, in which his "desertion" had been discussed, had lost the will to discipline him or even mention his willful independence.

On his arrival in Paris Napoleon was immediately contacted by the Revisionists, who publicly advocated revising the constitution to strengthen the executive. Actually they meant to replace the government of the Directory— by legislative action if possible, or by coup d'état, using military force, if necessary. The chief Revisionist was a director, the wily ex-Abbé Emmanuel Sieyès, a force in every government since 1789; the plotters included another director, Roger Ducos; the foreign minister, Talleyrand; the minister of police, Joseph Fouché; and Napoleon's brothers Joseph and Lucien. Sieyès picked Napoleon to be his "sword" (i.e., command the military), for which service Bonaparte was to be Grand Elector for Life in the new government, a surrogate king with ceremonial duties. Civilian consuls—Sieyès and others—were to rule.

Napoleon and the Revisionists had the support of most of the Council of Elders, the upper house of the legislature, and at least half of the Council of Five Hundred, the lower house. The intelligentsia (Madame de Staël, Benjamin Constant, René de Chateaubriand et al.) had been won over by Joseph Bonaparte, who was one of them. This didn't last, of course; Napoleon and the *idéologues* soon clashed. The propertied classes (bourgeois and noble)

---

effect, stranded. His communications with Paris were severed, and for a year he received almost no messages from the French government.

[5]What happened to Napoleon's army? Kléber took over, as ordered. He was assassinated by a Syrian fanatic in 1800. His post then was filled by General Jacques-François Menou, who, while serving in Egypt, became a Moslem and called himself Abd Allah Menou. Menou was defeated by a British expedition commanded by General Sir Ralph Abercromby in March 1801 and fell captive with his army. The survivors were repatriated during negotiations with the British which led to the Peace of Amiens (1802).

were generally supportive, since law and order had broken down and a strong government would benefit them. The officer corps and the army were convinced the war was being mismanaged. Most of the French people were merely weary, after ten years of revolution, one government after another, disorder, bloodshed, and war. When a strong leader appeared, they followed him; when he established a stable government, they gave him support.

The Revisionists' plot resulted in the coup d'état of 18–19 Brumaire (9–10 November 1799). On the first day, under threat of a fictitious Jacobin plot, the Elders gave Napoleon command of troops in Paris and called a conference of both councils for the next day. On the second day, meeting in the palace of Saint-Cloud, the Revisionists asked the councils for authority to write a new constitution. The Five Hundred had angry members, however, who crowded forward toward the podium when Napoleon tried to speak. He was surrounded and either fainted or, more probably, was knocked out by the press of legislators. He was carried out by grenadiers and recovered quickly.

It was Lucien Bonaparte, however, who became the hero of the day. He left the Five Hundred, of which he was president, when the ruckus started and ran into the courtyard, where lines of soldiers stood on guard. Jumping on a horse, he rode before them, shouting that the palace was full of assassins and Jacobins who must be driven out. They must save the Republic and trust General Bonaparte, he told them. Waving a sword, he promised to plunge it into Napoleon's heart if he betrayed the Republic. The troops went in and sent all the legislators flying, out doors and windows, through the gardens and away.

These actions were more violent than most of the plotters had wanted. To give the proceedings some semblance of legality, they recalled such legislators as would come to meet in evening session. This rump of the councils approved the writing of a new constitution by Sieyès, Ducos, and Napoleon, who were called provisional consuls.

Bonaparte then showed amazing political acumen by outwitting the veteran Sieyès. He insisted that committees of the two councils should approve the constitution and then the councils themselves, before the document was submitted to the people. This put the old legislators on his side. Napoleon then worked with Ducos and Sieyès on what was basically Sieyès's own constitution. At the same time, however, he encouraged the councils' committees to frame their own version, and they did, led by the liberal Pierre-Claude Daunou, heavily influenced by Napoleon. When the consuls and committees met, Daunou's constitution was approved. For all practical purposes it was Napoleon's. The French people shortly approved it overwhelmingly in a plebiscite.

The Constitution of the Year VIII, promulgated in December 1799, made Napoleon Bonaparte (by name) First Consul of France, the chief executive. Jean-Jacques Régis de Cambacérès and Pierre Lebrun were named

Second and Third Consuls but acted merely as Napoleon's advisers. Sieyès and Ducos were relegated to the Senate, which was appointive, but were allowed to help Napoleon choose the first thirty members. Universal manhood suffrage was established, but only for electors who, moreover, only supplied lists from which the Senate picked legislators for the new two houses, the Tribunat and Corps Législatif.

The government was Bonaparte. For the next fifteen years, as consul, then emperor, he ruled with his appointive Senate. He named advisers to his council of state, which proposed the laws. The laws were passed by legislative bodies chosen by the Senate, which he appointed. He chose ministers, prefects of departments, and administrators down to mayors of cities, officials of police, and commissioned officers of the army and navy. He had, in short, more power than the Bourbon kings. He was too canny a governor, however, not to have his major acts approved in national plebiscite, or to fail to cultivate his senators and legislators with praise and rewards. He did not believe in government by the people, or even by or with their chosen representatives, although he believed that he governed for the people. He thought any ruler a fool who did not listen to the people and their representatives.

From the beginning, he worked at improving his base of support among the leaders, eventually called the *notables*, of all sectors of society. Early on, he allowed political exiles to return—Jacobins and aristocrats alike—except for the former royal family, the Bourbons, and their most fanatic supporters. He then worked to form an amalgam of leadership among nobles of the Old Regime; new nobles, whom he created while emperor; and up-and-coming members of the middle class, whether in business or the administration. In this he was very successful. Toward the end of his reign as emperor, the business and banking communities were behind him, together with the great landholders, and the sons of old nobles, new nobles, and bourgeois *notables* were vying to serve him. But for his military reverses, beginning in 1812, his dynasty might have survived, a proposition which this book will not attempt to prove. We must concentrate on the campaigns.

# 4

# *OVER THE ALPS*
## *The Second Italian Campaign, 1800*

### The Hannibal Act

Once the Consulate was established, Napoleon returned to war. In the spring of 1800 he embarked on the Second Italian Campaign, again against Austria, the only power on the continent holding out against France. Napoleon decided to fight again in Italy, where he had been successful before and where he felt certain he was not expected. In fact, he hoped that the Austrians did not expect to see him at all. He had publicized the "fact" that, as first consul, he was prohibited by the constitution from going to war, which was not true— and if it had been, Napoleon probably would have gone anyway.

The Austrians indeed did not expect a French offensive in Italy. Their intelligence told them that the French already had all the troops they could muster in the field. Most were on the Rhine in Germany; those on the Italian front were besieged in Genoa; there were a few in the Alps between. The Austrians expected the French to concentrate on an attack in Germany, down the Danube, the traditional route to Vienna.

Napoleon conceived the circus play of taking an army across the Alps and dropping into Italy at the rear of the Austrian army, which was besieging Genoa. To hold Genoa, the anvil for his hammer, he sent Masséna, *"L'Enfant chéri"* of the First Italian Campaign. Bonaparte's inspiration, no doubt, came from ancient history: the example of Hannibal. No one had attempted quite such a march since Roman times. Strategically, Napoleon saw the French dispositions against Austria as on a single front stretching from the north of the Danube to Genoa, from Germany to the Italian Riviera and the Mediterranean. In that context, his strike across the Alps would be a penetration of the Austrian center, which, he expected, would throw all Austrian field forces into disarray.

He gave Berthier, his chief of staff, the task of finding and assembling 60,000 troops in the vicinity of Dijon, near the Alpine passes. Berthier, ever faithful, did the job. Furthermore, he equipped the army to cross the Alps with special clothing, shoes, snowshoes, and rations. Some items proved useless, for example, sledges manufactured to carry the cannon. They were too cumbersome, and the cannon instead were dragged in hollowed-out logs. Generally, however, the army was more than ready to march by late April 1800, when Napoleon arrived on the scene.

On 15 May, after the snows began to break in the mountain passes, he ordered the army to march. The main body crossed the Great Saint-Bernard Pass, with Bonaparte following on a mule, a beast hardy and sure of foot, not the fiery grey stallion of the David painting. The army reached the crest of the pass with relative ease and was treated to cheese and wine by the monks of the Abbey of Saint-Bernard. Beyond, however, Austrian garrisons had to be dislodged, which was no great task except at Bard, where a fort on a commanding pinnacle dominated the road. In the end it was bypassed, but all the guns except six had to be left behind, along with some cavalry, which could not travel the narrow ledges and paths with the infantry. It was two weeks before the fort at Bard was reduced and Napoleon's artillery, essential to his functioning, could follow.

Meanwhile, the first consul emerged onto the plain of Lombardy on 30 May. On 2 June he was in Milan, where he restored the Cisalpine Republic (now styled the Italian Republic) and received the cheers of the multitudes, who hated the Austrians. He also directed the scrounging up of additional cannon and put available forces on the march toward the Po and Lodi, on the Adda. Above all, he did not want the Austrians, pinned down at Genoa by Masséna's resistance, to escape to Mantua again.

## Masséna Loses Genoa

Masséna meanwhile had held tenaciously to Genoa, tying up the major Austrian field army until Bonaparte crossed the Alps. He personally had commanded the Genoa garrison of 10,000 men; the rest of his Army of Italy (17,500) was at Nice. When Napoleon began his march over the Alps in mid-May, the Austrian commander in Italy, Field Marshal Michael Friedrich Melas, had 51,000 men fighting Masséna: 21,000 surrounding Genoa and 30,000 between Nice and Genoa. (Melas had a total of 128,000 troops in Italy, but most were in the Quadrilateral forts and garrisons across northern Italy.) By 31 May, on news of Napoleon's approach, he had pulled some of his troops back from Nice (they would not be visiting France after all) but kept the pressure on Masséna at Genoa.

Masséna's men were wasting away on a daily diet of a few ounces of horsemeat and bread laced with straw. On 4 June, he took his last chance to surrender on good terms—to march out with his men under arms—and gave over the city to the Austrians. Only 6,500 of his original 10,000 men had survived, and many were barely able to march. In a few days they would have had to surrender unconditionally. Melas guessed as much, but he was willing to grant terms because he wanted to garrison Genoa himself, so that he would be more free to concentrate on Bonaparte. Masséna's troops from Nice, reduced to 14,000 but in fair shape, were moving to join him; his army constituted a psychological threat to the Austrians who, when they learned Napoleon was in Milan, feared being caught between the two forces. This, in fact, was what Bonaparte had hoped for. But Masséna could not deliver with his half-dead troops. Napoleon would have to fight this campaign without his old comrade.

Napoleon, in Milan, did not hear of Masséna's loss of Genoa until 8 June, four days after it occurred. At first, he refused to believe it. *L'Enfant chéri* had carried out his orders, but Bonaparte had expected more—a miracle. When he did accept the fact, however, he accelerated his plans to move south and west, toward Genoa, so as not to allow Melas to escape. Napoleon was not deterred from moving by the fact that he had only 28,000 of his troops available out of 60,000 in northern Italy. He wanted a quick and spectacular victory to strengthen his new government and nail down his control of France.

On familiar ground, his ego inflated by the plaudits of the Milanese, Bonaparte was not as wary as he might have been. He badly underestimated his Austrian opponent. Field Marshal Melas was seventy-one, but his brain had not rotted. Leaving 10,000 men at Genoa and garrisons at Turin and elsewhere, he ordered the rest of his army to concentrate at Alessandria, about half way between Genoa and Milan. By 10 June he had 34,000 men there, heavy on cavalry and artillery, and was ready to give battle.

Napoleon, in a fairly leisurely fashion, took off from Milan and swept to the south and west, in the general direction of Genoa. He arrived east of Alessandria, on the far side of the Bormida River, late on 13 June. He had reports from cavalry scouts and French divisions, who had captured Austrian prisoners, north of him and in the Alps, that Melas was directing his units to Alessandria, but he had a fixed notion that the Austrians did not believe he meant to give battle there. To be safe, however, Napoleon sent out scouts to see if the bridges over the Bormida were up. Reports came back that all the bridges had been destroyed or removed.

Napoleon accepted the scouts' word without ordering a double check because it confirmed what he already thought: Melas would not fight. Knowing the slow and cautious ways of the Austrian army as he believed he did, he did not see how the force in Alessandria could be ready to fight. With Genoa in Austrian hands, he expected Melas either to make for that city, where he might be protected indefinitely by the British fleet, or east toward the Quadrilateral. With that in mind, he dispatched two sizable forces to block the two routes: a reduced division (about 3500) to Piacenza, a crossing point of the Po River, and Desaix's corps (2 divisions) to block the roads to Genoa. One division (Monnier) went toward Garofoli, while Desaix personally led his second division toward Novi. Napoleon thus deprived himself of some 12,000 men. On 14 June, when Melas hit Napoleon with 34,000 Austrian troops,

Napoleon had only 15,000 men: two corps (Victor on the Bormida, Lannes three miles to the east); some units of Murat's reserve cavalry; and the Consular Guard (1100), some of it as far as eight miles from the battlefield.

## Battle of Marengo

On 14 June 1800 at dawn, therefore, Victor's corps on the Bormida was hit by Austrian troops in force. For over four hours, Napoleon still refused to believe that the Austrians meant to give battle. Meanwhile, Lannes's corps became fully engaged and, off and on, the reserve cavalry and even the Consular Guard. At about 10:00 AM, Napoleon began sending out urgent messages for his detached divisions to return. That to Desaix said in part, "Return, in the name of God, if you still can." Neither commander received the messages; they were sent too late, and some copies were taken by Austrian cavalry, who vastly outnumbered the French. But Desaix, without orders, marched to the sound of the guns and, as it turned out, saved the day for Bonaparte.

Beginning in mid-morning and continuing all day, the French were forced steadily eastward. The strongpoint of Castel Ceriolo, on the French right, fell at about noon, and Napoleon shortened his lines and continued the retrograde action, backpedaling toward San Giuliano. At 5:00 PM they were at the village. The retreat had covered some five miles in the course of the day; Napoleon had been reinforced along the way by about 4000 men, including his Consular Guard infantry and Monnier's division, but had not been able to stem the Austrian tide. Melas, who had sustained a minor wound early in the day, had already judged the battle won, turned the command over to General Zach, and repaired to Alessandria to rest. In the face of ever-weakening French resistance, the Austrian forces had fallen into a lazy formation which Zach did not discourage. This placed only a few regiments in contact with the withdrawing French; the remainder were strung out along the road to San Giuliano.

At this juncture Desaix arrived, ahead of his troops, looked over the battlefield, and said to Napoleon, "This battle is lost, but there is time to win another one." His division was close behind, and its relatively fresh men moved into the line, steadying the corps of Lannes and Victor. Napoleon waited until Kellermann could consolidate the scattered cavalry and Marmont could form an artillery battery and then ordered the attack. The infantry, supported by Marmont's artillery, which moved as the situation demanded, drove straight into the overconfident Austrians. Meanwhile, Kellermann charged through gaps in the line and into and through the rear of the enemy, then reformed and charged again and again. The Austrians gave ground, and as they retreated into the packed ranks in the rear, their retreat turned into a rout.

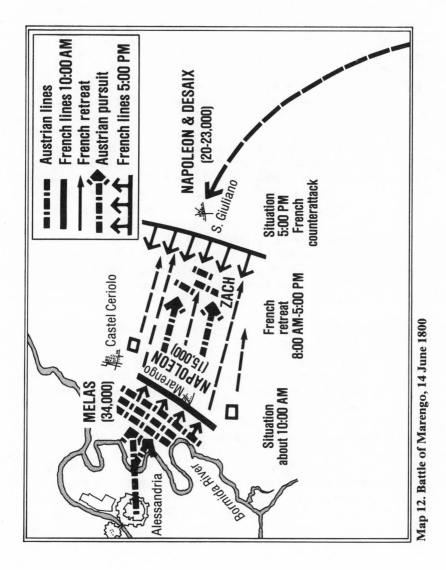

**Map 12. Battle of Marengo, 14 June 1800**

The French pursuit was tired. Therefore, under cover of darkness, the bulk of the enemy made it back across the Bormida. Austrian casualties were about 1000 killed and 5500 wounded, plus 3000 prisoners—not bad for a major battle. The French lost 1100 killed (including Desaix, the hero of the day), 3600 wounded, and 900 captured. Whereas the French were exhilarated and confident, however, the Austrians were totally demoralized. Melas decided his troops were beyond effective reorganization, and on the next morning (15 June), he asked for an armistice. Napoleon granted it, and on 18 June Bonaparte turned his army over to Masséna and returned to Paris. The war in Italy was over.

Napoleon's after-action bulletin on Marengo told the story much as it had transpired. He gave full credit to Desaix and expressed deep grief for his fallen comrade ("Why am I not allowed to weep?"). He gave credit to Kellermann, and others as well. Naturally, he did not say that Desaix had snatched him from the jaws of disaster, but while maintaining that his army was never out of control (which it was not), he was fair to his subordinates:

> [In late afternoon] the enemy advanced along his whole line following the fire . . . of more than a hundred cannons. The roads were jammed with fugitives, wounded, debris; the battle seemed lost. . . . [But at] San Giuliano the division of Desaix was arrayed for battle. . . . All the fugitives formed behind it. . . . To cries of *Vive la République! vive le premier consul!* Desaix attacked the enemy at the charge. . . . Kellermann . . . with his brigade of heavy cavalry . . . charged with full force. . . . All the army followed.

Marengo preyed on his mind, however. It remained a dark episode on his record because Desaix had saved the day and, worse, on his own initiative, since Napoleon's orders had not reached him. Moreover, although Marengo had ended the war in Italy, it had not brought the Austrians to the peace table. General Jean-Victor Moreau's victory at Hohenlinden later in the year would do that.

In 1803, therefore, Napoleon ordered the staff of the Dépôt de la Guerre to produce a new account. They were to begin their research with the report by General Pierre Dupont, Berthier's staff chief at Marengo, and interviews with other participants. The result was not altogether pleasing to the first consul, although it expanded his role in the victory. In 1805, after touring the area, Napoleon ordered the history of Marengo revised yet again. This time he gave more specific instructions, since he had convinced himself that he had had a plan, after all, which had won the battle.

In the 1805 account the Austrian force jumped to 45,000, with 200 cannon. It said that Desaix had been sent toward Novi, but with orders to return if a major engagement developed near Marengo. Moreover, the new version had it that the village of Castel Ceriolo had been held all day long

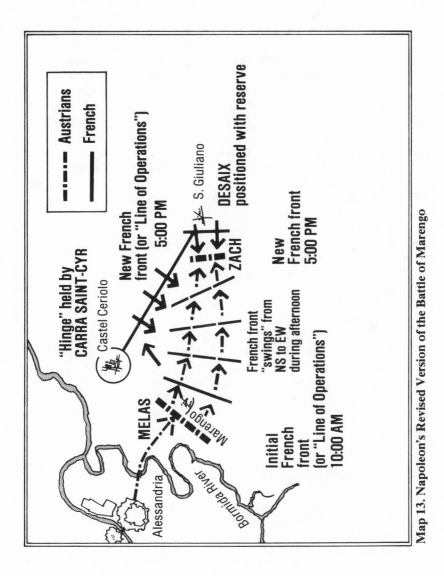

Map 13. Napoleon's Revised Version of the Battle of Marengo

by the brigade of Carra Saint-Cyr, part of General Monnier's division. The part about Desaix's orders was false, except that implied in every order is the possibility of change. The business about Castel Ceriolo ignored the testimony of witnesses that the town had been lost early in the day and recaptured only after the French counterattack had begun. Finally, Castel Ceriolo was presented as a pivot on which the French line had shifted, changing the front against the Austrians from one running roughly north-south to an east-west line. Instead of a disorderly retreat, "our echelons made their retreat in checkerboard fashion by battalion in profound silence; one could see them, under the fire of eighty cannon, maneuver as in an exercise."

This maneuver, Napoleon now claimed, plus the *planned* arrival of Desaix, had allowed the French to take the Austrian army in the flank and rear, by planned envelopment, and destroy it. General Monnier was not mentioned. General of Brigade Carra Saint-Cyr—who was following Napoleon's orders to the letter, of course—became a hero of the battle. Desaix's status was reduced from that of *the* hero to *a* hero, a valiant general also following Napoleon's orders. In fact, the report now read, "Bonaparte went several times to [control the retreat] in order to give Desaix time to take the position he had designated [in San Giuliano]."

Napoleon stuck to this account and, at St. Helena, even composed a maxim to explain his victory:

> *Le grand art des batailles* is to change, during the action, your line of operations. . . . That is how I won a victory at Marengo: The enemy threw himself on my line of operations to cut it; I had changed it, and he found himself cut up instead.

All this is hardly testimony to Napoleon's good character, even if he believed his amended account.[1] However, it has nothing to do with his stature as a military commander.

### Peacemaking and the Uses of Peace

Following Marengo, in the summer of 1800, Bonaparte did not march on Vienna, as in 1797. Austria seemed certain to seek peace, since General Moreau, commanding 120,000 French troops in Germany comprising the Army of the Rhine, was making steady progress against the Habsburg army.

---

[1] Still another account appeared under the Bourbon restoration. The Dépôt de la Guerre made a study of the various accounts of Marengo, published as *Rapprochement entre diverses relations de la bataille de Marengo* (1828). At that time, the royal government was combating the Napoleonic legend and used the Marengo accounts as a weapon. More recently, David Chandler took up the subject, and he is renowned for his impartiality. See "Tuning the Record," *Proceedings of the Consortium on Revolutionary Europe: 1981* (Athens, GA, 1982).

After Marengo, he could be reinforced from Italy. At first, the plan seemed to be working. After Moreau took Ulm and Munich, the Austrians agreed to an armistice on 15 July 1800. However, the British had given Austria a hefty subsidy to fight on, so that the Austrian emperor avoided making terms while he rebuilt his forces. At one point he introduced delays by demanding that the British be included in the negotiations. In mid-November, Napoleon ordered the war resumed. The Austrians, under the Archduke John, struck first and surprised the French east of Munich. But Moreau recovered and scattered the Austrian army at Hohenlinden on 3 December.[2]

Austria immediately agreed to serious talks and made peace by the Treaty of Lunéville (February 1801). Meanwhile, to restore religious peace in France, the Concordat of 1801 was negotiated with Pope Pius VII. Finally, the British, suffering from war weariness, came to terms by the Treaty of Amiens (March 1802).[3] All Europe was at peace for the first time in ten years, and First Consul Bonaparte had time to consolidate his government in France—and prepare his armed forces for greater triumphs.

Napoleon used the time bought by peacemaking to annex Piedmont, Elba, and part of Switzerland to France; to make himself president of the Italian (formerly Cisalpine) Republic; and to bully Holland and Naples into attenuating their trade with Britain. He ignored his promise in the Treaty of Amiens to negotiate a trade agreement with Britain. He simultaneously demanded that Britain surrender Malta, recaptured from the French in September 1800, as promised at Amiens. The British declined. Napoleon also began implementing a grand colonial scheme by which Louisiana, secured

---

[2]The French had celebrated the victory of Marengo, but when the war did not end, they turned sour and insulting. Moreau at Hohenlinden had achieved peace, for which the people had waited so long. He returned to Paris a hero. The city gave him interminable fêtes, which inflated his ego and that of his wife even more. Moreau soon became a rival personality to Napoleon, which the first consul (soon to be emperor) could not countenance. Therefore, in 1804, Moreau was implicated in a royalist plot and imprisoned. His co-conspirators were condemned to death, but he was merely exiled, which indicates that he probably was not guilty but had been entrapped by Fouché's police. Napoleon wanted to be rid of him.

[3]By the *Treaty of Lunéville* (9 February 1801), Austria reconfirmed French possession of Belgium and the left bank of the Rhine; princes who had lost lands were to be compensated in Germany. It recognized the French "sister republics"—the Cisalpine (Italian), Helvetic (Swiss), Ligurian (Genoese), and Batavian (Dutch). Austria further put the Grand Duchy of Tuscany at Napoleon's disposal. The *Concordat* (signed 15 June 1801, promulgated at Easter 1802) recognized the Roman Catholic faith as the religion of the great majority of Frenchmen, but not as the established church in France; thus, Napoleon could guarantee freedom of religion in his civil code. The head of state was to nominate bishops, the pope to consecrate them, if he approved. The government was to pay the clergy; the pope agreed not to challenge confiscations of church property during the Revolution. The Concordat reunited the Catholic clergy in France, in schism since 1790, when 50 percent had refused to take an oath of loyalty to the Revolutionary government. It finally brought an end to the peasant revolt in the Vendée, which had flared up repeatedly since 1790. In the *Treaty of Amiens*, Britain agreed to return all its conquests except for Ceylon and Trinidad and to evacuate Elba and Malta. Malta was to revert to the Knights of St. John. France promised to respect the independence and integrity of Naples, Portugal, and the Batavian Republic. Neither side respected the terms of the treaty, which lasted only a year.

from his ally Spain, would be the breadbasket for the sugar islands of the French West Indies, a scheme which failed because of the revolt of the blacks in Haiti and the fevers which killed the French army sent to subdue them. It was at this point that Napoleon gave up his colonial ambitions and sold Louisiana to the United States: "Damn coffee, damn sugar, damn colonies!"

Meanwhile, Bonaparte's consolidation of power in Italy and blocking of British trade with Europe were sufficient to outrage the British. They withdrew their ambassador from Paris in April 1803 and resumed war at sea without the formality of a declaration. Napoleon retaliated by moving troops into Germany to occupy Hanover, a family possession of King George III. He also began assembling at Boulogne the Army of England, which trained at camps along the coast for a cross-Channel invasion. It was at Boulogne, and the posts referred to under that name, that Napoleon reorganized the strike force of the French army, the body of 200,000 men which became the *Grande Armée* of 1805.[4]

## The *Grand Armée*

At Boulogne, Napoleon restored to the army all the glamour of the Old Regime and added more. Regiments, and in particular the cavalry, were given distinctive uniforms in blazing colors, often three or more different ones but at least two for parade and field, the one as splendid as the other. Napoleon's own uniform was that of a colonel of Imperial Guard cavalry (1st *chasseurs à cheval*); on campaign it was the green coat with red facings and gold epaulets. The emperor made a fetish of always appearing before the troops in the same faded green coat, by which they knew him and which became famous; it was part of his style. The uniforms, and new flags with eagles atop the flagstaffs (thus, "the eagle" of the regiment) added to morale. Even more did restoring the identity of all foreign regiments: Poles, Swiss, Hanoverians, and others. Some provincial regiments were reformed as well.

No new weapons were introduced, however, nor were tactics in the basic, drill sense. As noted in the Introduction, the weapons were inherited from the Old Regime: the .69 caliber Charleville musket (often .70 or .71, tolerances were not close), the .69 carbine, the .69 pistol, and the Gribeauval artillery consisting of 12-, 8-, 6-, and 4-pound field guns and heavier siege pieces. The tactics were inherited from the Revolution: the attack in battalion column or in *ordre mixte*, column and line. Contrary to what one might expect, Napoleon did not add power to the artillery to better serve his infantry. At Boulogne and throughout his wars, he maintained an average of 3 cannon per 1000 men, about the same ratio as his enemies.

---

[4]From 1805 onward, the French standing army numbered between 500,000 and 600,000 men. It is the field army which is described here.

Napoleon's emphasis was on organization, discipline, morale, training, hardening, and better use of weapons (which did not include marksmanship for the infantry, however). The effectiveness of his work was fully demonstrated in the 1805 campaign, the subject of Chapter 5. This discussion will be limited largely to the basic organization of the army and closely related matters.

Napoleon's major innovation was to make the corps the standard unit of all arms, replacing the division, now subordinated to the corps. It numbered 20,000 to 30,000 men, usually commanded by a marshal or lieutenant general (a temporary grade), and was capable of giving battle unsupported. It comprised two or more infantry divisions of 8000 to 12,000 men, a brigade of light cavalry of 2000 to 3000 men, six to eight companies of artillery, engineers, medics, trains, and headquarters. The infantry division was divided ideally into two brigades of one or more regiments (3500+ men). The regiment, after some experimentation, had a standard complement of four battalions of six companies of 140 men each, or 3360 line troops, plus headquarters and a military band. The total corps artillery support was 48 to 64 guns (6 cannon and 2 howitzers per company of 110 men), of which two or more companies were under corps control, and the rest attached to divisions or brigades. Corps guns were mostly 12-pounders; those at lower level 8-, 6-, and 4-pounders, with the 6-pounders disappearing by 1812.

The infantry battalion had one company of *voltigeurs* or *tirailleurs* (skirmishers), one company of *grenadiers*, and four companies of *fusiliers* (ordinary infantrymen). The skirmishers were chosen from the smaller and more agile men; they led the attack, advancing like Indians to disorganize the enemy. Casualties were high, and after 1809 artillery preparations more often did the skirmishers' job. The *grenadiers* were the taller men and were used as shock troops; despite their name, they did not carry grenades, which had proved too dangerous. The cavalry was of two types, light and heavy. The light cavalry were called hussars, *chasseurs à cheval*, dragoons, and (after 1809) lancers; the heavy cavalry were the *cuirassiers* and *carabiniers à cheval*. They differed in that the heavy cavalry had bigger men who wore body armor (the cuirass) front and back and steel helmets with roach and plume, and who rode heavier horses. The two sorts of heavy cavalry differed only in regimental colors; the light cavalry by headdress (helmet for dragoons, bearskin shako for hussars, etc.) and regimental colors. All were armed with sabers, carbines, and pistols.

Army headquarters (Napoleon) controlled 150 or more guns in the field, which brought the army average to 3 guns per 1000 men. Army also controlled the cavalry reserve of 20,000 (1805) to 60,000 (1812) men, usually commanded by the "First Horseman of Europe," Marshal Murat. Marshal Berthier was the chief of staff on every campaign save Waterloo.

Finally, there was Napoleon's trump card, the Imperial Guard, which grew from the Consular Guard of 1800–1804. The Guard was much more than a bodyguard; it was a small, elite army with its own infantry, cavalry, artillery, engineers, trains, and headquarters. It grew from 8000 in 1805 to 80,000 in 1812. It was commanded personally in battle by the emperor, though headed by a marshal (later two, one each for infantry and cavalry). The Old Guard, of regiments formed in 1800–1806, was composed of combat veterans of three or more campaigns. The Middle Guard, formed in 1806–1809, had the same requirements. The Young Guard, formed after 1809, was filled with veterans but then, increasingly, with merely promising and usually tall, imposing soldiers. The Guard was above having to prove itself in battle, so Napoleon could hold it back as his ultimate reserve. He delighted in using the artillery but seldom committed the infantry, the *grognards* (grumblers), who stood in intimidating mass behind the lines, often in full-dress uniform. When he did commit his infantry, it never failed him—until Waterloo. The Guard was privileged in every way. Privates ranked with sergeants of the line, sergeant-majors with lieutenants, colonels with generals or marshals of the line.

Napoleon fought with a regular army for most of his career, contrary to the usual view, which is of an army of draftees. The officers and noncommissioned officers were career men and professionals, although many had entered through the National Guard or started as conscripts. Until 1813, after the Russian disaster, even the rank and file was regular—otherwise Napoleon's draft quotas would have had to be higher. Manpower was available by military conscription, a system inherited from the Revolution and Carnot's *levée en masse* (modified by the Jourdan-Delbrel Law of 1798). Men registered at age 18, and were subject to call between ages 20 and 25; men who turned 20 in a given year were called the "class" of that year. Napoleon used conscription modestly, however. Between 1800 and 1810, he called an average of only 73,000 men per year. Only in the crisis years of 1812–1814 did he use it heavily, calling then 1,500,000 men.

Admittedly, the presence of foreign troops in Napoleon's army also helped to keep down draft quotas in France. The *Grande Armée* of 1805 was the most French of any Napoleon ever led, and about one-quarter of it, or 50,000 troops, was foreign: Polish, German, Italian, Irish, and some others. (This counts only men in French uniform; there were also allied troops, in 1805 almost all from the German states, and the Italian army—half-Italian, half-French—which fought largely in Italy.) The numbers of foreign troops increased with every year. For example, in the *Grande Armée* of 1812, no less than two-thirds of the troops were foreign. That army was different, in that it was organized as a "European" force. Nevertheless, of the 600,000-odd men who marched into Russia, only 200,000 were French from the territorial departments of 1789. The *Grande Armée* formed at Boulogne was decidedly professional, as the 1805 campaign would demonstrate.[5]

---

[5] A few facts may be in order here about the armies of the major enemies of Napoleonic France: Austria, Prussia, Russia, and Great Britain. All had in common aristocratic officer corps.

Austria and Prussia had many ancient generals. Austrian commanders in their seventies were common, e.g., Beaulieu and Wurmser of the 1796–97 Italian Campaign and Melas of Marengo; in Prussia, of 142 generals active in 1806, 60 were over sixty, 13 over seventy, and 4 over eighty. Not all Austrian and Prussian commanders were inept, but all suffered from an eighteenth-century syndrome and tended to oppose change. Russia had a large number of foreign officers, mostly on staff, but also in the field. Of the major commanders (ignoring the czar) who faced Napoleon later, only Mikhail Kutuzov and Piotr Bagration were native Russians. All countries commissioned nonnobles in the artillery and engineers, and Austria in the border forces on the Ottoman frontier.

Britain had a purchase system by which commissions went to commoners and nobles alike, and by which even Wellington became an officer, and a more open aristocracy; nevertheless, the officer corps was still dominated by aristocrats of relatively old title. Parliamentary committees and cabinet officers, however, oversaw the army and continually investigated alleged misconduct, ineffectiveness, or failure, which tended to force oldsters to retire, so that commanders on average were relatively young. Wellington was the same age as Napoleon. The Prussian officer corps was purged after 1807 (all but 22 of 142 generals were dismissed) and replaced by younger men. Pairing effective old commanders with bright young staff officers greatly improved efficiency. The combination of Field Marshal Blücher and General Gneisenau in 1815 is a classic example.

All armies were enlarged to meet the French challenge, so that on the battlefield, Napoleon usually found an equal or greater number of enemy troops facing him. The British, who fought largely on the high seas, expanded their army the least—to 200,000 in 1812, of whom only 50,000 were in Europe (under Wellington in Spain and Portugal). None of the powers resorted to conscription, which was judged too democratic and dangerous by the monarchs. (The yearly Russian levy of serfs would not seem to count.) Austria resorted briefly to a *Landwehr* (National Guard) in 1809, then abolished it. After 1807, Prussia used the *krümpersystem* (rotating men in and out of the regular service) and produced a *Landwehr* in 1813, but there was no universal draft of manpower. Britain expanded its militia and recruited from it. All countries hired foreigners; the Austrians filled vacancies largely from the German states, as did the Prussians, who began with an army one-half non-Prussian but reduced it to one-quarter by 1813. The Russians confined their hiring mostly to skilled European officers and noncommissioned officers. The British had the fewest foreigners—the King's German Legion (Hanoverians), some Hessians, and some men recruited on campaign in Spain. The British furnished officers and men to reorganize the Portuguese Army, which ultimately made up over half of Wellington's field forces in the Peninsula.

All the powers except the British tried to copy the organization of the *Grande Armée* of 1805, described above, invariably after defeats by Napoleon's forces. Austria adopted the corps after 1805; it was sometimes the size of the French (20,000 to 30,000 men), but usually smaller since, with some exceptions, it had no divisions but had directly under corps command varying numbers of brigades of infantry and cavalry (each about half the size of the French), plus inadequate numbers of battalions of light infantry and squadrons of light cavalry. The Austrian army remained as unwieldy as before. There was one great improvement, however. Most artillery was taken from battalions (the 6-pounders) and put in corps reserve (together with 12s and 18s), so that in 1809, the Archduke Charles often had more guns at his direct disposal than Napoleon. It prompted the French emperor, for once, to copy the Austrians and increase the size of batteries in the Guard and under independent command. The Prussian corps was similarly formed after 1807. Wellington organized two corps at Waterloo, but only temporarily, and for convenience; the largest British unit was the division of 4000 to 7000 troops, composed sometimes of two brigades, sometimes one plus a regiment, sometimes several regiments. Bagration introduced the corps, exactly modelled after the French, in the Russian army in 1812. It served only to cause confusion in that critical year.

The weapons of the powers were similar and of about equal range and effectiveness, except that the French artillery was lighter and more maneuverable. Russian muskets and carbines were of nonuniform caliber, though generally about .74; the Austrian and Prussian muskets were about .74, compared to the French .69. Many Russian infantry units, and some Austrian and Prussian, were equipped with British weapons. The British standard was the .75-caliber "Brown Bess," with Baker rifles in the 95th and part of the 60th Regiments only.

In short, Napoleon's opponents managed to match him in numbers, without risking the enrollment of the untrustworthy masses through conscription. They also matched him, roughly, in weapons. They were never really able to use the model of his corps organization, however, or to introduce sufficient light infantry and cavalry to give themselves equal freedom of maneuver. And in Napoleon's victory years, none was able to match his officer corps or the discipline and enthusiasm of his rank and file.

# 5

# THE SCRAMBLER ON THE DANUBE

## The Ulm-Austerlitz Campaign, 1805

### The Infuriation Game

Between 1803 and 1805, Napoleon made a great show of preparing to invade England, but at the same time he seemed intent on provoking a war in Europe proper. His occupation in 1803 of Hanover put French troops on the Elbe River, deep inside the German (Holy Roman) empire, ruled by the Austrian Francis II. King Frederick William of Prussia was nervous over the French presence, although Napoleon promised to give him Hanover if he cooperated. The Imperial Recess (*Reichsdeputationshauptschluss*) of February 1803, remapping Germany according to Napoleon's treaties with Austria, was an affront to the Holy Roman Emperor and to German princes as well.

In 1804, Bonaparte gave them worse. He was ready to make himself emperor and to found the French Empire, and he gave European monarchs and peoples a few shocks to emphasize his determination and to condition them to accept it. He outraged the courts of Europe by having the Bourbon Duke d'Enghien kidnapped in Baden, brought to France, and shot for treason, an act of terror calculated to intimidate the Bourbons and all hereditary monarchs. At the same time Fouché's secret police closed in on royalist spies and conspirators in Paris, which resulted in the deaths (one executed, the other a suicide) of the two major leaders, Georges Cadoudal and General Jean-Charles Pichegru. General Moreau at this time was sent into exile.

In May 1804, the French Senate, duly prompted, proclaimed Napoleon Emperor of the French; the people, in plebiscite, overwhelmingly approved. On 2 December Napoleon crowned himself "in the name of the French people and the Army," using the crown of Charlemagne brought from Aachen. Pope Pius VII, whose predecessor had crowned Charlemagne Roman emperor in 800 AD, watched passively. All this was to demonstrate that Bonaparte was the successor of Charlemagne, not of the Bourbon kings. He ignored the fact that Charlemagne already had a successor, the Austrian Holy Roman Emperor, Francis II. Who would now rule in Germany?

To compound the injury to the Austrian ruler, Napoleon made himself king of Italy, another traditional Habsburg title. He named Eugene de Beauharnais, Josephine's son, as his viceroy. For the coronation in the Cathedral of Milan in May 1805, he had the iron crown of the Lombards brought from Monza and also had struck a commemorative medal, bearing his profile and the Lombard motto *Rex Totius Italiae* (King of All Italy). This greatly alarmed Pius VII, who was the ruler of central Italy as well as a spiritual leader, and the Bourbon king and queen of Naples. Moreover, en route back to Paris in July, Napoleon annexed Genoa to France.

Russian opposition to Bonaparte, meanwhile, had grown. Czar Alexander I had ordered his court into mourning when he heard of the execution of the Duke d'Enghien. The czar was vocally and emotionally opposed to the illegitimate Bonaparte dynasty in France. His interests in the Mediterranean were challenged. The Ionian Islands off Greece had been taken by France in 1797 by the Treaty of Campo Formio, and although they had become a Russian protectorate in 1799, French determination to recover them was obvious. Moreover, Alexander saw that Russia's interests in the Balkans were threatened by a Napoleonic kingdom in northern Italy. Most importantly, he wanted Russia to play a great role in European affairs. Thus the czar led Russia into an alliance with Austria and Great Britain, initiating the Third Coalition against France.

### Charade at Boulogne

Napoleon was aware of the coalition against him, which all but guaranteed a war in Europe in 1805. Yet, since 1803, he had been noisily training the Army of England at Boulogne, ostensibly for the invasion of Britain, and he continued to play that game despite the fact that he surely had abandoned the plan by mid-1805. Considering the might of the British navy, even if he got his army across the Channel, he might be trapped in England.

Solid evidence that he was thinking of fighting in Europe, not invading England, is that his last act before departing from the new Kingdom of Italy had been to inspect the fortresses of the Quadrilateral in view of a possible Austrian attack across the Alps. En route to Paris, Napoleon ordered Marshal Masséna to Italy to command the Army of the Kingdom, for which he considered Eugene too young and inexperienced—a further indication that he expected war.

Once back in France, however, he made straight for Boulogne in August 1805 and seemed to turn his back on the Continent, undoubtedly to deceive his European enemies and the British. For weeks his most public pronouncements concerned the imminent invasion and the war at sea. For his enemies' benefit (there were spies under every rock), he gave ostentatious attention to the movements of Admiral Pierre-Charles de Villeneuve, who was to clear the English Channel for the invasion. The naval strategy would result in October in the Battle of Trafalgar, a disaster for the French navy. Meanwhile, however, Napoleon's charade at Boulogne had kept British attention riveted on their own shores and confused Austrian planning.

In August, while seemingly rooted at Boulogne, Napoleon was dispatching units of his army toward the Rhine. On 22 August, he signaled to Villeneuve, "Enter the channel, England is ours." On 23–24 August, he ordered the whole Army of England (now the *Grande Armée*) to march for Germany. His intention was to surprise the Austrians (soon to invade Germany, his diplomats in Vienna told him) by attacking them and the Russians, if they came up fast enough, long before they expected him.

The Austrian War Council thought that Napoleon again would make his main effort in Italy. Thus they ordered to Italy 90,000 men under the Archduke Charles, their best commander. Napoleon, of course, planned his major offensive in Germany, not Italy. He wrote Eugene, "I will lead the enemy such a dance that he will not bother you in Italy." He was marching for Germany with his first *Grande Armée*, totaling almost 200,000 men. It comprised seven corps under veteran marshals, 40,000 reserve cavalry under Murat, and an 8000-man Imperial Guard. France's allies, Württemberg, Baden, and Bavaria, would supply 50,000 more excellent troops.[1]

In Germany, Napoleon faced an army of only 70,000 under General Karl Mack von Leiberich. Mack had built-in command problems; his army was nominally commanded by the young Archduke Ferdinand, a rotten soldier, there only because the Russians insisted that their aristocratic generals deal with a Habsburg prince. Mack's nearest Austrian support was the 25,000-man army of the Archduke John in the Tyrol. The Russians were moving to reinforce the Austrians with some 95,000 troops. Field Marshal Mikhail Kutuzov, with 35,000, was supposed to join Mack by 20 October; 60,000 more men were ten days behind him.

The Austrians had overestimated the time required for the Army of England to reach the Rhine by three weeks, and they underestimated by two weeks the time required for the Russians to reinforce Mack in Germany.[2] Mack invaded Bavaria, France's ally, on 13 September 1805. The Bavarian army moved north, out of his way, to await Napoleon's coming and perhaps

---

[1]These states had acquired territory in the Imperial Recess of 1803, thanks to the French, on whom they depended to keep it. The rulers also were emotionally pro-French (pan-German nationalism existed only in the minds of select intellectuals). Furthermore, the larger states of Germany perennially had opposed the power of the Holy Roman Emperor, whereas the smaller states, which needed his protection, were loyal. The French-inspired settlement of 1803 eliminated small and ecclesiastical states in favor of larger ones and was part of Napoleon's plan to destroy the Holy Roman Empire, which succeeded in 1806.

[2]The staff may have ignored the fact that the Russians were still using the Julian calendar with dates twelve days earlier than the Gregorian, in use in the rest of Europe.

to be in a position to declare neutrality if he fared badly. Mack moved up the Danube to Ulm, on the border of Württemberg. He was in no hurry, merely hoping to discourage Napoleon's German allies. He expected no French army east of the Rhine before mid-October and expected to have Russian reinforcements by that time.

### Blitzkrieg to Nowhere

Napoleon, however, began wheeling his huge army across the Rhine on 25 September, and by 30 September six corps (one was behind in reserve) and Murat's cavalry were swinging east and south in long arcs toward the Danube River. The first corps crossed the Danube on 7–8 October, and the last on 11 October. As Map 14 shows, the crossing points on the Danube were all east of Ulm. The first corps went across at Donauworth, Münster, Neuburg, and Ingolstadt. Early historians of the campaign, plotting the routes of the French corps with the foreknowledge that Napoleon trapped Mack at Ulm, thought they saw a master plan in execution: the envelopment or encirclement of Mack's army. This interpretation keeps reappearing, but it is in error. Napoleon had no such plan to trap Mack at Ulm. He expected Mack to detect the approach of his enormous and noisy army and to drop south of the Danube, then retreat to a defensible river line—the Lech, Ammer, Isar, or Inn—where he could be reinforced by the Archduke John from the Tyrol. On this assumption, Napoleon had issued orders on 4 October directing his army toward the Lech River line, then shortly toward the Ammer, with Marshal Jean-Baptiste Bernadotte heading for Munich, on the Isar. For the next week, until 11 October, he urged his corps in that direction. But Napoleon had overshot his enemy, who was still near Ulm, and was conducting a blitzkrieg into thin air.

Mack, at the same time, was in a position to charge through Napoleon's rear along the north bank of the Danube, tearing up his communications and supply lines almost at will. Mack owed his advantage not to skill but to the fact that his cavalry had not detected the approach of the French. They had been watching the roads out of the Black Forest; the French skirted to the north. Nevertheless, he had Napoleon at a terrible disadvantage, and he knew it, but, as it turned out, he could not act accordingly. Mack wrote on 7 October that Napoleon was playing the Marengo game by crossing the Danube and marching between his army and Austria. "It would be easy to make him pay dear for that foolish audacity, for one would only have to descend [go east] along the left [north] bank."

On 9 October, Mack ordered a march through Günzburg and along the north bank of the Danube, a move which would have devastated the French. The Archduke Ferdinand, however, paralyzed his headquarters with arguments and counterorders, and at day's end Mack merely ordered a closer

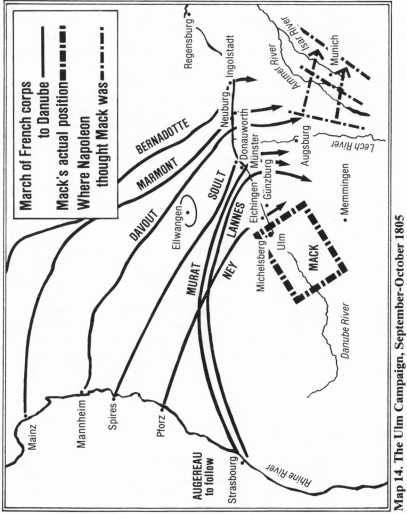

**Map 14. The Ulm Campaign, September–October 1805**

concentration on Ulm. For some days, Ferdinand had been pressing for an all-out retreat on the Tyrol, which would have been a safe move not damaging to the French. On 12 October, after the last French corps, led by Marshal Michel Ney, crossed the Danube, Mack made a final effort for unanimity among his commanders for a march through the French rear, this time all the way to Regensburg, where he hoped to meet the Russians. Ferdinand, as usual, opposed positive action, and the last chance to take the offensive against the French was lost.

Napoleon, meanwhile, moved his headquarters to Donauworth on 8 October and pressed on toward Augsburg; he persisted in the belief that the Austrians were to his southeast. On 9 October he directed Ney to expedite his crossing of the Danube. The marshal was to send one division only to Ulm, to bag stray Austrian troops and make them prisoners. On 10 October Napoleon refused to be alarmed by reports from both Ney and Davout of Austrian units south of Ulm; he was certain that they were marching for the Lech River line via Memmingen. On 11 October Ney crossed the Danube, the last corps across, by Napoleon's orders, leaving only Dupont's under-strength division north of the river.

Dupont, with a force of 4000, mostly cavalry, marched on Ulm only to be met on the hill of the Michelsberg by 25,000 Austrians, commanded by Mack himself. Dupont was cut to pieces, but he managed to fight until nightfall, then escaped eastward. Mack had been wounded during the battle and went to Ulm, which may have saved Dupont. Neither the Archduke Ferdinand nor anyone else gave any clear orders to the Austrian generals. Dupont made good his escape and reported to Ney, who reported to Napoleon, who heard the news late on 12 October. At almost the same instant, Mack was in a council of war with his generals, trying to launch a march across Napoleon's rear to Regensburg. He went nowhere, as noted above, thanks to the Archduke Ferdinand.

**Scrambling Back to Ulm**

In the middle of the night of 12–13 October, the Emperor of the French finally realized his errors. The thought of what Mack could do almost overwhelmed him. Among other problems, the army treasury, siege guns, and ammunition trains were all near Ellwangen, 40 miles north of Ulm. And on the north bank of the Danube Napoleon had not even a full division to protect either them or his communications and supply lines. In the predawn hours of 13 October, with torrents of freezing rain pummeling his carriage, Napoleon, accompanied by the Guard, rushed west to Günzburg. En route, he issued orders to Murat, Ney, and Lannes to recross the Danube and engage the Austrians at Ulm. His orders were accompanied by accusations of stupidity for having crossed the Danube in the first place—for having missed the Austrians. Napoleon was blaming everyone but himself, and his abuse, although it made them angry, somehow inspired the marshals to outdo themselves. He also sent Marshal Jean Soult through Memmingen to Ulm and Marmont westward on a more northerly track.

On the 14th, the Austrians made it easier for Napoleon. The Archduke Ferdinand, making for Prague, fled Ulm with 6000 troops—to deprive Napoleon of the satisfaction of capturing a Habsburg, he said. Napoleon dispatched Murat and the cavalry in pursuit; the Gascon cut down over half of Ferdinand's men before dropping south a week later to lead the *Grande Armée* toward Vienna. Three of Mack's corps had encountered the French south of the Danube and had fled for Austria or the Tyrol, where there were friendly forces. Of the 70,000 troops in his original army, Mack was left at Ulm with some 27,000 men.

Ney had a tough fight for the half-demolished Elchingen bridge but took it late on the 14th. On the 15th he drove the Austrians from their positions on the Michelsberg and, together with Lannes, sealed them into Ulm. By the morning of the 16th Soult and Marmont had arrived south of the Danube to make escape across the river impossible. On 16 October Napoleon began the bombardment of Ulm with all the guns he could muster. Mack refused to surrender or negotiate. His generals, however, defied him and offered to parley. On 20 October, Mack surrendered, and his entire force of 27,000 marched solemnly out and laid down their arms.

Napoleon had learned long before to make the best of good and bad events, in action and in propaganda. He gave Talleyrand, his foreign minister, the official version of the Ulm campaign on 17 October: "My plan has been executed just as I conceived it. I totally deceived the enemy, and of his army of 100,000 men more than half have been captured, killed, wounded, or deserted. The discouragement of the enemy is extreme. . . . I march against the Russian Army in a few days." On 19 October, he wrote Josephine: "I have accomplished my design; I have destroyed the Austrian army by simple marches." But before the campaign was quite finished, Bonaparte defensively exaggerated an accomplishment which was startling enough as it stood: he got his version on the record first. His vilification of his marshals on 12– 13 October was also defensive. He burdened them with guilt before they had time to consider that perhaps their leader himself had blundered.

Mack, the loser, was sentenced to twenty years in prison by an angry court-martial. He was paroled by the Austrian emperor, but his military career was at an end, while Napoleon's military career had begun again on an imperial scale. But what if Mack had not been interfered with by the Archduke Ferdinand? What if his officers and men had been just a little more aggressive and alert? What then? After all, Mack knew what moves he should have made. He had tried twice, on 9 and 12 October, to set his army in motion to the east along the north bank of the Danube. What if he had marched? Napoleon might have been destroyed; at the very least, he would have had no easy strategic victory.

The spectacular victory at Ulm was a result of both Austrian bungling and Napoleon's ability to scramble. He pulled it off despite his initial gross mistakes. Again, however, we must give some credit to his commanders, particularly to Ney, Lannes, and Murat, and to his troops, who carried out his orders with alacrity. There was another factor as well, one which Napoleon had never enjoyed before: superior numbers. From 1805 through 1812, he always had more troops than his enemies, which enabled him to commit greater tactical and strategic sins and survive with greater ease. Greater numbers were made possible simply by the expansion of France proper—from 98 departments in 1799, when Napoleon took over, to 130 in 1810–and by the multiplication of satellite and allied states which, in 1810, would include all of Europe, even Russia. In 1812, only Russia and Sweden (and of course Britain) would not be allied with France.

**Battle of Trafalgar**

The news of the victory at Ulm overwhelmed that of the Battle of Trafalgar, fought on 21 October 1805, the day after Mack's surrender. It was a result of Napoleon's naval strategy, mentioned earlier, conceived initially to clear the Channel for an invasion of England.

In March of that year, Admiral Villeneuve, with a French fleet, had set sail from Toulon. His mission was to lure Admiral Nelson, the victor of the Battle of the Nile, and the British Mediterranean fleet to the West Indies, "lose" him, race to the Channel, and, in combination with French fleets from Brest and Rochefort, cover Napoleon's invasion of England. To a point, the strategy worked. Villeneuve reached the West Indies in mid-May; Nelson followed, arriving on 4 June. Villeneuve escaped being sighted and sailed back to Europe on 9 June. Nelson belatedly followed on 12 July but made an amazingly quick seven-day crossing to Gibraltar. En route he sent a fast frigate to warn the admiralty in London that Villeneuve was Europe-bound. By accident, the ship sighted the French fleet and was able to report its position.

Villeneuve, meanwhile, had met nothing but disappointment. Neither the Brest nor the Rochefort fleet made its rendezvous with him; the British navy kept the one at Brest bottled up, while the Rochefort fleet broke free but missed Villeneuve and returned to port. Moreover, Villeneuve blundered into Admiral Sir Robert Calder's fleet and was mauled in a confused battle in deep fog. He was not beaten, but he considered it impossible to reach the Channel, much less control it. He put in at El Ferrol, then sailed to Cadiz

(Spain was an ally), arriving on 20 August. There he was joined by a Spanish fleet of old and rotten ships manned by uninspired crews.

When Napoleon heard that Villeneuve was in Cadiz, he called him a coward and sent orders relieving him of command. The admiral ignored the orders. Determined to save his honor, he sailed from Cadiz to meet Nelson at Trafalgar on 21 October. The result was a disaster for Villeneuve, who lost 22 of 33 vessels, including his flagship. Nelson, with 27 ships, lost not a single one. Ironically, Villeneuve, who probably wanted to die in battle, survived, while Nelson was killed. Lord Nelson's body was transported to London where he was entombed in St. Paul's Cathedral with all the honors of state.

The victory at Trafalgar established British control of the seas for the remainder of the Napoleonic period. It is another irony that Napoleon himself, still playing out his Boulogne charade, caused this climactic confrontation of French and British naval power. Villeneuve was in a no-win situation and had long since served his purpose, since Bonaparte had called off the invasion of England.

**On to Vienna**

On the German front, Marshal Kutuzov, with 38,000 Russians, arrived at the Inn River on the Austrian-Bavarian border in mid-October, but he went no farther after hearing of Mack's surrender. He received various Austrian units which had eluded capture at Ulm, but the Emperor Francis would not place them under his command. The next contingent of Russians, 40,000 under Field Marshal Friedrich Buxhöwden, had just entered Moravia. Kutuzov thus decided to retreat east and north into Moravia where he hoped to unite the whole Russian army of 90,000, and where he could be reinforced in safety by Austrian forces, perhaps even by the Archduke Charles, from Italy.

Kutuzov burned the bridges over the Inn and withdrew east along the Danube, apparently making for Vienna. Actually he intended to cross the Danube at Krems, 30 miles short of Vienna. Napoleon put Murat and the cavalry on the road to Vienna on 26 October with orders to pursue the Russians. That meant all the way to the city, as the orders were understood by Murat and by Lannes, whose corps was ordered to follow Murat. In fact, five corps followed him along the south bank of the Danube; Marshal Edouard Mortier's corps moved parallel on the north bank. Marshal Ney had been sent into the Tyrol to guard the army's south flank.

Murat went forward, overtaking the enemy and finding more Russians to put to the saber by the day. On 6 November, he learned that Kutuzov planned to cross the Danube at Krems and make for Moravia. He so notified Napoleon, who sent him orders to go after the Russians with "your swords on their asses" (*l'épée sur les reins*). But Murat did not get the message in time and, instead of following the Russians, galloped for Vienna, leaving Napoleon the message, "I see nothing that would delay Your Majesty's march for Vienna for a minute." The French emperor was livid with anger. He damned Murat and even his messenger, whom he called "such a brute (*bête*) that he can explain nothing." By the time the messages reached Murat, he and Lannes had entered Vienna (12 November), happy as two schoolboys. They paraded in with thousands of splendid cavalry; Francis had declared the Austrian capital an open city.

Napoleon blamed Murat for leaving Mortier exposed, alone, and unsupported, on the north bank. It was really Napoleon's fault, however; he had given Mortier little thought for some days but, on hearing of Murat's position, suddenly realized that Kutuzov might annihilate him. The Russian, instead, was intent on retreating north. He bruised Mortier once to slow him down and marched away.

Meanwhile, Napoleon ordered Murat to seize the bridges north of Vienna. He did so bloodlessly by announcing that a truce was in effect and ordering the Austrians out of the way. Murat and Lannes, two swaggering and spectacularly dressed Gascons, walked forward alone, intimidated the Austrian prince commanding the main bridge, and waved their men across. But Murat failed to exploit his advantage. Rather, he allowed Kutuzov's representatives to talk him into signing a real armistice, which he had no authority to do. When Napoleon heard about it, he angrily ordered Murat to negate the truce and pursue the enemy—but the enemy had escaped.

Kutuzov united the available Russian armies (71,000 men) at Olmütz. Francis reinforced him with 15,000 Austrians, bringing allied strength to 86,000. At this point, however, Czar Alexander relieved Kutuzov and took command himself. He was a tall, athletic figure of twenty-eight years who fancied himself a general and decidedly looked the part.

Napoleon paused briefly in Vienna, then moved north to Brünn, 40 miles southwest of Olmütz. The Imperial Guard, under Jean-Baptiste Bessières, was with him; nearby were the corps of Lannes, Bernadotte, and Soult, all dispersed for provisioning; Murat's cavalry patrolled between Brünn and the Russians. Napoleon thus had direct command of fewer than 67,000 troops. Davout and Mortier were near Vienna, backing up Marmont, who was south of Vienna to block the Archduke Charles if he approached. Ney was moving through the Tyrol to Carinthia with the same mission.

The Archduke Charles had invaded the Kingdom of Italy from the east in late September 1805 but had proceeded cautiously, anticipating the appearance of Napoleon. His greater numbers pushed back the Franco-Italian army commanded by Marshal Masséna, who moved warily as well. At the end of October, however, Charles heard the news of the capitulation of Ulm and began a withdrawal over the Alps. Masséna struck at his rear at Caldiero on 29 October. The next day Charles counterattacked, and a full-scale battle ensued. The outcome was indecisive, except that Masséna emerged so disorganized that Charles was able to continue his withdrawal with relative ease. On 26 November, therefore, Charles joined his forces with those of the Archduke John at Marburg in Styria. Both had left garrisons behind to delay the French and had suffered erosion of forces, common in the generally uninspired Austrian army. However, their combined army numbered 80,000 and, although it was 180 miles from Vienna and 255 miles from Brünn, posed a threat to Napoleon.

At Olmütz, meanwhile, Kutuzov reminded Czar Alexander that if he waited, he might be reinforced by the Archduke Charles and even by Ferdinand, who had assembled 18,000 men in Prague. Alexander thus could throw 184,000 men against the French. Napoleon might be able to assemble 100,000 troops in short order, but he probably would have to fight with 70,000 or fewer. The Russians, however, were running low on supplies and food. On that score, Kutuzov suggested that, if the situation became critical before Charles arrived, the army withdraw into Poland, resupply, and then link up, perhaps even as late as spring, with the Austrian armies again. Time, Kutuzov argued, was on the side of the Allies; they should use it to ensure victories. If they won battles, King Frederick William had agreed to bring Prussia into the alliance, which would mean greater Allied numbers.

Alexander would have none of this. He had Napoleon outnumbered, he was certain, by 86,000 to 70,000 men. His younger advisers told him he could win, and he was determined to try. On 27 November, therefore, Alexander began his advance on Brünn. Both sides had gone through pretenses of peace negotiations as an excuse to send observers through enemy lines. Thus Napoleon anticipated the Russian movement and, in fact, had encouraged it by showing as few troops as possible. On 28 November, when the Russians approached Brünn, Napoleon withdrew Marshal Soult's corps from the Pratzen, a high plateau west of Austerlitz which was key terrain. Alexander's conviction that the French were weak was confirmed. His advance continued.

When, on 1 December, Alexander found Napoleon's army arrayed behind the brook of the Goldbach, he finalized his plans. He would strike at the French right (south) flank, held lightly by part of Soult's corps, penetrate to the Vienna road and cut the French supply line. He then would drive through the French rear, destroying the army or, at least, turning the south flank, forcing the French to retreat toward Prague. On that road, they would be blocked by the army of the Archduke Ferdinand, while Alexander came up from behind and destroyed them.

On the day of 1 December, Napoleon had fewer than 57,000 troops, which made the Russian czar heady with hopes of victory. The French emperor had ordered 6000 men of Davout's corps from Vienna, but it would not arrive until dawn of the next day. He had ordered Bernadotte, with 10,000 of his corps, south from the Prague highway, leaving Karl Philipp von Wrede's division (Bavarian) to guard against the approach of Ferdinand from the north. Bernadotte was moving into reserve some two miles west of Lannes's front but was out of sight.

## Battle of Austerlitz

The Allied army began its attack at dawn on 2 December. By 7:00 AM Alexander had committed 40,000 of his 86,000 men to the south flank. He had another 16,000 on the Pratzen and some 14,000 advancing along the Olmütz-Brünn road. The Russian Imperial Guard and reserve cavalry (10,500 and 5500) were between the two northern columns. The French line, still along the Goldbach, was being reinforced by Davout (6,000), who had marched 70 miles from Vienna. Also, Bernadotte had moved forward into reserve with 10,000 men, bringing Napoleon's strength to 73,000. Davout, in the predawn hours, had taken over the French south (right) flank with 3000 infantry and 4000 cavalry from Soult. At 6:00 AM only half of Davout's reduced corps was in place, some 3000 men protected by Soult's cavalry; the remaining 3000 came into line between 10:00 and 11:00. Napoleon gambled that Davout would arrive in time to hold his right flank. Davout accomplished the mission, which made Napoleon's victory possible, but it was too close for comfort, and a lesser commander might not have done the job.

Davout took over the southern front of the army—three of seven miles—by deploying his men west of the Goldbach, driving such Russians as had forded the brook back across, and establishing a stable line. The enemy outnumbered him 4 to 1, but his men were determined and the terrain was on his side. There were lightly frozen marshes on the enemy side of the Goldbach, and the masses of Russian infantry crashed through and found themselves bogged down in mud and freezing water. Davout's infantry and close-support artillery cut them down as they came. The Russians, however, kept advancing in ever greater numbers onto the bloody killing ground. The czar stuck doggedly to his plan, ignoring the cost and the fact that he was weakening his right (north) flank.

From 10:00 AM onward, Davout's corps became the anvil on which Napoleon could hammer the Russian army at will. At about 9:30 AM, Napoleon had ordered Soult to retake the Pratzen, and his corps, which had been waiting for the order, sprang into action. (The marshal cockily promised to deliver in fifteen minutes.) Russian Imperial Guards counterattacked, however, and broke one of Soult's divisions, but Napoleon committed the cavalry of the Imperial Guard under Bessières, who drove them off. Meanwhile Soult was reinforced from other corps to form, with the Guard cavalry and artillery, a "mass of decision."

At about 11:00 AM the French attacked southward from the Pratzen, driving the Russians toward the frozen ponds, marshes, and rivulets to the

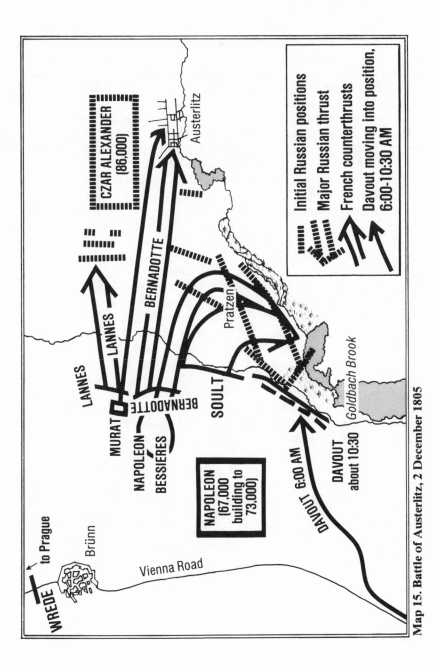

Map 15. Battle of Austerlitz, 2 December 1805

south. At about 1:00 PM, Davout's corps moved into the attack. The Russians were pressed into a more and more constricted space and finally broken and thrown into flight across the marshes and ponds, where the ice broke and hundreds of men were drowned. The firm ground between the larger ponds was enfiladed by the French artillery, including that of the Guard, and became a hideous killing ground in itself.

Simultaneous with Soult's drive to the south, Lannes's corps moved east along the Olmütz highway and Bernadotte drove toward Austerlitz, followed by Murat and the cavalry. By 4:00 PM, when the sun of Austerlitz began to set and the snow began to fall, the Russian army was in totally disorganized retreat. Murat found pursuit impossible. The czar had lost 25,000 men, 10,000 of them killed; the rest were so scattered that Murat's cavalry could not find a major track to follow. Except for his Guard, Alexander's army was no more. The French only had 2000 killed, 7000 wounded. Czar Alexander refused to make terms and merely marched away. The Austrian emperor, on the other hand, anxiously sued for peace, for which he would pay dearly. Napoleon's victory was overwhelming.

"You engage, and then you wait and see," Napoleon had said, describing his tactical "art." Austerlitz was the prime example of this system. Napoleon met the Allies, held back a large reserve (the Guard, Murat's cavalry, and for many hours, Bernadotte's corps), waited for Alexander to make gross mistakes, and then threw in his reserve to seal a total victory. It showed a master tactician at work, but also one who was dependent on skillful subordinates, especially Soult and Davout, and on superbly trained and highly motivated troops, who executed his orders without faltering.

Mark well that Marshal Davout, the "Bald Eagle," ordered in very late, marched all night and arrived on the morning of Austerlitz to shore up Napoleon's right wing. He already was known as a tough disciplinarian and total professional. He was a poor noble, like Napoleon, who also had been granted a royal scholarship to military school. As we shall see, Davout would emerge in 1806 as a superb independent commander and in later years would repeat his Austerlitz feat time and again—sweeping in to roll up the enemy's flank, at Eylau (1807) and Wagram (1809), for example—and perform other tasks as well, such as deploying the *Grande Armée* of 1812. During Napoleon's later campaigns, Davout would become to him what Masséna had been in 1796–97 in Italy: the man who could be counted on to deliver the blow that won battles. Ever faithful, he was ready to serve Napoleon in 1815 upon his return from Elba.

## Postscript

The tactical victory of Austerlitz, coming after the strategic victory of Ulm, marked Napoleon as one of the all-time masters of the art of military command.[3] There is one curious fact about Austerlitz, however, which is often overlooked. Napoleon did not use all his available troops to combat the czar or even bring them into a back-up position, such as that of Wrede's division of Bernadotte's corps, which remained on the Prague highway. Over half of Davout's corps remained at Vienna. Marmont was not recalled from south of Vienna, nor was Ney from the Tyrol. Granted, the mission of Marmont and Ney was to prevent the Archduke Charles from reinforcing the czar. By 27 November, however, Napoleon knew that Charles could not join Alexander, and he was faced with a force superior in numbers. The explanation would seem to be either that Bonaparte was contemptuous of the Russians, or that he was uncomfortable as yet with large armies or, more bluntly, had not learned how to use them. The latter explanation seems more valid. The French army at Austerlitz was the largest Napoleon had ever deployed on a battlefield. During the campaign of 1806–07, he would learn better how to use the advantage of numbers and even to depend on that advantage.

---

[3]Napoleon wanted both the public and posterity to believe that he could read the enemy's mind. An order in the Dépôt de la Guerre, dated 1 December 1805, the day before the Battle of Austerlitz, reads: "When they march to turn my right flank, they will expose their flank to me [and I will attack and destroy them]." This is what happened. Henry Lachouque discovered, however, that the order was amended on 2 December, after the battle began. (Lachouque was an honest historian, though an admirer of Napoleon; his best-known book was *Napoléon et la garde impériale*, published in 1957.) The original order ran: "They will attack my batteries, and I will take them on the flanks." Such deception was unworthy of a great commander, but it was typical.

# 6

# OVERKILL IN THE EAST

## The Jena-Auerstädt-Friedland Campaign, 1806–07

> With few exceptions, victory is
> assured to the army with the
> greatest numbers.
> —Napoleon to Arnault

## Fomenting More Conflict

"To win is nothing, you must profit from success," Napoleon once wrote to his brother Joseph. That had been his constant policy. After Austerlitz, by the Treaty of Pressburg, he made Austria give up Venice, most of Istria, and Dalmatia to the Kingdom of Italy. Francis II also was forced to cede the Tyrol and other alpine lands to Bavaria and lesser territories to Württemberg and Baden, and to recognize as kings the rulers of Württemberg and Bavaria, Napoleon's allies. Generally, by this treaty Napoleon was punishing Austria and rewarding his friends. Taking Venetia and the Balkan lands removed the last vestige of Austrian power in Italy. Losing the Tyrol, a Habsburg crown possession since 1363, was an especially hard blow for Austria. At the time Talleyrand warned Napoleon that he was making of Austria an eternal enemy, but the French emperor paid him no heed.

In early 1806, Napoleon punished another feckless enemy. He ordered Marshal Masséna, commanding the reinforced Army of Italy, to march south and conquer Naples; he named Joseph to be king, and on 15 February he was in his capital. For the invaders, except at Gaeta and a few other strongpoints, the campaign was a walk in the country; the Neapolitan Bourbon army fled to Sicily.

Napoleon had acted because the Kingdom of Naples had been led into the Allied coalition by its queen, Marie-Caroline,[1] who loathed Napoleon and called him a crowned Jacobin, when her vocabulary of profanity failed her. After she heard of Napoleon's victory at Austerlitz, however, she addressed a letter to the "Emperor of Europe" and asked for mercy, but got none. Napoleon decided to take over Naples, if not Sicily, which was protected by the British navy. The Neapolitan Bourbons, with a lapse during 1799–1800, had cooperated constantly with France, but Napoleon did not care to deal with them further.

At the same time, by threatening to annex the Batavian Republic to France, he induced the Dutch to request a Bonaparte king and then created the Kingdom of Holland for his brother Louis. Napoleon simply wanted better control of the Netherlands. The Dutch had cooperated with all French governments since 1795, and their navy had served Napoleon especially well, but he was not satisfied. Moreover, he was convinced that the Dutch had "all the money in the world" and wanted Louis to get him a greater chunk of it.

By July 1806, Napoleon completed the work begun by the Imperial Recess of 1803, which he had forced, by establishing the Confederation of the Rhine (*Rheinbund*). This included most of the German states and, soon, all but Prussia. He thereby usurped the power in Germany traditionally held by the Holy Roman Emperor. Recognizing this, Francis II abdicated the ancient title and henceforth styled himself Francis I of Austria. The Holy Roman Empire thus disappeared from the map.

Francis, nevertheless, meant to take revenge on Napoleon. He appointed the Archduke Charles commander-in-chief of the Austrian army and head of the War Council (*Hofkriegsrat*), with instructions to reform and expand the army. The archduke could work no quick miracles, however, and Austria shunned any alliance against France in 1806. Charles began by replacing the arms and equipment destroyed and horses killed at Ulm, Austerlitz, and elsewhere in 1805; refilling the ranks and increasing pay; and expanding the standing army to 300,000 men. He also began planning for a National Guard (*Landwehr*) to be called in wartime. Most vital and difficult, he next began easing elderly and ineffective officers out of the service and replacing them with younger and better educated officers. Unhappily, he did not complete his work before war hawks pushed Austria into conflict again in 1809.

Prussia, on the other hand, was spoiling to fight by mid-1806. Before Austerlitz, it had been about to ally with Russia and Austria, but afterward (December 1805) it allied with France and in return was allowed to occupy Hanover. In early 1806, however, Napoleon told the Prussian minister in Paris that his king would have to renegotiate the treaty. Frederick William

---

[1]Marie-Caroline was the wife of King Ferdinand V of Naples; he was a Spanish Bourbon and a nonentity. She was the sister of Marie-Antoinette, queen of France, who had been sent to the guillotine in 1793.

felt humiliated and robbed but could only comply. By the new treaty, he retained Hanover but gave up lands in Germany and Neuchâtel, in Switzerland. In June 1806, moreover, the Prussian king heard rumors (and they were true) that Napoleon was offering to return Hanover to Britain if that country would make peace. This was the last straw for Frederick William. His kingdom had already been truncated; now he stood to lose Hanover, which he had been given in compensation. If that happened, he might well lose control of his independent and bellicose nobles. Furthermore, he and the nobility were angry and apprehensive over the creation of the Confederation of the Rhine. Prussians had resented Austrian dominance in Germany, but French dominance was intolerable.

## Prussia Attacks

In July 1806, therefore, Frederick William allied with Alexander I of Russia, who was still at war with Napoleon. In August, the Prussian king mobilized his armed forces—250,000 men—with field armies totaling 145,000. The Russians were assembling two armies of 60,000 men each to reinforce the Prussians. Saxony allied with Prussia, as did smaller states such as Brunswick (Braunschweig) and Hesse-Cassel. Frederick William, convinced that he commanded the invincible "army of Frederick the Great," decided to strike at the French in Germany without waiting for the Russians. On 12 September he ordered his armies into Saxony, where they picked up Allied contingents and marched southwestward. On 4 October, Prussian armies were at Jena and Erfurt, very near the border of the *Rheinbund*. Meanwhile, on 26 September, Frederick William sent an ultimatum to Napoleon to either evacuate Germany or face war.

Napoleon, meanwhile, anticipating Prussian actions, had already left Paris on 21 September to take command of the *Grande Armée*, most of which had remained in Germany after Austerlitz. Since French ambassadors with their staffs and military attachés were still at the Prussian and Russian courts, he knew through those sources that Prussia was about to attack his forces in Germany, that the Russians would not reinforce them for many weeks, and that he had the Prussians vastly outnumbered. Napoleon radiated confidence; it was part of his style. However, in his heart of hearts, he was apprehensive about meeting the Prussian army face to face. Later, on St. Helena, recalling the campaign for Montholon, he would refer to the Prussians as "the finest troops in the world." Indeed, Frederick the Great was the only eighteenth-century general he respected. He disdained all living Prussian commanders, but he was unsure whether Frederick's glory might not still inspire the army. His stomach knotted a little at the thought.

Before Napoleon reached it, the *Grande Armée* had been south of the Main River, generally, with some units south of the Danube. In August, he had written to Berthier to "announce that the army will soon march [for France]," but not to move a man. On 19 September he had ordered the army concentrated in the vicinity of Bamberg, on the Main. On 6 October he actually took command at Bamberg. He had 180,000 French, reinforced by some troops of his German allies, of which 100,000 were ultimately available.

Napoleon, at age thirty-seven, then was at the height of his powers; Marshal Davout, destined for a crucial independent role, was thirty-six. In command of his six corps were marshals already famous and some destined to be legends: Lannes, the handsome, hot-tempered Gascon; Ney, the towering, redheaded "Bravest of the Brave"; Davout, the cool, efficient "Bald Eagle"; Augereau, a hero of the First Italian Campaign; Mortier, the valiant giant; and Bernadotte, "*Sergent Belle-Jambe*," a favorite of the troops. The flamboyant Murat commanded 20,000 reserve cavalry. The rough old Lefebvre led the Imperial Guard infantry (6000), and the Gascon Bessières the Guard cavalry (2500).

The Prussians technically were under King Frederick William, who accompanied the armies, but they actually were commanded by the Duke of Brunswick with excessive advice from the king, the army staff, and the ranking commanders. Brunswick (age seventy-one) had three armies, the largest (75,000) under himself, one of 40,000 under the Prince von Hohenlöhe, and another of 30,000 under General Ernst Rüchel. Brunswick had begun his march in late September with the plan of driving through the Thuringian Forest to the Main and destroying the *Grande Armée* before it organized. However, his movement had been too slow. Decisionmaking and coordination were difficult, especially since he and Hohenlöhe detested each other. Thus, on 8 October, when Brunswick became aware that he would not surprise the French and that, in fact, they were moving on him from the south, his army had advanced only to the vicinity of Gotha, with Hohenlöhe to the east along the Saale River and Rüchel to the west at Eisenach.

Brunswick ordered the armies to withdraw toward Berlin and consolidate behind the upper Saale or the Elbe River. Instead, there was much dispute at headquarters over where the Prussians should make their stand. Before they could mass their armies, Napoleon was upon them. He had struck northeastward without knowing exactly where the enemy was. He referred airily to his army as "the battalion square," ready for anything. His general direction was toward Leipzig; his plan was to neutralize Saxony and knock it out of the war, envelop the Prussian army, and cut it off from retreat to the key fortress of Magdeburg on the Elbe. (Napoleon was astonished that the Prussians had not stood on the Elbe and waited for the Russians. They had not because Brunswick had hoped to surprise the French and because they overestimated their own strength.)

The corps of Lannes and Augereau made for the valley of the Saale. The corps of Soult and Ney were some 35 miles to the east, eventually on the line of the Elster River, followed by Jerome Bonaparte with one Bavarian

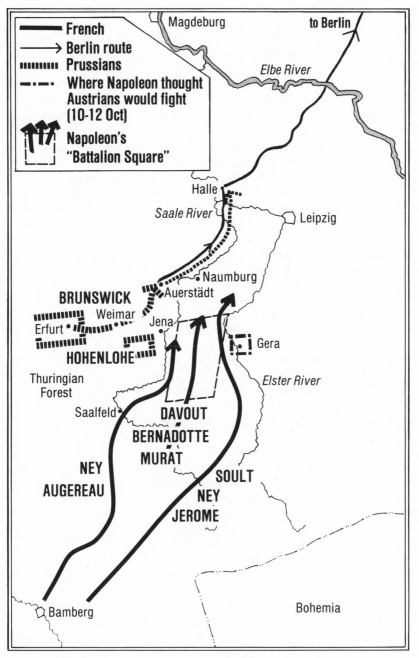

**French**

→ **Berlin route**

▪▪▪▪▪▪ **Prussians**

–·–· **Where Napoleon thought Austrians would fight (10-12 Oct)**

**Napoleon's "Battalion Square"**

Magdeburg

to Berlin

*Elbe River*

Halle

*Saale River*

Leipzig

Naumburg

**BRUNSWICK**

Auerstädt

Weimar

Erfurt

Jena

Gera

**HOHENLOHE**

*Elster River*

Thuringian Forest

Saalfeld

**DAVOUT**

**BERNADOTTE**

**MURAT**

**NEY**

**AUGEREAU**

**SOULT**

**NEY**

**JEROME**

Bamberg

Bohemia

**Map 16. The Jena Campaign, 6-12 October 1806**

division. Between these two sides and a little ahead of the "battalion square" was the cavalry of Murat, followed by the corps of Davout and Bernadotte. On 10 October, at Saalfeld, Lannes encountered Prince Ludwig of Prussia, overaggressively commanding what had been Hohenlöhe's advance guard, and attacked. The prince, pinned against the Saale by superior forces (25,000 to his 9000), tried to save the situation by charging at the head of a mass of hussars. He was killed. Reported Napoleon laconically in the Second Bulletin of the *Grande Armée*: "One can say that the first blows of the war have killed one of its instigators."

On 10 October Napoleon based his planning on the incorrect assumption that the Prussians were in retrograde along the Elster toward Leipzig and would probably stand at Gera. The clash at Saalfeld gave him pause, and he rushed Augereau forward to backstop Lannes. Once Lannes reported victory over only a small advance guard, however, Bonaparte returned to his fixation on Gera. He ordered Murat and Bernadotte to Auma and Soult to Gera; Soult and Ney were to follow. Lannes and Augereau were to continue their movement along the east bank of the Saale. On the 12th, the army went on its way undisturbed, as it reached and overreached all objectives.

There was no Prussian concentration at Gera. Lannes, on the Saale opposite Jena, reported that there were large Prussian armies between Jena and Weimar. So did Augereau and Davout, all basing their intelligence on statements of prisoners, spies, and local residents.

"The veil is lifted!" proclaimed Napoleon when the reports reached him early on 13 October. The Prussian army was at Jena and would soon attack Lannes. He directed Augereau, Ney, and Soult to march for Jena and recalled Murat and the cavalry from near Naumburg to Jena. He marched for Jena himself with the Guard. Davout was ordered to move from Naumburg to Apolda, "in the enemy rear" along with Bernadotte. The order read: "If the Prince de Ponte-Corvo [Bernadotte] is with you, you can march together. The Emperor hopes, however, that he will be . . . at Dornburg." On the morning of the 13th, Lannes crossed the Saale, took Jena (from which the last Prussians were withdrawing), and the Landgrafenberg, a commanding hill west of the town. Napoleon joined him at about 4:00 PM, confirmed his misconception that the whole Prussian army of 100,000 or more was before him, and began preparations for a major battle.

But Napoleon had made one gross misjudgment. The largest Prussian army (64,000 men) was not before him but was marching for Auerstädt, en route to Halle and the Elbe. It was bearing down on the single corps of Marshal Davout, whom the French emperor had sent into the enemy rear. Facing Napoleon (but not massed) were 38,000 men under Hohenlöhe, supported by 15,000 under Rüchel at Weimar. Hohenlöhe was the flank guard of Brunswick's army and was to become the rear guard when the main army was well to the north. His right (22,000) was at Capellendorf, five miles from the French front; his left was at Dornburg, also five miles away. Facing the French directly was a single division (8000 men) under Tauenzien.

Napoleon's greatest fear was attack by superior forces before all his units arrived; that is, before noon on 14 October. The most dangerous period, he judged, was the late afternoon and night of 13 October. He accepted the risk which, in retrospect, was no risk at all. For the morning of the 14th, he planned an offensive which would disconcert even a numerically superior enemy—an attack on his center with troops massed almost shoulder to shoulder. As he wrote to Soult: "You sense that my will is to hazard nothing and attack the enemy . . . with double his forces."

The emperor spent the night packing available troops (Lannes's corps and the Guard, 22,000 and 8500) onto the Landgrafenberg. He personally supervised the building of a road to get his artillery to the highest point, where he rested, surrounded by his splendid Guard. This famous preparation has been much marveled at. However, Napoleon's massing of troops on the Landgrafenberg surely reflected a certain fear of the "army of Frederick the Great" and the fabled robot-like advance of its lines of infantry. And considering that only one enemy division was actually facing him directly and that his vaunted artillery (range: 1/2 mile) could barely reach the front ranks of that one division, the whole exercise seems comic. But we enjoy the privilege of hindsight and of knowing that the Prussian army was something of a paper tiger.

## Battle of Jena

At 6:30 AM on 14 October, in dark and fog, Napoleon, reflecting his fear of being beaten to the punch, sent Lannes forward. He and the Guard remained in reserve on the Landgrafenberg. The attack began raggedly. Lannes was expected to attack through Closwitz, but because of poor visibility, his corps veered to the left; one division took the village but lagged behind; the rest of the corps blundered through the fog toward Vierzehnheiligen. As the fog cleared about 9:00 AM, Tauenzien's division attacked the French flank, marching as in Napoleon's nightmares in steady, drill-field lines. Momentarily, they split the advancing French, but they were too few. Moreover, Augereau came up on Lannes's left; Ney with his advance guard suddenly appeared between the two, was bloodied and almost cut off, but finally linked up with the others. By 10:00 Vierzehnheiligen was in French hands.

Hohenlöhe mustered maximum forces and at about 11:00 counterattacked, but he was stalled for lack of manpower before Vierzehnheiligen and decided to wait for 13,000 reinforcements under Rüchel, marching from Weimar. However, Rüchel, as it turned out, took four hours to cover six miles and arrived too late to matter. (Why the march took so long is still a

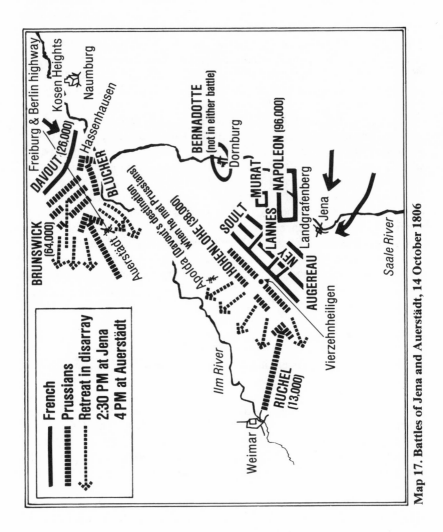

Map 17. Battles of Jena and Auerstädt, 14 October 1806

mystery, although the Prussian high command clearly blamed Rüchel, who was retired after 1807, when reform of the army began.) Meanwhile, Soult's corps moved up on Lannes's right, and Murat arrived with most of the cavalry. At 12:30 the French attacked in force, and Hohenlöhe's army fled in total disarray. Rüchel, with some 13,000 of his men, arrived at 2:30 PM and attempted to counterattack through the remnants of Hohenlöhe's army. The attempt was impressive—again with the Prussian infantry in drill-field order— but it was swept away by Hohenlöhe's retreating masses, and Rüchel joined the pell-mell flight.

The Battle of Jena was over. Napoleon with 96,000 men (40,000 actually engaged) had downed Hohenlöhe (38,000; 33,000 engaged) and Rüchel (13,000) separately, as it were. The French sustained 5000 casualties; the Prussians, 11,000 plus 15,000 captured. It had been a walkover.

### Battle of Auerstädt

Ten miles to the north, at Auerstädt, a more serious battle was nearing its end. Marshal Davout, with a single corps of 26,000 men, had met the bulk of the Prussian army (64,000 men), initially under the Duke of Brunswick. At about 6:30 AM, Davout, marching on Apolda from Naumburg via the Kosen bridge over the Saale, as ordered, encountered the Prussian advance guard at Hassenhausen. He quickly brought Gudin's division into line. Forming squares, it was able to counter the attack of a Prussian division and twelve squadrons of cavalry, brought forward by General Blücher von Wahlstatt, who had ridden all night.

Blücher, a hard-drinking and aggressive sixty-four-year-old, attacked at will, accomplished little, and went into reserve. At 9:00 AM, Davout was able to bring up Friant's division and a brigade of cavalry, but the Prussians had four divisions forward and attacked frontally. The time of crisis had come. At about 9:30, however, the Duke of Brunswick was mortally wounded, and although King Frederick William personally assumed command, things went badly for the Prussians. At 11:00 AM, when they seemed to have mass and momentum and were about to turn the French left flank, Davout's last division (Morand) arrived, threw the Prussians back, and turned the enemy flank. By 1:00 PM the Prussian army had broken completely. Davout's infantry pursued until 4:30, the cavalry until 6:30.

The victory was Davout's, and it was complete, but the cost had been high. Davout had 8000 casualties, almost one-third of his corps. The Prussians suffered more, but not proportionate to their numbers, with 12,000 killed or wounded and 3000 captured. Few organized units of any size escaped. When Napoleon, at 2:00 AM on the 15th, heard of Davout's victory over 64,000 Prussians, he refused to believe it. "Your marshal . . . saw double today," he roared at the messenger. By the 16th, however, he had accepted the facts and wrote Davout a letter of congratulation to be shared by his generals and men.

Major credit for destroying the Prussian army must go to Davout. Had he been overrun on 14 October, Brunswick might have escaped to join the Russians, thus making a final victory over the Allies much more difficult and, considering the drubbing the French would take at Eylau (February 1807) from the Russians, perhaps impossible.

As for recognition, Davout got little at the time. Napoleon's bulletin called Jena and Auerstädt one battle, that of Jena, where he himself commanded against the Prussians. On the streamers of battle flags of regiments which fought at either battle, *Jena* was emblazoned. In 1808, in belated acknowledgment, he gave Davout the title of Duke d'Auerstädt, two years after the events, when the French public had other campaigns to think about. When it came to sharing reputations, Napoleon was not generous. Davout, all the same, wasted no energy on jealousy; he was a thorough professional, proud of the job he had done and convinced that no one outside the army would understand his performance anyway.

Without question, the major battle was fought at Auerstädt, not at Jena. Napoleon misjudged where the major Prussian army lay and thus gave his whole attention to the action at Jena and none to that at Auerstädt. He must have credit for striking at Hohenlöhe on 14 October—otherwise, more of the Prussian army might have moved northward to attack Davout, or to escape. However, Napoleon moved on the false assumption that the Prussian army was before him. In a way, Bonaparte was misled by Lannes's reports of the 13th; when the estimates of enemy numbers reached 20,000, Napoleon's imagination took over, and in late afternoon he was convinced he had 60,000 or more before him. But false intelligence is always a factor together with the "fog of battle." Neither can excuse a commander, especially a Napoleon. The commander takes credit for victory and blame for defeat; there are no excuses.

Napoleon benefited at Jena from the actions of good subordinates, notably Marshal Lannes. But there is also the ineptitude of Napoleon's opponents. The Prussians went far toward defeating themselves, both at Jena and Auerstädt. As noted above, they had grossly overestimated the strength and effectiveness of their own army. They advanced without waiting for the Russians, extended their forces westward, and made themselves vulnerable; they had no effective centralized command; Brunswick's and Hohenlöhe's armies were separated; and there was little coordination between the two.

Like Marengo, Jena and Auerstädt preyed on Napoleon's mind. On St. Helena, he reinterpreted the battles for Montholon. The crucial action, he said, was at Jena. Davout merely blocked the enemy's escape across the upper Saale at Kosen. Even if Davout had been pushed back to the Saale, he could have held the bridge at Kosen with as few as 6000 men. Bernadotte marched to Dornburg, as ordered, putting himself on Brunswick's flank and confusing his actions.[2] Bernadotte's absence allowed Davout "to cover himself with immortal glory and to carry the reputation of the French infantry to the highest point," but "in any case the victory was assured at Jena." If that is not an outright falsification, it is an interesting piece of self-deception.

## Berlin and the Continental Blockade

Napoleon directed Davout to march on Berlin and gave his corps the honor of entering first, on 24 October 1806. Napoleon arrived the next day after paying his respects at the tomb of Frederick the Great in Potsdam. Meanwhile, various corps columns, joined at crucial junctures by Murat's cavalry, pursued the few remaining organized units of the Prussian army. The Prussian reserve, under the Prince von Württemberg, was shattered at Halle on 17 October. The remnants of Hohenlöhe's main body surrendered on 28 October at Prenzlau. Blücher valiantly tried to defend Lübeck, but he had to surrender on 7 November. The fortresses from Magdeburg to Stettin surrendered without much of a fight; on the Baltic, however, some fortresses held for months, with Danzig and Königsberg, especially, becoming factors in the war. Similarly, Prussian fortresses in Silesia had to be reduced. Of the mobile forces of Prussia, hardly anything remained. Only Lestocq, with 15,000 men (by February only 9000), joined the Russians and fought on. The king and queen of Prussia took refuge with the czar.

On 21 November, Napoleon turned his hand to economic warfare on a grand scale. He issued the Berlin Decree, which initiated the Continental System—a self-blockade of Europe, or as much of it as Napoleon could command—directed toward bankrupting Britain by destroying its trade with the Continent. It proclaimed a blockade of the British Isles (in fact unenforcible) and closed European ports to British vessels, ships carrying British goods, or ships which had taken on cargoes at British ports, including colonial ones. The Berlin Decree (and the supporting Milan Decree of 1807) also made a bid for the support of neutrals, notably the United States, by championing freedom of the seas and denouncing the British blockade of the European coast as illegal. Napoleon's actions toward the United States did not jibe with his words. French privateers shot up American merchantmen, and French customs officials seized and impounded U.S. vessels until mid-1811. Nevertheless, Napoleon's propaganda in part helped to lead the United

---

[2]Bernadotte's behavior was astounding and amounted almost to treason. He had refused to march with Davout and, although he could hear the guns of both Jena and Auerstädt during the day of 14 October, he moved stolidly to Dornburg and fought in neither battle. His behavior can be explained by vanity—his unwillingness to serve under Davout—plus the fact that he technically was protected by orders directing him to Dornburg. He was chastized by Napoleon but not punished, perhaps because he was a member of the imperial family. He had married Desirée Clary, with whom Napoleon had once thought himself in love and who was the sister of Madame Joseph Bonaparte.

States into the War of 1812 against Britain. Thus, in world perspective, the United States took the side of France in the year when Napoleon launched his invasion of Russia.


## On to Warsaw and the Countess Walewska

At the end of 1806, troops of France and its allies, Bavaria and Württemberg, invaded Prussian Poland and called on the Polish people to rise up against their Prussian rulers. Meanwhile, on 11 December 1806, Elector Frederick Augustus of Saxony deserted Prussia and allied with France. Napoleon named him king of Saxony and shortly made him temporary ruler of the new Duchy of Warsaw.

Napoleon created the Duchy of Warsaw, it seemed to the Poles, as an earnest of intent to restore the Kingdom of Poland. He probably was sincere, but he kept waiting for the right time to hand it over to a Bonaparte king (his brother Jerome was the most likely candidate), and that time never came. However, the Poles saw Napoleon as their savior and their only hope. The Kingdom of Poland had been destroyed in 1795 by partition among Austria, Prussia, and Russia. France, under Napoleon, was the only power that seemed capable of imposing its will on all three. The French appeal to Polish patriotism thus drew a great response. High Polish nobles, the most prominent of whom was Prince Josef Poniatowski, took leadership, and thousands of Poles rallied to fight beside the French.[3]

Davout's corps and Murat's cavalry led the way to Warsaw. On 10 December Davout's corps entered the city first, in parade order, to the cheers of the populace. Poniatowski appeared to greet him, and the Polish aristocracy outdid themselves in entertaining the French commanders. Napoleon himself, soon joined by Talleyrand to deal with diplomatic problems, took up headquarters in Warsaw on 1 January 1807.

When Napoleon dismounted at the steps of his residence in the city, a group of beautiful, rosy-cheeked little girls came forward to give him flowers. He was charmed and responded with smiles and hugs, but his real attention was on a dazzling blonde who silently managed the children. Michel Duroc, his grand marshal of the palace, made inquiries and reported that she was Countess Maria Walewska, age eighteen and married to a nobleman forty-odd years her senior—but very faithful to him all the same.

The French emperor's desire to meet Madame Walewska was broadcast among the gentry, and Prince Poniatowski made sure she was at his next

---

[3]Poniatowski, a cavalier out of legend, was made a Marshal of France in 1813, the only foreigner to achieve that grade; he was drowned during the retreat from Leipzig a couple of days later. Some Poles were still with Napoleon at Waterloo—some, admittedly, out of preference for France over Russia, then dominating Poland, as it has since, except for twenty years between the two World Wars.

party. She was tongue-tied when introduced to Napoleon, but he was even more intrigued. He wrote her love notes, which she found shocking. But the Polish nobles, and reputedly even her elderly husband, urged her to try to please the emperor for the sake of her country. Only Napoleon, she was made to understand, could restore the ancient Kingdom of Poland. Maria consented, and in short order she was Napoleon's mistress. When he moved his head-quarters north to Finkenstein, she went with him and was his comfort during the terrible winter campaign.[4] (Josephine, who had come up to Mainz, was sent back to Paris on the excuse that Poland was too dangerous for her.)

## Chasing the Russians

Let us return to December 1806. In that month, the Russians began to come at the French armies; the Prussian king, his will stiffened by the beautiful Queen Louise, refused to talk terms. The war promised to be a long one. Despite the delightful Walewska, Napoleon regretted having to fight in Poland during the winter of 1806–07. He had been away from Paris too long; the politicians back home were up to their usual plotting, and the business community was nervous.

Among Napoleon's troops, moreover, morale was poor; they were surly and moved sluggishly. There was no system of rotation: men were sent home only when wounded severely, and whole units were sent back only when judged useless or a liability. Food was in short supply: Poland was too bare and sparsely settled for an effective program of living off the land and, although the army trains carried four days' rations of hardtack and dried beef, they were seldom issued unless a major battle loomed. Peace was what the men had expected after the sweeping victories over the Prussians; instead, they found themselves ordered into the frozen wastes of Poland. They had not been able to rest, and they had not been fully re-equipped. Their officers, and even the marshals, had lost some of their enthusiasm. Napoleon's appearance still brought cries of "*Vive l'Empereur!*," but they were echoed weakly among the troops. Even from the Guard regiments Napoleon heard muttered obscenities and some bold complaints. The *grognards* marched, as did the rest of the army, but woodenly. This may account in part for Napoleon's limited success during the winter.

In December 1806, as the French entered Poland, Marshal Count Alexander Kamenski directed the Russian army of 70,000, plus Lestocq's 15,000 Prussians, toward Warsaw in widely dispersed columns. Napoleon, still in Prussia, concocted a plan to trap the Allies on the Narew River, northeast of

---

[4]Maria became something more than a mistress to Napoleon. When he returned to Paris, she went with him and was given a house near the Tuileries. Their son, Alexander Walewski, born in 1810, was recognized by Napoleon as a natural son and made one of his heirs. Madame Walewska was the only one of Napoleon's loves to visit him in exile on Elba.

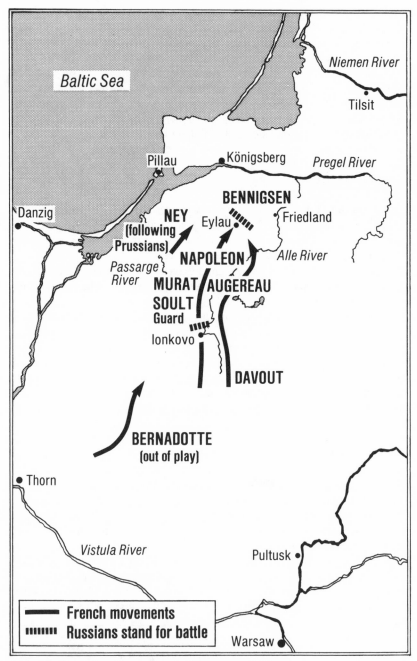

**Map 18. The Eylau Campaign, 1-7 February 1807**

Warsaw. It required a blitzkrieg by his disspirited troops, however, and they were not up to it. As a result, on 26 December, Lannes's corps of 20,000 came up against General Theophil von Bennigsen's Russian corps of 37,000 at Pultusk. Lannes got the worst of it, but he was rescued late in the day by Davout, whose corps evened the odds. Bennigsen withdrew northward under cover of darkness.

The elderly Kamenski, age seventy-five, meanwhile had resigned his command. Bennigsen, sixty-two, took over the Allied army in Poland, and in January 1807 ordered an offensive to the south. It was a good move, since Napoleon, confident that there would be no major action until spring, had spread his corps for wintering and had assigned the largest area to Bernadotte, who was to support the sieges of Danzig and Königsberg. Bernadotte and Ney fell back southward before the Allied columns, and Napoleon, on 27 January, ordered a counteroffensive in force. Bernadotte received no orders to join the main army until 3 February, however, and therefore he was two days' march away when the major battle of Eylau occurred.

Moreover, the Russians were forewarned of the French offensive. Berthier sent Bernadotte orders on 30 and 31 January, in multiple copies by different couriers, but atypically in the clear rather than in code. Bennigsen had them the day they were sent, thanks to the Cossacks, the Russians' superb scouts, marauders, and light cavalry. Bennigsen knew not only Napoleon's line of advance, but also that the French corps were widely separated and that he might take Napoleon at a numerical disadvantage. Nevertheless, on his first encounters with the French—Murat's cavalry and Soult's corps—he fell back into East Prussia, generally along the valley of the Alle River. On 3 February, at Ionkovo, Napoleon forced Bennigsen to make a stand, but he could not bring enough men together fast enough to win before the sun set and the Russians withdrew. Napoleon angrily ordered pursuit at all speed.

On the afternoon of 7 February 1807, Murat and Soult were before Eylau, well into East Prussia. They were shortly joined by Augereau, and then Napoleon, with the Guard. Dark had come early, and it was bitterly cold; to gain shelter for his men, Napoleon allowed Murat and Soult to take the town, which they did in a costly night battle. The next morning, when the mists rose after a night of zero temperatures and sporadic snow flurries, Napoleon saw Bennigsen's main force deployed on a long ridge east of Eylau.

Napoleon was surprised but pleased. Since Austerlitz he had disdained Russian leadership, and nothing had happened to alter his opinion. He thought that the French were outnumbered, but he was unruffled. Napoleon had only 45,000 men and 200 guns on the spot. But the night before he had ordered Davout (15,000), 15 miles southeast at Bartenstein, to march at dawn for Eylau. Early on 8 February he sent orders for Ney to join him. Bernadotte also was ordered to close on Eylau, but at two days' march, or more, he was really unavailable. As it turned out, only Davout reinforced Napoleon, and not until the afternoon. In fact, Bennigsen had at least 67,000 men and 460 guns and was reinforced to 75,000 before the battle ended.

## Battle of Eylau

At about 8:00 AM on 8 February the Russians opened the battle with an artillery bombardment of the town. At 8:30 Napoleon sent Soult's corps, with divisions north and south of Eylau, against the Russian right. He hoped to goad the Russians into committing themselves on their right, against Soult. When they were deeply involved, he meant to throw the weight of his army— the corps of Augereau, Davout, and Murat's cavalry—against the Russian left, collapse or envelop it, and win the battle. But Davout, an important part of the *masse de décision*, was not present.

Soult's divisions went forward over the snow and frozen creeks, only to be bloodied and disorganized by massed Russian artillery and then thrown back on Eylau by determined infantry attack. To protect Soult, Napoleon ordered Augereau to attack with his corps. The marshal, his head wrapped in a huge scarf under his hat, was very ill but went forward with the troops. He was not well organized; the order had come quite prematurely. Moreover, the way ahead was obscured by sudden, heavy snowfall. Augereau's men marched headlong into a Russian battery of 70 guns, which opened up at point-blank range and cut them down by the hundreds. One regiment was able to form a square, but it was overwhelmed by enemy infantry. At 10:30 AM Napoleon was well on the way to being beaten. Soult was back in his original position at Eylau; Augereau's corps was destroyed as a fighting unit, with survivors altogether disorganized.

Napoleon ordered Murat to shore up the center of his line by attacking the Russians with 11,000 reserve cavalry, followed by the cavalry of the Guard led by Bessières and such corps cavalry as could be mustered, a total of some 16,000 horse. The Gascon rode at the Russians with his usual bravado, waving his gold cane and disdaining to draw his sword, one of his vanities. The maneuver worked. Bennigsen was taken totally by surprise, and instead of pressing forward his attack against a French center bereft of infantry—one he was sure to break with his masses of stolid footsoldiers—he merely held fast and did nothing.

How easily Bennigsen might have won is illustrated by the fact that, just before Murat was ordered forward, Russian infantry actually overran Napoleon's command post in the Eylau cemetery. The emperor was saved by his escort of 100 men, who sacrificed themselves; then a Guard battalion commanded by Napoleon himself pushed the Russians back. Bennigsen was unaware that he had forced Napoleon to use his last reserve, the Guard.

By the time Bennigsen regained his composure, Davout was coming up on his left. It was now about 1:00 PM. Napoleon ordered Davout to attack,

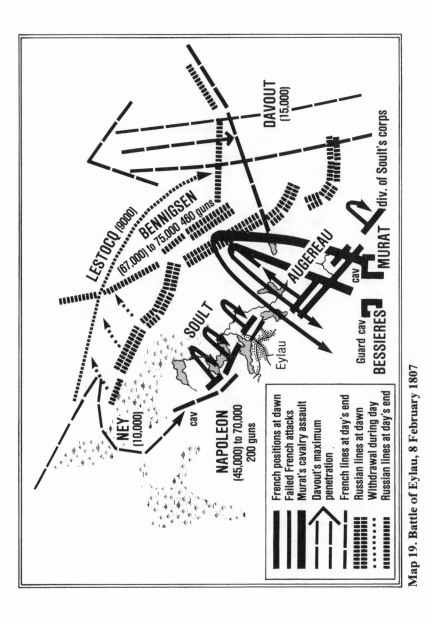

Map 19. Battle of Eylau, 8 February 1807

DAVOUT
(15,000)

div. of Soult's corps

MURAT

AUGEREAU

LESTOCQ (9000)

BENNIGSEN
(67,000) to 75,000 460 guns

SOULT

cav

Guard cav
BESSIERES

Eylau

NEY
(10,000)

cav

NAPOLEON
(45,000) to 70,000
200 guns

French positions at dawn
Failed French attacks
Murat's cavalry assault
Davout's maximum penetration
French lines at day's end
Russian lines at dawn
Withdrawal during day
Russian lines at day's end

while Soult, Augereau, and Murat held fast. Davout, ever dependable, turned the Russian flank, and by about 3:30 the French seemed to have the upper hand. However, Davout's men were exhausted, frozen, and hungry, and at their seeming moment of triumph, Lestocq's 9000 Prussians, who had marched in from the north, reinforced the Russian left, forced Davout to give some ground, and stabilized the Allied line. Ney, who had been following Lestocq until he received orders in the afternoon to reinforce Napoleon, arrived at 7:00 PM and attacked the Russian north flank, but then, as night came on, he fell back and lined up north of Soult's corps.

Neither side had won, but the French had suffered more devastating blows. Two of four corps were decimated, demoralized, and probably ineffective. The cavalry had been badly mauled, and its ranks were thin; there were more men than horses, since the horses had been killed by the hundreds by enemy fire or had fallen and broken legs and had to be destroyed. The remaining corps were understrength; only the Guard was reasonably intact.

Bennigsen had at least 60,000 organized effectives and a 2-to-1 advantage in artillery. However, he was bone-tired, uncertain of the condition of the French, and fearful that Napoleon had more tricks up his sleeve. He could not see that the odds were in his favor if he fought a second day. Although many of his generals urged him to stand, he ordered the Allied army to withdraw during the night. That left Bonaparte in possession of the field, if hardly triumphant. "War," Napoleon would say in 1808, "is three-quarters an affair of morale. The balance of other factors counts only for another quarter." That certainly applies here. The Russian commander gave up.

Napoleon admitted 7600 casualties; he probably had 25,000 killed and wounded. The Russians had 15,000 killed and wounded. In the dark, frozen dawn of 9 February, the French saw a battlefield littered with corpses as far as they could see: men and horses in contorted positions among the wreckage of artillery caissons and wagons. "What a massacre," said Ney, "and with no result." The sight shocked even Napoleon, who wrote to Josephine, shading the truth a little: "The victory is mine, but I have lost many men; I am not consoled that the losses of the enemy were greater."

The Battle of Eylau settled nothing; for practical purposes it was a draw, made so by Bennigsen's lack of fortitude. Napoleon might have won it if he had adhered to the maxim he formulated in 1806: "The art of placing troops is the great *art de guerre*. Always place your troops in such a way that, whatever the enemy does, they can be united within a few days." He thought his corps were close enough together to be united for a major battle, but they were not. He had failed to consider the condition of the roads, the Cossacks' ability to interdict communications, and the poor morale of his commanders and men. He was lucky that he was not defeated at Eylau and captured in the bargain. Davout saved him and almost won the battle for him late in the day.

## Dragging Through Winter and Spring

Both the French and Russian armies, weary, torn, and bleeding, went into winter quarters. Napoleon spent much time during the cold months with Madame Walewska in the castle of Finkenstein. From there he ran the French government and even composed detailed instructions for organizing a school for young ladies at Ecouen. Still, reorganizing, re-equipping, and refilling the ranks of his army was his first priority.

The emperor ordered Marshal Augereau, who was still very ill, back to France and called Masséna to the *Grande Armée*. He set French conscription quotas higher than at any time since 1799; over 100,000 men were drafted. At the same time, all the states allied with France, including Italy, Westphalia, and Holland, were asked for new contingents of troops. The *Grande Armée* in Poland was brought to over 200,000 men, backed by 100,000 more in Germany and 300,000 in France. New men meant fresh enthusiasm. The morale of those present had been raised by dispatching to France the wounded and the psychologically unfit. The veterans were given plenty of rest and better rations. Fresh horses were secured for the cavalry, better than those lost earlier: massive Prussian Trakehners and muscular, steady warmbloods from Bavaria, Hesse, and Württemberg. By the spring of 1807, the *Grande Armée* was ready to fight again.

Napoleon's plan for the spring was to annihilate Bennigsen. To destroy the enemy's army was always his major purpose; other objectives were merely intermediate. He had kept Marshal Lefebvre's corps battering away at Danzig only because it threatened his rear (the British might land Allied troops there) and because the Allies shipped in supplies through the port. By 27 May, Danzig was in French hands, and Napoleon believed he could mount a new offensive. His corps were still widely separated, however, and Bennigsen knew it from the reports of his ever-swarming Cossacks.

Bennigsen, meanwhile, had rebuilt the Russian (Allied) army as well and had 90,000 men under his (and Lestocq's) command, with 30,000 in the Tilsit area and 20,000 keeping pressure on Masséna's corps near Warsaw. He planned to throw 90,000 men across the Passarge River and scatter the French before Napoleon could consolidate his forces. But Lestocq attacked prematurely, and the plan failed from lack of coordination. The attack was intended for 4 June, but Bennigsen postponed it until the 5th; Lestocq did not get the word, attacked Bernadotte on the 4th, and was thrown back. Both he and Bennigsen attacked again on the 5th, but by that time Napoleon was alerted and moved up heavy support forces. And besides problems of coordination, there were two other complications. First, communication was difficult; although Lestocq and Bennigsen knew both German and French, their subordinates spoke to each other largely in pidgin French. Second, Lestocq was as impetuous as Bennigsen was plodding; his vanity and impatience were very great. Thereafter, Lestocq's mission was to cover Königsberg, the Allies' remaining major port on the Baltic, while Bennigsen himself stalked the French.

Napoleon, meanwhile, directed five corps, the reserve cavalry, and the Guard on Heilsberg with the hope of separating Bennigsen from Lestocq and cutting him off from Königsberg. The French took the town and Russian fortifications on 10 June, after an all-day battle and 8000 casualties, so that Napoleon announced a victory. Nevertheless, Bennigsen continued to move freely northward, although he kept the Alle River between his army and the French. Napoleon chose to ignore the fact that Bennigsen was veering to the east and so directed his army northward, generally on Königsberg, where he was sure the Russians were bound. He ordered two corps and much of the reserve cavalry (Soult, Davout, and Murat)—over 60,000 troops—to march at all speed on Königsberg. The corps of Victor, Ney, Mortier, and Lannes were 30 to 50 miles behind, with Lannes on the extreme right of the army, which was extended over a 40-mile line between Gutstadt and the upper Alle. Bennigsen in the meantime had reduced his army to 60,000 in order to reinforce Lestocq in Königsberg to 25,000 troops. (Napoleon did not know this, however, until he was battling Bennigsen at Friedland.) Bonaparte at this point again violated his maxim about keeping his troops together and made himself vulnerable to an attack from the east by Bennigsen.

## Battle of Friedland

On 13 June 1807, Bennigsen was moving north along the east bank of the Alle when his Cossacks reported chasing a few French cavalry from Friedland, just across the river. They estimated that west of the town was a single French division, reinforced by cavalry and some artillery. Bennigsen decided to cross the river and destroy this isolated French unit. It was, in fact, Lannes's corps of 18,000, but that would have made no difference to the Russian commander. The opportunity was too much to resist. In late afternoon, he began moving his army over three narrow bridges, a process which took all night.

By 9:00 PM Lannes had informed Napoleon, who was at Eylau, 15 miles west. The emperor immediately ordered Mortier's corps to reinforce Lannes, knowing full well that he could not arrive before the next morning. At 10:00 he also ordered Ney to march for Friedland. Mortier had to come from 15 miles to the southwest; Ney had to travel about 25 miles. For some hours Napoleon then turned his attention to the attack on Königsberg and dictated detailed instructions for Murat, who was in overall command. Until well after midnight Napoleon was still convinced that Bennigsen would stand for a major battle only to protect Königsberg. By about 2:00 AM, however, after reading report after report of growing Russian masses in Friedland, he finally concluded that some action was developing there. Napoleon sent orders

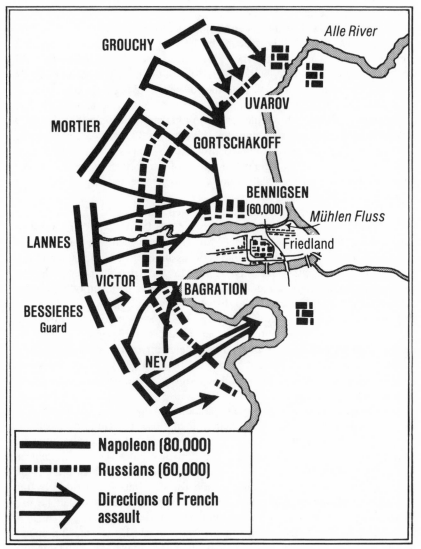

Map 20. Battle of Friedland, 14 June 1807

to Lannes to hold as best he could, and at 4:00 AM he marched with the Guard, Victor's corps, and three cavalry divisions.

Lannes, meanwhile, had been battling the Russians long since. To meet the hordes that filed steadily over the bridges, he deployed his infantry in a semicircle, concealed by high wheat. He placed his cavalry, led by General Emmanuel de Grouchy, on the flanks, most of it on his left opposite Platoff's Cossacks. So deployed, Lannes held the Russians, giving little ground, until a division and some cavalry from Mortier's corps arrived at about 7:00 AM on 14 June to shore up his center and bring his strength to 26,000. By 9:00 AM Mortier's other units brought his numbers to 32,000. As the morning wore on, the Russians began to make inroads into Lannes's left, where Prince Piotr Bagration was attacking along the edge of the Sortlack Forest. At noon, however, Napoleon arrived with almost 50,000 men behind him, all of whom would be on line by 5:00 PM.

The French emperor at first was alarmed, since he had been listening to the thunder of Russian bombardments since 3:00 AM. His first view of the masses of enemy troops convinced him that Bennigsen was there with his "whole order of battle," which Napoleon assumed to be 80,000 or more, since he did not know of the men sent to Lestocq in Königsberg. Had he again committed the same blunder as at Eylau? Was he again outnumbered because of the 60,000 men he had dispatched to Königsberg? Napoleon had Berthier write Murat to take Königsberg at all speed—allowing himself no theatrical charges—and to march with Davout's corps for Friedland. He might, he said, content himself with bombarding the enemy until the morrow, so he hoped Murat and Davout would be present by 1:00 PM without fail, which would give him undoubted numerical superiority. He already had superiority but did not know it.

Napoleon personally reconnoitered the enemy position, first with binoculars from the high ground at Posthenen, then closer up. He also dispatched every available aide to check the enemy positions. The more familiar he became with the Russian dispositions, the more incredulous he was. Bennigsen had trapped himself! His back was to the Alle River, over which there could be no quick withdrawal. In addition, the Russian line was divided by the sizable stream, the Mühlen Fluss. Finally, Napoleon realized that he had Bennigsen outnumbered. There was no reason to delay a battle.

By 5:00 PM, when the last of his troops arrived, the French emperor was in jubilant spirits. "It is a good day! It is the anniversary of Marengo!" he shouted to the troops as he rode about. They responded with cheers. Napoleon was certain now that he could crush the enemy with superior mass, and he did not propose to play sporting games. There would be no subtleties; he would merely roll forward and push the Russians into the river.

Ney, whose corps had virtually missed the Battle of Eylau, was ordered to make the main attack on the Russian left (south) flank and drive the enemy on the south side of the Mühlen Fluss into and through Friedland. The corps of Lannes and Mortier, flanked on the north by Grouchy's reinforced cavalry, would hold fast. Victor's corps and the Guard were in reserve. By 5:30, Ney's infantrymen were storming through the Sortlack Forest, followed by the cavalry of Latour-Maubourg. By 6:00 all the enemy south of the Mühlen Fluss were jammed into Friedland, where the town and the bridges were set on fire. The Russians to the north were bravely attempting a counterattack, but to no avail. A half-hour later Lannes and Mortier moved forward, while Grouchy stood on the high ground and watched the Cossacks he had battled so fiercely retreat up the Alle. At 10:30 the battle was over, with Russian survivors still trying to swim the Alle. Russian losses were at least 30,000, half of them killed, burned alive, or drowned. What remained of Bennigsen's main force was demoralized, scattered, and ineffective. French casualties were not light—10,000 with 1400 killed—but this time a climactic battle had been won.

On 15 June, the day after Friedland, Lestocq abandoned Königsberg and tried to link up with the remnants of Bennigsen's army. Further fighting was impossible, however. Murat's cavalry moved swiftly east from Königsberg, with the corps of Davout behind him and Ney, from Friedland, close behind. The campaign was, in effect, over.

Without doubt Napoleon scored a triumph at Friedland. It was made possible by the errors of Bennigsen, who had divided his forces and put himself into an impossible position with his back to the Alle. Napoleon also had divided his forces, but, as Friedland proved, he had sufficient corps close enough together to beat the Russians. If, on the other hand, Bennigsen had attacked Lannes at Friedland with all his forces, Napoleon might not have been able to save him and win the battle. At worst, from the Russian viewpoint, Friedland would have been another Eylau. That probably would not have been very damaging to the Russians, but it could have been fatal for the French emperor, whose nation might not have tolerated another great bloodletting.[5]

That Napoleon had 80,000 men on the field and could roll over Bennigsen at the end is to the credit of Lannes, who held the field through the night of 13–14 June with 18,000 against 60,000. General Grouchy, commanding the cavalry on Lannes's left flank, kept the Cossacks at bay and prevented them from getting any accurate idea of Napoleon's strength. The French emperor himself displayed the ability to muster his forces in relative concealment and thus to achieve some surprise when he hurled his masses against Bennigsen. He had the numbers; he tried no razzle-dazzle play but merely crushed the enemy against the river. He had learned to use mass, finally. He had divided his forces, but not so disastrously as before Eylau.

---

[5]Napoleon's hold on the French people was not that tenuous, but it was on the politicians and *notables* who ran the country. Even an extended campaign could start them making contingency plans to save themselves, if not actually set them to plotting. This will be illustrated in discussing the last campaigns.

## Tilsit

After the Battle of Friedland, Bennigsen made his official reports as optimistic as possible, but he wrote privately to the Grand Duke Constantine, the czar's brother: "Ask him [the czar] if he does not want to stop the effusion of blood; it is not combat any more, but a veritable butchery." On 19 June Alexander I asked for a truce. Napoleon assented and requested a personal meeting with the czar. It was staged (there is no other word for it) at Tilsit on 25 June on a raft anchored in the Niemen River—the dividing line, as it were, between Russia and Europe. Napoleon turned on all his charm, leading with the bright smile he seldom revealed and a warm embrace. The czar, flattered, responded in friendly fashion, the more so when he discovered that Napoleon had no demands on him, only on the Prussian king, on whom he found it convenient to blame the war. Fêtes were given for the members of royalty present, and their ministers and military commanders. French units entertained their opposite numbers on the Russian side (the grenadiers of the Imperial Guard the grenadiers of Alexander's Guard, and so forth).

Together, the tall, blond Alexander and the small, dynamic Napoleon inspected each other's armies, Napoleon especially delighting in Alexander's more exotic troops: the Cossacks, Kalmouks, and Baskirs. While they thus enjoyed themselves, Napoleon proposed a division of power between Russia and France in Europe and a future division of the Ottoman Empire between them. The czar was enthralled with his newfound "friend."

The traitorous Talleyrand, summoned from Warsaw to Tilsit, privately told the czar that Napoleon could not be trusted, but Alexander was under the Bonaparte spell. Moreover, since he had to make peace anyway, the terms offered were incredible. He would lose no territory; all he had to do was join the Continental System (which meant war with Britain, but only Russian commerce would suffer). Napoleon even allowed Alexander to delay his decision until he had tried to mediate peace between France and England, which, of course, failed.

As for Prussia, Napoleon was much taken with its queen, Louise, who was beautiful, spirited, and an outspoken patriot. "The only man in Prussia," he called her, reacting to the bland resignation of her husband. However, Napoleon's fascination did not deter him from robbing Prussia blind. The country was required to give up its part of Poland, which became the Duchy of Warsaw as Napoleon's earnest to the Poles that he would resurrect the Kingdom of Poland. Prussian lands west of the Elbe River, plus those of its allies—Brunswick, Hesse-Cassel, and lesser states—plus part of Hanover (the rest went to France) became the Kingdom of Westphalia, to be ruled by Napoleon's youngest brother, Jerome. Murat's Duchy of Berg was enlarged and became a grand duchy. Prussia was forced to join the Continental System and, finally, to pay an indemnity of 140,000,000 francs. Thus Prussia, like Russia, became an ally of France, if a reluctant and surly one.

# 7

# THE "AFFAIR OF SPAIN"
## The Peninsular War, 1808–1813

> That miserable Spanish affair . . .
> is what killed me.
> —Napoleon at St. Helena

## The Peninsular War

Napoleon's power in Europe was at an all-time high, but he was not satisfied. He meant to extend his control to Spain and Portugal. The decision to seize Iberia was probably the most disastrous of his career because of the 300,000 casualties his armies sustained in the five-year war which ensued, the enormous cost in money and materiel, and the effect on French morale. Nevertheless, the emperor himself was in Spain for only two and one-half months (4 November 1808–16 January 1809). Command of French forces in the Iberian Peninsula was delegated. Although Napoleon did try, to a degree, to direct the war from Paris, the Peninsular War is not valuable in analyzing his performance as a commander. It therefore will be given short shrift.

## Sins of the Spanish Ally

In 1807 Napoleon's empire was larger than that ruled by Charlemagne a thousand years before, but he had an appetite for more. He exerted power in the Iberian Peninsula only through an alliance with Spain, dating from 1795. This had to change if he were to perfect his control of Europe and enforce the Continental System. By the fall of 1807, he was taking steps to seize both Spain and Portugal. As for excuses, Spain had proved dangerous by "betraying" him in 1806. During the tense night before Jena, while Napoleon rested fitfully in the midst of his Guard, he received the astounding news that Spain was mobilizing. In the order, Prince Manuel Godoy, the first minister to King Charles IV, urged unity against "the Enemy" (unnamed). However, after the French won at Jena and Auerstädt, Godoy called off the mobilization. He professed surprise that it had disturbed the French ambassador and protested that the enemy was Portugal. Napoleon thought that droll, but he did not react at the time. After Tilsit, he was ready to deal with the danger of Iberia to the French Empire.

Spain and Portugal were not military powers, but Portugal had been a British ally for centuries, and the British Navy could land enemy troops at will on the shores of either. Both were trading with the British: Portugal openly, Spain under very transparent guises. Moreover, from Napoleon's point of view, Spain had otherwise been a poor ally. King Charles had furnished him unreliable troops, antiquated warships (most of them shot to pieces at Trafalgar), and promises of money (but no cash). And, too, Iberia offended Napoleon's sense of order. As he saw it, Spain and Portugal belonged in his empire and the Continental System for their own good. Their governments were medieval, their dynasties degenerate (especially the Spanish Bourbons), their people under the twin tyrannies of feudalism and the Church.

Napoleon was certain the people would be grateful to him if he intervened. That was a primary misconception. The people would fight for king and church. A strong nationalism would move the people to resist an invader, although it was not really devotion to country. Rather, it was a zealous loyalty to the crown, which was identified with the hero kings who had freed Spain from the Moors, and the Church, whose clergy had marched with the kings to replace Islam with Christianity. The Inquisition still was seen as the protector of the Christian state against Moslems and Jews. The vast majority of Spaniards were illiterate peasants, who had been taught and believed that the French were agents of the Devil, with Napoleon as his representative on earth. They did not even approach understanding that he (and later King Joseph Bonaparte) wanted to reform Spain and enlighten the Spanish people as well as dominate the country.

## Bourbon Spain

Since 1795, when Spain had been defeated by the French Republic, it had been allied with France. From the Spanish point of view, the alliance had brought nothing but grief. Spain had been relieved of Santo Domingo by the Republic, and of Louisiana and Italian territories by Napoleon. It had lost men and ships in Napoleon's wars. It had been forced into war with the

British, whose navy had devastated its commerce, almost severed its ties with the colonies, and shaken its control over them. Spain's economy was in shambles; the port cities seethed with labor unrest which often erupted in violence. The Spanish Church considered France, which had spawned the Enlightenment, a province of the Devil. The Spanish people generally felt humiliated and blamed all their miseries on the French.

Napoleon had no sympathy for the Spanish or their rulers, whom he found disgusting. Queen Maria Luisa was the mistress of the prime minister, Godoy. King Charles was a gentle, doddering nobody, more interested in hunting than in government, and at intervals insane. Ferdinand, the crown prince, continually was plotting to overthrow his father and/or murder his mother. He regularly betrayed his followers when found out. He was a generally devious and unsavory character, and ugly too, with a stubby body and startlingly jutting jaw. Nevertheless, in a country with a medieval devotion to the monarchy, he was the hope of Spanish liberals and the millions of common people who hated Godoy's regime.

It was Godoy who had negotiated the treaty of 1795 with France, for which he acquired the strange title "Prince of the Peace." The prince was also first minister, generalissimo of the armies, and grand admiral of the navy. He had reached these heights largely because of his liaison with the queen, begun when he was a handsome young Guard officer and she already aging. Napoleon thus saw Godoy as the key to Iberia. He knew that the prime minister would be finished when Charles IV died, or if he were overthrown. The French emperor played on the weakness of Godoy's position. He secretly promised the minister a kingdom in Portugal, guaranteed by himself, in return for the Treaty of Fontainebleau (27 October 1807). This treaty authorized Napoleon to send an army across Spain to invade Portugal and to station a 40,000-man reserve at Bayonne, on the Spanish border. Godoy knew that the mission of the reserve was the conquest of Spain, but he neglected to tell the generals of the Spanish army. In November, General Andoche Junot, with a French army of 28,000, marched to Lisbon almost unopposed and began restructuring the government of Portugal, while the royal family and thousands of followers fled to Brazil on board British battleships.

At the end of 1807, French troops began to inch into Spain. In March 1808, Marshal Murat was designated Lieutenant of the Emperor in Spain and commander of the Army of Spain. By that time there were nearly 100,000 French troops over the border.[1] The French approached Spanish fortresses and posts as allies, in march order, with flags flying and bands playing. Their reception depended on individual Spanish commanders. In Catalonia, they

---

[1]Bessières, 22,000, guarding the Bayonne-Madrid route; Duhesme, 20,000, in Catalonia; Verdier, 16,000, in Aragon; and Murat (Dupont's and Moncey's corps), 40,000, advancing to Madrid.

fought. (The Catalans were by tradition fierce, independent, and jealous of their freedom; they had "shown the knife" to invaders as far back as Charlemagne.) On the high road from Bayonne to Madrid, however, they generally welcomed the French. Murat paraded to the Spanish capital.

Napoleon had called Murat "a hero and a beast," and in Spain he meant to exploit the beast. The French emperor expected little trouble, except perhaps in Madrid. If the city rose against the French—and he hoped it would—he knew that Murat would give the Spanish a "whiff of grapeshot." That done, he expected the whole country to be cowed and submit to his authority. He was right about Murat, but he was dead wrong about the Spanish.

At first, all went well in Madrid. Cheering crowds greeted the French, who entered in a spectacular procession led by a division of the Imperial Guard, each regiment preceded by eagle bearers, trumpeters, and drummers— French horsemen in red, green and silver; Polish cavalry in grey and cerise, mounted on grey chargers; *gendarmes d'élite, chasseurs*, artillery, and infantry, and a detachment of turbaned Mamelukes. But Murat outshone them all. In a green velvet uniform and red boots, white plumes waving over his black shako, jewels glittering from his cap, belt, scabbard, and saber hilt, he sat effortlessly on a prancing, capering black stallion and waved a gold cane to roars of delight from the Madrileños.

The honeymoon was to be short. Murat was unaware that the people cheered partly because they thought he supported King Ferdinand VII. The former crown prince had overthrown his father on 17 March 1808, at the royal summer residence in Aranjuez, south of the capital. Six days later (23 March) Murat entered Madrid, and the populace assumed there was a connection. On 27 March Ferdinand, accompanied by only four bodyguards, rode into Madrid and presented himself to Murat. He begged for Napoleon's recognition and repeated an old request for a Bonaparte bride. He asked Murat to tell the French emperor that he had spared the life of Godoy, because Napoleon would have wished it.

Charles IV and Maria Luisa, meanwhile, sent via Murat messages of devotion to Napoleon and asked his help in recovering their throne. The queen included an extra note begging him to save Godoy, "the innocent and affectionate friend of the Emperor, the Grand Duke [Murat] and all the French." Napoleon was overjoyed. He considered Charles a genial idiot, his queen a slut, and Ferdinand potentially a more untrustworthy ally than the old king. He directed Murat to dispatch all the Bourbons to Bayonne "for talks": both the kings, the queen, all the royal children, and anyone else with a claim to the throne. The old king and queen went happily, as did Godoy. Ferdinand hesitated, encouraged by Spanish supporters and British agents to "disappear" and lead an armed resistance. In the end, however, he lacked the courage and went along peacefully. A few at a time, the other Bourbons were dispatched very quietly.

**Dos de Mayo**

On 2 May (*Dos de Mayo*), French cavalry escorted a carriage up to the royal palace to take away Don Francisco, the last of the royal children. Crowds gathered and assailed the cavalrymen, who cut their way out. Frustrated, the people tore the carriage to shreds. As the news spread, people took to the streets in rebellion against the French.

Napoleon had sent Murat instructions, including placement of cannon for best effect, on how to handle a mob action in Madrid. The marshal had his troops poised on the outskirts of the city, ready to move down streets that ran to the center of the capital like spokes to the hub of a wheel. The French converged from all directions on the central plaza, the Puerta del Sol, driving the Spanish before them. A few strong points held by Spanish regulars were bypassed and taken later. Plazas en route and finally the Puerta del Sol were swept by cannon fire and then overrun by cavalry. The Madrileños were unarmed but fought valiantly with household implements, tools, sticks, and stones. They rained chamber pots, cookware, furniture, and roof tiles on the French from upper stories and housetops. But all was in vain. By mid-afternoon Madrid was quiet. Next morning French firing squads cut down alleged leaders and Spaniards caught with weapons. Madrid would never rise again against the French, but other parts of Spain took the example to heart.

Atrocities committed on the *Dos de Mayo* have remained part of Spanish folklore—especially those of the Mamelukes, although there were only eighty-six of them. These barbaric warriors, pummelled from above, entered buildings and beheaded men, women, and children, rolling their heads down the stairs. Moreover, they were Moslems. Napoleon had brought back the Moors to persecute Spanish Christians, and they never forgave him for that. He had a war on his hands.

Almost unnoticed by the French, a grass-roots rebellion blazed up and spread over Spain. (Such news as reached Bayonne was not taken seriously.) With enormous effect, the Spanish clergy rallied the people to oppose the "Devil's servants." Some friars actually took up arms and raised bands of guerrillas. Provincial juntas formed; country nobles, fearful that Napoleon would eliminate their privileges, joined the juntas and cheerfully raised and led troops. Many liberal nobles, disposed to support a Bonaparte dynasty in the hope of reform, were swept up in an irresistible tide of popular enthusiasm against the French and fell into positions of leadership, hoping somehow to give the rebellion progressive goals. Many of all classes, as we know, equated patriotism with loyalty to the Bourbon dynasty and the Church. In the provinces not occupied by the French, volunteer armies were formed around regiments of the old Bourbon army. In the north, the most important Spanish generals were the elderly Gregorio Garcia de la Cuesta and the young Don

José de Palafox, an officer of Irish descent, and in the south, General Francisco Castaños. Elsewhere, guerrilla bands were organized.

## King José Napoleon

With the royal family dispatched to Bayonne, Napoleon called Joseph Bonaparte from Naples to take the throne of Spain. The emperor expected Joseph's charm and reputation as an enlightened monarch to appeal to the Spanish. (Joseph was handsome, socially adept, and very intelligent, but a soft personality who had little interest in the military or wars.) Marshal Murat and his wife Caroline Bonaparte replaced Joseph in Naples. As it turned out, Napoleon would have been well advised to leave the soldier in Madrid and the reformer, Joseph, where he was. But the emperor refused to believe that the Spanish would dare to oppose his forces.

Napoleon's misconception was strengthened by the Spanish National Junta which he called to Bayonne. In a country where nobles and clergy dominated society in medieval fashion, many of the highest grandees and most of the liberal nobles—including the Dukes del Parque and de Albuquerque, Count Francisco Cabarrus, and Manuel Romero—appeared, as did the heads of the Dominican and Franciscan orders and a bevy of archbishops and cardinals. Many who did not appear sent Joseph wishes for success. The National Junta cheerfully approved a constitution which was astoundingly liberal for Spain.

Joseph was crowned on 7 July by the Archbishop of Burgos and, determined to govern for "his people," took the road to Madrid with an all-Spanish ministry, escorted by Imperial and (mostly French) Royal Guards. En route to the capital, Joseph wrote Napoleon several times a day, and the letters made the emperor angry. The Spanish were hostile, Joseph said. He was passing through villages where people either stared at him sullenly or were gone; they had left their windows and doors boarded up. Napoleon tried to reassure him: Cheer up! Remember the Spanish at Bayonne. "All the better people are on your side."

Joseph broke his whining pattern to ask for command of troops in Spain. Napoleon was pleased; his brother was showing a little spirit. Murat had been replaced at Madrid by General René Savary, a veteran of no great distinction; Joseph complained that Savary was not even keeping him informed. Napoleon gave Joseph the command, never dreaming that his gentle brother would have to make important decisions. The new king, however, soon found the burden almost overwhelming.

On 20 July 1808, Madrid greeted Joseph in silence. Rags rather than banners—a sign of contempt—hung from windows and balconies. The few spectators watched in vacant curiosity. Almost immediately, some of the king's Spanish followers began deserting him. Polite excuses for leaving were made by the more prominent men—the Duke d'Infantado, Don Pedro de Cevallos, Joseph's minister of foreign affairs, and Sebastian Peñuela y Alonso, his interior minister. Minor officials and servants just disappeared. Joseph was very puzzled; it was a week before news arrived to clarify matters.

On 19 July at Baylen, to the south, General Dupont's corps of 20,000 had been surrounded and captured by Castaños's rebel army. The Spanish general had only 30,000 men, partly untrained volunteers, but stiffened by regiments of the old Spanish army; one division was under a superb Swiss general, Theodor Reding. Dupont had expected no resistance and gotten careless; when he heard Spanish armies were approaching, he signaled Madrid for help (his messengers were massacred by peasants) and went into defensive positions. When, after two weeks, the Spanish appeared, he stayed in place. After another week, however, with no reinforcements in sight, he tried to retreat, but his hungry men were out of condition from idleness and shortly out of water in the blazing July sun. Reding headed them off, and Castaños closed in to make the capture.

To add to Joseph's consternation, Marshal Jeannot de Moncey, whose mission had been to seize Valencia on the east coast, appeared in Madrid after being threatened by "huge" rebel armies from the south. Joseph had to decide whether to stand or retreat. In fact, the king's forces outnumbered the rebels in the south, who could muster fewer than 40,000, while Joseph had 35,000 in Madrid and 20,000 on the highway to Bayonne, many of them Imperial Guards. Joseph preferred to take no chances (nor did his generals, in fairness to him), and on 31 July he evacuated the capital and went into retreat. By early August, he had withdrawn the French army north of the Ebro River.

Napoleon, outraged, accused Joseph of retreating "all the way into France." The imperial temper was not improved by news that 17,000 British, under Sir Arthur Wellesley (later Duke of Wellington), had landed in Portugal and defeated Junot disastrously at Vimiero (21 August 1808). Junot, hoping to surprise him, had rushed into the attack with only 13,000 men. Wellesley had chosen good defensive positions and hidden many of his men on the reverse slopes of hills. (This would be his specialty from Vimiero to Waterloo.) Junot attacked with dash and valor, again and again, and was shot to pieces. The French lost 2500 men, the British 700. Junot, demoralized, had agreed to evacuate Portugal; the British Navy transported his army to France.

At this point, General Mathieu Dumas, en route for Spain, saw Napoleon before he left Paris. "This coat must be washed in blood!" the emperor shouted, seizing Dumas by the lapels and shaking him. Then he turned away, muttering, "I can see that I must go myself and set the machine in motion again." He began preparations. In a hastily arranged interview at Frankfurt, Napoleon persuaded Czar Alexander to keep the peace in northern Europe while he went to Spain. He then ordered most of the *Grande Armée*, still quartered in Germany, to march for Spain. By the end of October 1808, Napoleon had

300,000 troops awaiting his order north of the Ebro. Joseph, whose head-quarters was at Vitoria, was ordered to do nothing until the emperor reached him. His intentions were clear. During 1806–07, Napoleon gradually had learned to use the superior numbers available to him. Especially in Spain, where he wanted to show the people the price of resistance with quick and crushing blows, he could see no reason to use finesse. He would demolish all Spanish forces, and that would be that. So he thought.

### The Emperor!

On 3 November 1808, at 3:00 AM, Napoleon wrote Joseph from Bayonne that he would arrive soon, incognito. Around midnight on 5 November, he reached Vitoria. At dawn on 6 November, a sixty-gun salute announced his presence. The troops bivouacked for miles around began cheering at the twenty-second salvo. A king rated twenty-one; more meant that the emperor himself was there. The rumor that Joseph would command was false.

Napoleon greeted his brother affably, but he summoned him to no military councils, and very few on civil affairs. The new king was frozen out of his own headquarters. Between military orders, Napoleon issued angry proclamations designed to intimidate the Spanish. "I am here with the soldiers who conquered at Austerlitz, at Jena, at Eylau. . . . Who can beat them? Not your miserable Spanish soldiers." To an order of monks suspected of encouraging the guerrillas, he shouted: *"Messieurs les moines*, if you persist in meddling in war, I will cut off your ears!"

Bravado Napoleon could afford. Intelligence reports showed fewer than 90,000 troops opposing the *Grande Armée* across the Ebro. As he had planned, he was ready to crush the Spanish totally. He pretended to give them choices: between war and peace and "a King full of sagacity . . . just and good, or [conquest and military government]." Actually, he was there to teach them an unforgettable lesson, no matter what.

It would be easier than Napoleon thought. The Spanish were weaker than numbers indicated. Most of the troops were barely trained and extremely provincial (the Catalons would fight only in Catalonia), grouped according to their generals' preferences with large gaps between armies (really corps in size), and with no overall command. The generals were so vain and bound by promises to provincial juntas that they could agree only to cooperate.

### The *Grande Armée* Marches

The French army was set in motion on 9 November. Marshal Victor's corps, on the right wing, found the army of General Joaquin Blake and scattered it. On the French left, Lannes, Moncey, and Ney forced Castaños to retreat and

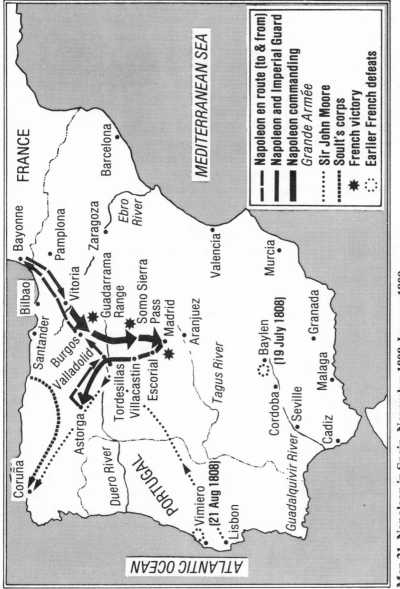

Map 21. Napoleon in Spain, November 1808-January 1809

drove Palafox into Zaragoza. In Catalonia, General Laurent Gouvion-Saint-Cyr battled against the only real resistance, on the road to Barcelona.

Napoleon drove for Madrid with the main army—corps of Soult, Junot, Mortier, Lefebvre, and Victor, plus the Imperial Guard and reserve cavalry numbering 50,000—almost as many horsemen as the enemy before him had troops. On 10 November his force rolled over Burgos, which was savaged and plundered, much to the dismay of King Joseph, who had appointed royal commissioners—pairs of clerics and laymen—to protect his people from the evils of war. Napoleon cheerfully took the blame; he wanted the Spanish to beg him to put Joseph back on the throne.

The imperial army advanced almost unopposed, in march order, except for cavalry flankers, as it approached the Guadarrama Mountains. It was a magnificent sight: infantry in legions with bayonets flashing, regiment after regiment of cavalry, each in distinctive uniforms, artillery rolling behind massive draft horses, the bands of the regiments playing or sounding the drums. Then suddenly, on 30 November, as the first troops climbed the Pass of Somo Sierra, the long column ground to a halt. Blocking the pass were 9000 men under Benito San Juan, who had cannon trained on the single road to the summit. Until it widened near the top of the pass, it was a narrow track carved into veritable cliffs flanking the rushing Duratón river. Thus the Spanish guns delivered a volley on the skirmishers leading the advance, who had fallen back. The whole army was stalled.

**Battle of Somo Sierra**

Napoleon rode forward to assess the situation with his escort of the day, the Polish *chasseurs* (later lancers) of the Imperial Guard: seven officers and eighty men, all young noblemen, mounted on grey chargers. The emperor peered through his field glass, muttered some curses under his breath, turned to Colonel Jan Koziutelski, commanding the Poles, and ordered him to charge the Spanish guns. Koziutelski formed up his squadron and charged head-on, but the cannon blazed and a third of the Poles, including the colonel, were shot from their horses before they had covered a hundred yards. They took cover behind some boulders. General Walther, commanding the Guard, and others urged Napoleon to leave the job to the infantry who, with time, could outflank the Spanish guns. But the emperor was angry: "My Guard will not be stopped by peasants!" He sent young Count Philippe-Paul de Ségur, his aide, forward with the order to charge again. The Poles formed and charged; Ségur, who had an acute sense of honor, charged with them. This time they overran the guns; in an instant, the battle was won. The Spanish fled; San Juan was killed by his own men while trying to rally them. The *Grande Armée* was free to march on to Madrid.

The Poles had paid a heavy price, however. Forty-four lay dead, sixteen were wounded seriously (including Koziutelski and Ségur), and hardly a man was without wounds. On the field, Napoleon decorated them all—living and dead—with the Legion of Honor. He celebrated their triumph in his bulletin of 2 December. The Poles of Somo Sierra became legendary in Poland, as they still are today.

On 2 December, the anniversary of Napoleon's coronation and of Austerlitz, the *Grande Armée* was before Madrid; the defenders made brave sounds, but could not resist. Napoleon entered the city on 4 December and personally assumed control of the Spanish government. He relegated Joseph to the Pardo, a royal hunting lodge nearby. Within a few days, the French emperor had abolished the Inquisition and seized its treasury, confiscated the property of rebels, and ordered his army to sequester goods he thought France needed—from *quinaquina* (for quinine) to prize Merino sheep to improve French flocks. For effect, he sent a few overt rebels before firing squads. He then announced that he would restore Joseph to the throne, *if* the population of Madrid would sign oaths of allegiance to the king. They rushed to do so. Still, Napoleon showed no sign of relinquishing power but worked steadily. He abolished the monastic orders; he confiscated the Bank of Saint Charles. What next?

Then, suddenly, just before Christmas, Napoleon was gone and Joseph was back in Madrid. The emperor had marched north to meet some unexpected enemies.

## Les Anglais

Unaware of the extent of French victories, Sir John Moore, with a British army of 30,000, had marched from Portugal to reinforce the Spanish rebels. On 19 December, Napoleon received word from General Dumas, at Burgos, of Moore's approach. *Les Anglais!* The English! (Napoleon never called the British anything else.) He had never fought the British before, except at Toulon, where he was not in command. His odds were wonderful: 10 to 1. He could hardly wait to get into action. "It is a gift of Providence!"

Moore, meanwhile, realized that he had blundered into the rear of an enormous French army and veered north and west, via Astorga, heading for Coruña, where his force could be picked up by the Royal Navy. Napoleon ordered corps already in the north into action. Soult was to pursue Moore, Ney to block the route to Coruña. Napoleon marched from Madrid for Astorga with his Guard on 22 December, leaving Joseph in command of the corps south of the Guadarrama.

On 24 December, the emperor was over the mountains, at Villacastin. He had crossed in a blinding snowstorm, on foot, leading his horse among the officers of the Guard. The winds had been so high they actually blew men and horses off the cliffs. He paused but briefly, then went into a forced march to link up with Soult. As he marched, however, alarming messages reached him from Paris. Austria was mobilizing for war. More maddening, a plot was brewing to make Murat his successor if he were killed in Spain; his sister Caroline (Madame Murat), Talleyrand, and Fouché allegedly were involved. At Astorga, he sent Soult orders to continue the pursuit and fired off a reprimand to Ney who, in the murderous winter weather of the Galician mountains, had failed to block Moore's retreat. Then he turned back to Valladolid.

Napoleon wrote to Joseph that he was again king in full power and in command of the Army of Spain—minus only some Imperial Guard units. He departed for Paris on 16 January 1809. On the same day Soult fought Moore at Coruña in a bloody battle in which the British stood their ground, but their general was killed.[2] On 17 January, the British Navy evacuated the rest of Moore's army. Soult had not won a victory, but he had cleared the Peninsula of the British—or so he thought.

On 15 January, Napoleon wrote to Joseph that "circumstances in Europe" compelled him to go to Paris. "If nothing prevents it, I shall return toward the end of February. . . . The court of Vienna is behaving badly. They shall live to regret it. Don't worry about anything." In fact, Napoleon never returned to Spain, which, it can be argued, made the "Spanish affair" into the blunder that finished him. However, discussion of that had better be deferred to the end of the chapter.

Marshal Soult, after the Battle of Coruña, moved into Portugal. Moore had left only 12,000 British troops in Lisbon, but by April 1809 they had been reinforced to 25,000; in addition there were 16,000 Portuguese troops available. On 22 April, Wellesley, recalled to London after Vimiero, arrived in Lisbon and took command. He marched north, surprised Soult at Oporto on 12 May, and drove him back into Spain. Wellesley then moved south, combined his force with a Spanish army under Cuesta, and marched on Madrid. By this time it was July 1809. Joseph devised a plan which might have trapped the Allied army. Three corps (60,000 men) were to march south from Salamanca and take Wellesley in the rear, while Joseph, with 45,000 men, marched out from Madrid to meet him head on. The marshals in the north responded sluggishly to Joseph's orders, however, and the corps from Salamanca did not arrive in time. Thus Joseph met Wellesley at Talavera (27–29 July) with less than half his maneuverable forces. The battle was indecisive, but Wellesley, warned by Spanish guerrillas of the approach of the French corps from the north, beat a retreat to Lisbon. There he built his

---

[2]Moore had lost 5000 men during the retreat; more were taken on board British vessels on 15 January. Thus he fought Soult on 16 January with 15,000 men, almost no cavalry, and 9 guns; Soult, however, arrived with only 16,000 men and 40 guns, so that the odds were about even.

base for the coming years, the Lines of Torres Vedras: a line of mutually supporting forts and prepared positions running from Torres Vedras on the coast north of Lisbon, east to the head of the Tagus Estuary, which protects the city on the south.

In 1810, Joseph, with Marshal Soult, conquered Andalusia, except for Cadiz, where the Spanish rebel government was protected by the British Navy. Meanwhile, with operations extending into 1811, Marshal Louis Gabriel Suchet conquered Aragon and Valencia. Thus at the beginning of 1812, the French held all of Spain except Cadiz. In the more remote mountain areas, guerrilla bands persisted and took a steady toll of Frenchmen by attacking poorly guarded convoys and isolated posts. In the absence of strong conventional armies, however, they presented no threat to French control.

### Napoleon's Marshals Attack Wellington

Let us return to the year 1810 and the campaign in Portugal. Napoleon decided that the key to victory in Iberia was the destruction of Wellesley's army in Portugal, but he saw no need to do so in person. Surely a veteran marshal could take care of "30,000 miserable Englishmen" holed up at Lisbon. In 1810, therefore, he gave Masséna command of the 60,000-man Army of Portugal with orders to destroy Wellesley, now Viscount Wellington. Masséna scored a victory over the English general at Bussaco in September 1810 and pursued him to the Lines of Torres Vedras. The lines proved impenetrable; for the entire winter, the French army battered at them in vain. In March 1811, his troops were hungry and in desperate need of supplies, so Masséna retreated back into Spain.

In May, Napoleon replaced Masséna with Marmont, who began another invasion of Portugal but could make no headway. Wellington consolidated his control of Portugal, moved to the border, and in January 1812 took Ciudad Rodrigo and in April Badajoz—the two key border fortresses—and was in position to invade Spain. In June, as Napoleon was invading Russia, Wellington, with 30,000 British and 20,000 Portuguese troops, drove into Spain, seized the forts at Salamanca, and drove Marmont northward. The marshal, who had 48,000 troops (making the odds about even), fought his way back to Salamanca, skillfully flanking every position Wellington took. At Salamanca, however, on 22 July, Marmont tried to outflank *les Anglais* once more, driving south of the city toward the Ciudad Rodrigo road. Confident and careless, he extended his army unnecessarily. Seeing the thin line of French to the south, Wellington, on the hills of Arapiles, ordered the attack. Marmont's army was scattered; the marshal was carried from the field unconscious after surgeons amputated his shattered arm.

Meanwhile, in March 1812, as he departed for the Russian campaign, Napoleon restored Joseph to command in the Peninsula. (In 1810, Napoleon, never pleased with Joseph's performance in Spain, had divided the country into six military governments under marshals or generals responsible directly to him. Joseph was left king only of Madrid and the surrounding area.) He probably did so because he thought the Russian Campaign would be short, he trusted Joseph more than any marshal, and he hoped he could keep the lid on in Spain for a few months. In fact, Napoleon made a cardinal error. Joseph had been marginally effective in 1809; in 1812, after three demoralizing years at Madrid as a do-nothing king, he was even less effective, and the marshals and generals were even more prone to ignore him. Marmont, however, prior to Salamanca, did call on Joseph for reinforcements (he had 18,000 troops at Madrid), but very late in the game. The king responded, moving north with 14,000 men, but arrived too late for the battle and scurried back to Madrid.

Wellington, however, marched on to take Madrid, which forced Joseph to withdraw to Valencia with his army and court—a comic-opera maneuver during which Joseph's troops had to give first priority to protecting spoiled, carping civilians while mounted Spanish guerrillas hurled insults from just beyond musket range. With the loss of Madrid, Joseph ordered Soult to evacuate Andalusia and reinforce him at Valencia. At year's end Joseph and Soult recovered Madrid but had not yet fought Wellington. The British general had avoided a second battle at Salamanca, where the French overtook him, had him outnumbered, but did not attack, probably because of the refusal of Soult to comprehend Joseph's orders. Wellington retreated to the border fortresses to await the new year.

At the end of 1812 Wellington was made Allied Commander in the Peninsula, an honor until then denied him by the stubborn Spanish. The tall, unflappable, handsome, and congenitally arrogant Lord Wellington had become a legend in the Peninsula. "The Peer" was a commanding figure, although he dressed habitually in civilian clothes and without insignia, even on the battlefield. He purported to despise his men, whom he called "scum of the earth who have enlisted for drink." He was a stern and occasionally brutal disciplinarian, yet his men respected and trusted him implicitly and would follow "Old Duero" anywhere. Astride a tall thoroughbred, he seemed to be everywhere during battles. He did not like the Spanish; he liked the Portuguese only a little better. The Spanish guerrillas he considered "scum and robbers." But they all came to count on him to win.

In the spring of 1813, Wellington invaded Spain with an army of 100,000 British, Portuguese, and Spanish regulars, supported by thousands of guerrillas. Napoleon ordered Joseph to abandon Madrid and mass his forces near Valladolid to prevent Wellington from marching on France. The king moved too slowly, and he was outflanked at Valladolid and forced to shift northward until he was behind the Ebro. Joseph finally stood to fight with about 70,000 men at Vitoria on 21 June 1813. The odds were not bad, since Joseph's forces were mostly French, whereas Wellington fully trusted only 80,000 of his men—50,000 British and 30,000 Portuguese. But Joseph and Marshal Jourdan, his chief of staff, disposed their forces haphazardly, and the Allies were able to exploit gaps between corps and unguarded bridges. Joseph was disastrously defeated; his troops fled by all routes into the Pyrenees; Joseph abandoned the army treasure, his carriages, and crown, and still barely escaped capture. Casualties on both sides were light, nevertheless—some 8000 for the French and 5200 for the Allies, which would seem to indicate that the French broke early, which is not true; they fought well as divisions and corps. However, the Allies were not prepared to pursue as they might have.

Wellington's victory, nonetheless, meant the end of the Bonaparte Kingdom of Spain and shortly enabled him to invade southern France. It influenced Austria to join the Allies in northern Europe. In 1814, after Napoleon retreated into France from Germany, he would have to concern himself not only with the pursuing Allies, but also Wellington in his rear.

## Why Napoleon's Absence?

If the Peninsular War was a major factor in Napoleon's defeat, why did he not take charge and win it, in person and early on? The answer is that Napoleon considered the problems of Iberia secondary, that the war could be won anytime. He did not appreciate the importance of the Peninsular War until too late, perhaps not fully until he could take a long view of it from St. Helena. In the beginning (1808), he considered Allied successes a fluke. He "proved" it by going to Spain with 300,000 troops, steamrolling the Spanish, replacing Joseph on his throne, and having Soult chase the British to their ships at Coruña. What was left? Surely Joseph could handle it.

In 1809, Napoleon was on campaign against the Austrians until his victory at Wagram on 5–6 July. Thereafter, he was occupied with expanding the empire, divorcing Josephine, and negotiating a marriage with a princess who could give him an heir. In 1810, Napoleon was absorbed with his marriage to Marie-Louise of Austria and the annexation of Holland and other areas to France. He also was very happy with his new bride and was expecting a child. The warrior and perpetual traveler had become a homebody.

Instead of going to Iberia—his best opportunity was in 1810—he sent Masséna to take out Wellington. Unhappily, L'Enfant chéri was old, battered, and war-weary. He told Napoleon that he did not want command of the Army of Portugal, but the emperor charmed and flattered him into accepting it. In the Peninsula, he showed all too much interest in finding comfortable palaces for himself and his twenty-year-old mistress. By simple neglect of duty he lost control of his subordinate marshals, and he failed.

In 1811, Napoleon's son was born, and he became even more reluctant to leave Paris. He also was building an army to chasten Russia, which had left the Continental System by the czar's *ukase* of 31 December 1810. Thus, rather than go himself to Spain, the emperor dispatched Marmont. He, like Masséna, did well initially, but Wellington had gained strength, and Napoleon made his task more difficult by subordinating him to Joseph. He, too, failed.

During the next three years, Napoleon had no chance to return to Spain. In 1812, he was in Russia, a fact of which Wellington took full advantage to pounce on Marmont and march to Madrid. At the end of 1812, Wellington withdrew to the Portuguese border, but in 1813 he emerged to scatter Joseph's forces, and the king became an "exile" in France. In 1813, Napoleon was fighting for his life in Germany and lost. In 1814, he fought a brilliant campaign in France, but again he lost to the Allies.

If Napoleon had returned to the Peninsula in 1810 or 1811, it seems more than probable that he could have won the war. French forces in Spain were always adequate. Moreover, victory over Allied conventional forces and the expulsion of the British from Spanish and Portuguese ports undoubtedly would have meant the end of the guerrilla war. The *partidos*, as well as Spanish conventional forces, were armed and supplied by Britain. Marshal Suchet, who subdued Aragon and Valencia, proved that the guerrillas could be tracked and defeated once Spanish regular armies were eliminated and the ports closed to the British.

Without Napoleon's leadership, however, no victory was possible. The marshals in Spain would not obey Joseph, nor would they obey one of their own. Thus, although Napoleon steadily kept forces in Spain at 300,000, they were unable to defeat 30,000 British and perhaps 30,000 British-trained Portuguese—all based in Portugal—or to rid themselves of Spanish armies, even though the Spanish alone never won a battle (after Baylen) against the French, no matter what the odds.

Without Napoleon, the war in the Peninsula lasted five years. It cost the empire 3,000,000,000 in gold; many times that in arms, materiel, and horses; and, most damaging, 300,000 casualties.[3] It was a demoralizing factor among French troops, and especially draftees, who deserted in droves if they were assigned to Spain. It encouraged Napoleon's enemies. It greatly weakened the empire long before the Russian Campaign began.

---

[3]Statistics on casualties among native Frenchmen in the French army are the most accurate available, and a guide to total casualties. Some 260,000 of the casualties in Spain were French (the rest mostly foreigners not enrolled in the French army, but the Neapolitan, Westphalian, and others). In the greatest disaster sustained by the *Grande Armée*, in Russia in 1812, French losses were 210,000, of whom 154,000 were listed as prisoners of war or missing in action. Casualties among foreign troops with the French army were about the same. Losses in other campaigns are almost negligible by comparison. In the Ulm-Austerlitz Campaign of 1805, French casualties totaled 14,000, including 2000 prisoners of war and missing in action.

# 8

# THE WAGRAM CAMPAIGN
## The Austrian War, 1809

### Austria in Ferment

On 24 January 1809, Napoleon hit Paris like a bomb. He had "finished" the war in Spain and was eager to act on the threat posed by Austrian mobilization. Impatient and angry, he demolished the succession plot against him with a barrage of invective, blaming it all on Talleyrand, calling him "dung in a silk stocking," and drumming him out of the imperial inner circle.

Austria was preparing for war against France as never before. A war party had appeared in 1808, spoiling to avenge the defeats at Ulm and Austerlitz. It was encouraged by French defeats in Spain and Portugal, the movement from Germany to Spain of thousands of French troops, and especially Napoleon's departure for Spain. The war hawks included beautiful young Empress Maria Ludovica (third wife of Francis I), Chancellor Philip von Stadion, and the Archdukes John and Ferdinand. They boasted as well a cheering section of foreign exiles with grudges against Napoleon—Heinrich vom Stein, Friedrich von Gentz, Pozzo di Borgo, Madame de Staël, and others. The German exiles loudly claimed that if Austria struck at Napoleonic France, Germans would rise and win their freedom.

The Archduke Charles was skeptical that the German states would support Austria. He was impressed by the nationalistic feeling the war party was generating in the Austrian empire (or at least the Austro-German heartland and Hungary), but he did not consider the Austrian army ready for a major war. He was disappointed by the progress of reforms he had introduced as head of the *Hofkriegsrat*, or War Council. He had introduced to the army a corps organization, generally on the French model, but was unsure that his officers could exercise the independent command required within an overall war plan. There were still too many ineffectives among the older officers, and too many dashing but untrained younger ones. Charles had built up the regular army to 300,000 men, and the *Landwehr* to some 150,000. He had numbers, even if Germany failed to supply more, but the troops were poorly trained.

In the end, Charles allowed himself to be won over because he was convinced Austria was bent on war no matter what he did, and he did not want to be left out. The Emperor Francis gave him command of the major army of 209,000, this time in Germany (rather than Italy, as in 1805). The Archduke John was to march on Italy with 79,000 men.

In March 1809, Charles proclaimed a War of German Liberation. On 9 April he marched into Bavaria, thus invading Napoleon's Confederation of the Rhine. As he had feared, the Germans showed scant interest in "liberation." Prussia, the most reluctant of Napoleon's allies, was still in shock from Jena and Auerstädt. King Frederick William disowned the one Prussian battalion, under Major Ferdinand von Schill, which invaded Westphalia, expecting to trigger a mutiny among Jerome Bonaparte's officers, but there was none. Schill marched for Stralsund, where he and many of his men were killed. In Bohemia, the younger Duke of Brunswick organized the volunteer Black Legion of Vengeance which also marched into the *Rheinbund*, but it was forced to flee to Hamburg, where the duke and some of his men were rescued by the British Navy. That was all. Napoleon's German allies stood firm against the Austrians, their loyalty strengthened by the early appearance of Napoleon and French troops. And, of course, there was thought of past and future rewards from the French emperor: keeping titles and lands. Bavaria, for example, had been handed the Austrian Tyrol, but it could not possibly hold it without French backing.

## Napoleon Takes the Offensive

In January 1809, from Spain, Napoleon called up the conscripts of the classes of 1809 and 1810. At the same time he ordered Berthier to Germany to reorganize the 90,000-man Army of the Rhine and troops from the Confederation of the Rhine. Corps were put under Davout, Masséna, and Nicolas-Charles Oudinot, and on their arrival from Spain, Lannes and Lefebvre; most of the Guard was also brought from the Iberian Peninsula, along with Bessières, who was given command of the cavalry reserve replacing Murat, king of Naples.

The French emperor took command of what he chose to call the Army of Germany (but may be called forgivably the *Grande Armée*) at Donauworth on 17 April. He had 200,000 men, including 50,000 Germans; however, half the French had never seen battle. The Archduke Charles's field army was slightly larger but divided north and south of the Danube. (Charles had originally planned to strike along the Main River but changed to the Danube. How he would have fared on the Main is a moot question, but his change of heart gave Napoleon time to get his dispersed forces together and put them on the march only eight days after Charles invaded Bavaria.)

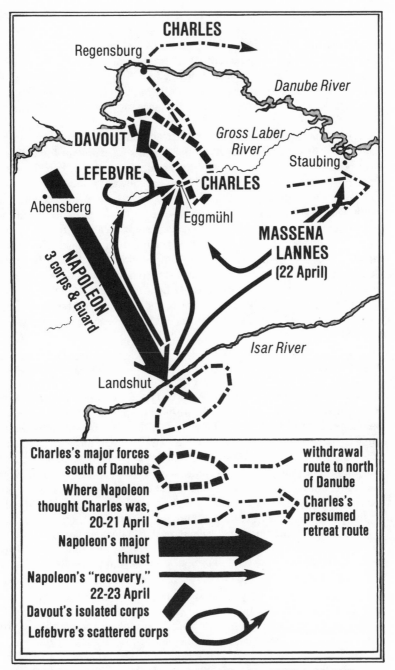

**Map 22. Napoleon Loses the Archduke Charles, 19-23 April 1809**

Napoleon struck south of the Danube, keeping his forces essentially together but, as usual, beginning operations with some blunders. (We shall ignore, for the sake of brevity, the errors of Berthier, which Napoleon had largely repaired before he marched.) After an initial minor victory at Abensberg on 20 April 1809, Bonaparte directed the *Grande Armée* on Landshut, and it thundered up to the place on 21 April, led by Bessières's cavalry. But the Austrian army was not there—only one Austrian division, which the French drove away.

In shifting south, Napoleon had left Davout's corps exposed near Eggmühl, where it was attacked by the Archduke Charles in force. It might have been destroyed, making way for an attack on the rest of the *Grande Armée* from the rear, if Charles had been fully aware of the French positions and moved more aggressively. This false move can be blamed on French intelligence, which depended on very suspect agents (double agents were almost the norm) and on field intelligence based on cavalry reports, prisoner interrogation, and local gossip. But Napoleon's orders make clear that the drive on Landshut was largely a result of his predisposition to believe that Charles would retreat south of the Danube, standing behind one of the river lines—the Isar, the Inn—if he chose to fight. Whatever Napoleon's reason, he was the commander and thus due blame as well as glory. He made a mistake. As he wrote to Admiral Decrès in 1805: "Excuses are vain; no battles are won with excuses."

At any rate, Charles was not at Landshut. Instead, he already had taken Regensburg (occupied earlier by a single French regiment), to link him with his forces north of the Danube and as an avenue of escape if needed, and begun attacking Davout at Eggmühl. As early as 2:30 PM on 21 April, Davout sent Napoleon, who then was at Landshut, a report that he was developing the main Austrian army near Eggmühl. The French emperor took the news calmly, because he believed that Charles was in retreat through Eggmühl and now might move south to Landshut, where he would intercept and destroy him; and if not Landshut, then Charles would surely march on Straubing and then retreat directly on Vienna along the south bank of the Danube. Thus he alerted two corps, Masséna and Lannes, to prepare to march for Straubing, on the Danube southeast of Regensburg.

During the afternoon and evening of the 21st, however, Davout's messages became ever more urgent. At 5:00 PM he reported his men exhausted and under heavy pressure. At 7:00 PM he sent General Henri Piré to emphasize to Napoleon that he was under heavy attack. At 11:00 PM, Davout wrote the emperor, "I will hold my positions, I hope, but the troops are too overcome with exhaustion to even dream of attacking positions with three times the artillery and troops that I have." Meanwhile, Napoleon had sent four divisions northward, with orders to be near Eggmühl by 9:00 AM on the next day, 22 April. At 3:00 AM on 22 April, however, when Davout's letter arrived, Napoleon finally was convinced that Charles was at Eggmühl. He ordered

Lannes to follow and assume command of the divisions marching on the town. At 4:00 AM, he wrote Davout that he was coming in person to his support with 40,000 men. He still predicted that Charles would retreat, however, since he had taken Landshut, and his advance regiments—Bessières's Guard cavalry—were half way to the Inn River on the Austrian border.

At Eggmühl, where Napoleon arrived in mid-afternoon on 22 April, Davout was saved from destruction, pell-mell, by Lefebvre, whose corps was closest to him, and by divisions of other corps from Landshut, which Napoleon belatedly had put under Lannes. Masséna arrived late, only to be ordered to Straubing again, since Napoleon still thought Charles was likely to go in that direction. The archduke, however, had decided to consolidate his forces north of the Danube. Leaving a minimal rear guard, Charles began his withdrawal through Regensburg on 23 April and on 24 April was at Cham, where he was shortly joined by his northern corps, bringing his field strength to 90,000. He withdrew east, down the north bank of the Danube, picking up scattered units, so that by the time he reached the vicinity of Vienna (but across the river from the French), he had 100,000 men.

On 23 April, Napoleon rejected a siege of the ancient fortress of Regensburg and ordered Lannes to storm the walls. The first attempt, about 1:00 PM, failed. Four hours later, Lannes succeeded. Meanwhile, the French emperor had been wounded. Frustrated that his army was stalled by the garrison (6000 men behind crumbling walls), he went too far forward and was hit in the right ankle by a spent musket ball. It was the last of only two wounds in his whole career. It barely drew blood, but rumors of his death began spreading. Napoleon spent the day riding about, sometimes recklessly, to show his men he was all right. He was in for much worse on this campaign.

Instead of following the archduke, Napoleon chose to march on Vienna. This violated his usual rule, which was to pursue and destroy the enemy army, no matter where it went, rather than to make his objective taking cities, whether capitals or not. In this case, he hoped that the Austrians attached such value to Vienna that they would ask for terms. If not, his men could get some needed rest before he went in pursuit of the Austrian army.

Napoleon took Vienna on 13 May and found no Austrian emissaries waiting. He had no clear idea of the location of the Archduke Charles's army but thought perhaps he was in Moravia, where he had found the enemy in 1805. This was a dangerous preconception. The permanent Danube bridges north of Vienna had been destroyed. Thus he began scouting the Danube for another place to cross, aware that he would be opposed, since some Austrian troops, mostly cavalry, were in evidence across the river.

He decided on Lobau Island, which divided the Danube five miles downstream, with the narrowest channel opposite the north bank. He seized and occupied the island on 18 May, and his engineers worked feverishly to erect a bridge between the south bank and Lobau—two spans—the first, 400 yards long, to a stepping-stone island; the second, about 300 yards long, from the island to Lob Grund, in effect a part of Lobau Island. Several separate bridges, of 125 yards or less, were thrown from the north end of Lobau over a more sluggish tributary to the north bank. Building the bridges—mostly on pontoons, with piles and trestles at intervals—and keeping them up was difficult. Spring rains had swollen the Danube, which was rising several feet per day; in addition, the Austrians continually sent barges, fireships, and the like down the river in attempts to destroy the bridges. Keeping them up, indeed, was essential, because Napoleon at this time meant to use Lobau for intermediate staging only.

Although there was room on Lobau, he did not mass his army on the island before crossing to the north bank. Thus, if either of the main spans went down, units on the north bank could not be reinforced. Why did Napoleon do this? Because he did not know how close he was to the enemy army. He was about to be surprised, and by superior forces. He had only three corps (Masséna, Lannes, and Davout), the reserve cavalry (Bessières), and 8000 of his Guard in the Vienna area—a total of 82,000 men. The Archduke Charles had almost 100,000 just north of Lobau Island and 16,000 more north of Vienna.

## Battle of Aspern-Essling

Charles had kept his cavalry busy observing French activity, and by late on 20 May he had posted five corps of infantry and one of cavalry in the hills west of Wagram, opposite Lobau but six miles away. He could not be sure Napoleon's move was not a feint. He knew that his men responded slowly to orders; he preferred to organize them after the French appeared in force, either crossing the Danube or on the north bank.

On 20 May the French completed pontoon bridges across the river. Cavalry under Lasalle led the way across, soon joined by a division of infantry. About midnight, the redoubtable Masséna completed the crossing with the rest of his corps, reinforced by Guard cavalry under Bessières. Masséna was fifty-one, and the years had been hard on him; he was stiff from the rigors of many campaigns and a dozen wounds. (After this campaign he wanted to retire, but Napoleon sent him to Spain, as we know.) Nevertheless, he climbed the steps to the church steeple in Aspern, made a judgment on the number and position of the enemy by his campfires, and supervised the alignment of his corps between Aspern and Essling, since the two towns, with brick and stone buildings, offered good anchors.

On 21 May, Charles unleashed his cavalry, then his infantry corps, against the French bridgehead between Aspern and Essling. Because of the slow march of the Austrians, the action was light until about 5:00 PM, when the weight of the enemy buildup began to tell. Charles had almost 100,000 men on the Aspern-Essling line with 260 guns. The French had fewer than

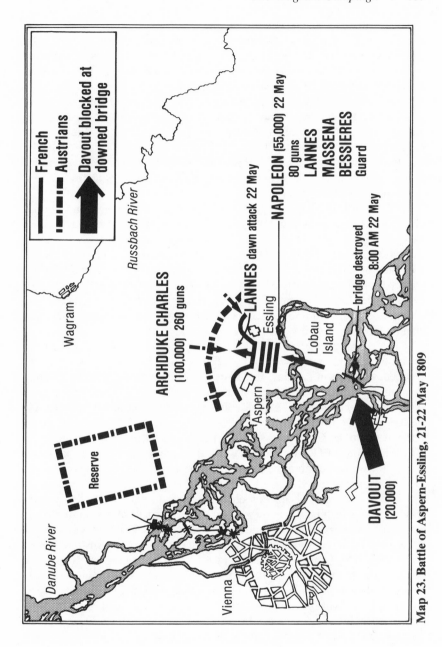

Map 23. Battle of Aspern-Essling, 21-22 May 1809

30,000 with some 80 guns. Masséna and Bessières nevertheless held their own, assisted for most of the day by Lannes, commanding one advance division under Boudet. About midnight, Lannes's whole corps was present and took over the central positions, bringing total French numbers to about 45,000, with the promise of more troops to come.

At dawn on 22 May, Napoleon was in the bridgehead, bringing along about 8000 Guard infantry and more of the cavalry reserve. Masséna gave him the opinion that the major Austrian army was before him. The emperor rejected the idea. Apparently, he could not shake the belief that the Archduke Charles had fled into Moravia (as had Kutuzov in 1805). Without waiting for Davout's corps to cross the Danube, he ordered an offensive, led by Lannes, between Aspern and Essling.

With 55,000 troops, Napoleon blindly attacked 100,000, and Davout (20,000) was destined not to reinforce him; even if he had, the French would have numbered only 75,000. Lannes's offensive caught the Austrians by surprise, however, and by 7:00 AM he had pushed their center back over a mile, and by 8:00, two miles. However, the French ran low on ammunition, and the cavalry dangerously outran the infantry. At this juncture the Archduke Charles seized the standard of the Zach regiment of his reserve grenadiers and led them forward into the teeth of French fire. Lannes's attack stalled at about 8:00 AM.

At almost the same instant, Napoleon heard the news that one span of the bridge over the main stream of the Danube had been totally wrecked.[1] In the predawn hours of 22 May, the Austrians had cut loose a massive, floating flour mill which had been anchored some eight miles upstream. It came inexorably down the river, gaining momentum, and smashed to splinters the bridge just south of Lobau. Davout's corps, massed on the south bank, could not move onto the island. Masséna and Lannes, with Bessières's cavalry and a few battalions of Guard infantry, were left alone on the north bank. Moreover, they would get no more artillery and only such supplies as small boats could ferry across.

At mid-morning, Napoleon ordered Lannes to fall back to the Aspern-Essling line, which he did in good order. The Austrians closed in quickly in full force and fury. Masséna, personally commanding at Aspern, lost the village twice but recovered and held it. In the center, dogged Austrian attacks were stopped by Lannes's infantry, aided by repeated sweeps of Bessières's cavalry. On the French right, Essling fell about 2:00 PM, but Napoleon sent in four battalions of the Young Guard, who took it back. Charles pulled back his infantry in favor of murderous artillery fire on French positions. Napoleon could not reply, since he not only had fewer guns (less than 80 to 260) but he also was short of ammunition for those he had.

---

[1]Napoleon might be forgiven for taking his bridges for granted if they had not been broken four times before 8:00 AM on 22 May: once on the 20th for four hours, twice on the 21st for over three hours, and once between 3:00 and 6:00 AM on the 22d, before the fatal breach.

At about 3:00 PM, Napoleon turned the command over to Lannes and retired to Lobau Island. Hardly had he left when a cannonball smashed Lannes's legs. He was rushed to the rear, where Napoleon's surgeon, Baron Jean Larrey, amputated one leg. It did not occur to Napoleon that Lannes would die. (He did, nine days later.) His first question to Marshal Masséna was, "You don't think [the loss of Lannes] has demoralized the troops, do you?" The marshal said no, but they could not hold against such odds.

At about 5:00 PM Napoleon reluctantly ordered the evacuation of the beachhead. From fatigue or disorganization, the Austrians made no move to interfere and did not even use their artillery. By about 3:00 AM on 23 May, the French withdrawal was complete. Masséna was the last man over the pontoon bridge before it was pulled back onto Lobau; the rear guard followed in rowboats. French casualties had been at least 15,000: Lannes lay dying, his corps barely existed; General Saint-Hilaire had been killed, as had General Espagne, incomparable leader of heavy cavalry; Napoleon's aide, General Durosnel, had been captured. Austrian casualties were higher, perhaps twice as many, but the French had left the field. Napoleon's first attempt to cross the Danube had failed.

The loss of Lannes was an extra blow to Napoleon. He was the first of the unkillable marshals to die (in battle, of wounds, or otherwise), and the last anyone expected to die. Lannes had survived more wounds than any soldier or officer in the French army. Perhaps the most handsome of the marshals, not tall, but broad-shouldered and blond, with the build of a lifelong horseman, he was quarrelsome and violent but showed unexampled bravery in battle. Wrote Napoleon to his widow: "I [have lost] the most distinguished general in my army, my companion in arms for sixteen years, and . . . my best friend." The army mourned. The emperor wept openly.

After the withdrawal, Napoleon pronounced that his army had been defeated by the Danube, not by the Austrians. He would not even give the enemy credit for destroying the bridges. "It was not Prince Charles who cut the bridges, it was the Danube, which rose fourteen feet in three days." The Austrians saw it differently; they celebrated a victory. They ignored the fact that Charles had failed to punish the French as they withdrew and had not even bombarded Lobau.

Fearful of further tarnishing his myth of invincibility, Napoleon refused to order the evacuation of Lobau and rejected any suggestion that he fall back to or west of Vienna or seek another crossing site. "I would as soon return to Strasbourg right now as to recross the Danube; would you sell the honor of our arms so cheaply?" He dictated a bulletin depreciating the importance of the Battle of Aspern-Essling, exaggerating enemy strength and casualties and giving low estimates of his own. He then turned to preparing for another crossing from Lobau.

Napoleon gave first priority to ensuring that the Danube would not ruin his next attempt. He set engineers, aided by sailors called from the French fleet, to build a barrier of piles over 1300 yards long across the main channel of the river to stop fireboats, mines, and any floating mills. This was to protect the bridges downstream; this time there would be two (not one) to Lobau from the south bank. On the north bank of the island, he ordered no less than twenty pontoon bridges readied to be extended over the Danube at all usable locations. To protect all of this, he formed a fleet of six gunboats and a floating, armored battery of 18-pound guns. He also was determined to have superior numbers during the second crossing, evidence that he had developed greater respect for the Archduke Charles. As the bridges fell into place after some three weeks, he began assembling his army, drawing in the maximum number of corps detached earlier. He also called on Eugene de Beauharnais's Army of Italy, which had been fighting a war of its own.

### The War in Italy and Hungary

At the beginning of the war, the Archduke John, with some 50,000 men, had marched on the Kingdom of Italy. (His whole army numbered 72,000, but he had sent 10,000 into the Tyrol and 12,000 into Dalmatia.) On 16 April 1809, he roundly defeated Eugene, commanding some 35,000 Italians and French, at Sacile in Venetia. (The whole Army of Italy comprised 37,000 Italians and 15,000 French, but Eugene too had sent men into the Tyrol and elsewhere.) Eugene kept his army together but was forced to retreat first behind the Piave River and then the Adige. When John became aware of Napoleon's victories in Germany, he began withdrawing over the Alps to reinforce the Archduke Charles. Eugene went into pursuit, inflicting huge casualties at the crossings of the Piave and Tagliamento rivers, and kept on John's heels until he retreated into Hungary.

Eugene then put General Jacques Macdonald, with 15,000 men, on the trail of John and rode for Vienna, joining Napoleon on 27 May. The French emperor received him warmly and issued a bulletin praising both him and the Italian Army. "The Viceroy displayed . . . the *sang-froid* and perception that mark a great captain." But there was more serious business for Eugene. His army was reinforced to 45,000 and given the mission of preventing the Archduke John from making junction with the Archduke Charles. John had marched north along the Raab River, which flows into the Danube sixty miles downstream from Vienna. He expected to be heavily reinforced by Hungarians at the town of Raab, near the confluence of the rivers, but a rally of nobles (the traditional "Insurrection") produced few troops.

On 14 June, Eugene caught John at Raab, where the archduke was forced to turn and fight with some 35,000 men, a mixture of raw recruits and soldiers exhausted from their long march and demoralized by their losses. The viceroy went straight to work, leading his infantry forward, supported by the artillery of Sorbier (later commander of the artillery of the Imperial

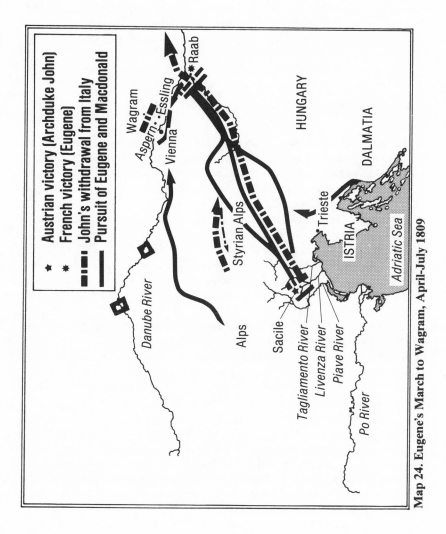

**Map 24. Eugene's March to Wagram, April-July 1809**

Guard). As night fell, Eugene led cavalry charges which dispersed the Austrian army. Although John made it across the Danube with 12,000 men, he was forced to retreat southeast, away from Vienna, to reorganize. He was not able to join with Charles before Napoleon had crossed the Danube and forced him into a major battle. Eugene, on the other hand, joined Napoleon with about 30,000 men.

## Battle of Wagram

At the end of June, therefore, Napoleon had built his forces on and adjacent to Lobau to 190,000 men and 480 guns. Opposite him, the Archduke Charles had 140,000 men and 450 guns. Rains, which had continued since the spring, increased in frequency, and the Danube rose accordingly. The new bridges held up well. Once Eugene arrived with the Army of Italy, Napoleon was ready to attack the Austrians. In the first days of July, he crammed as many troops as possible onto Lobau and moved up the others to the south bank of the river.

Across the Danube, Charles had withdrawn most of his men onto the plateau behind the Russbach River, about six miles north of the Danube. Only some 25,000 were left on the fortified line of Aspern-Essling, which was extended to Enzersdorf. The mission of those troops was to delay the French. The archduke wanted time to array his forces after Napoleon's army debouched onto the north bank of the Danube. He knew that his troops maneuvered ponderously; his officers transmitted orders slowly, and the men responded slowly. It seemed clear that Napoleon would cross from Lobau, but it could be anywhere along five miles of north shoreline. If he crossed at Aspern and Essling, then Austrian forces could buy time (he thought) until he put his army into position to fight. If he crossed elsewhere, then he could act accordingly. This was a good plan, except that he should have left either fewer or more troops on the Aspern-Essling-Enzersdorf line, where the fortifications were very weak, especially near Enzersdorf. Fewer might have observed the French, briefly delayed them, and then moved back; a greater number was needed to hold them. As it was, Charles's advance detachment quickly was overrun and lost.[2]

Charles hoped to be reinforced by the Archduke John's 12,000 men, who were near Pressburg, but he would be disappointed. John did reach the vicinity of Wagram, but too late. There was an Austrian army of 20,000 under the Archduke Ferdinand in Bohemia and Galicia, but it could not help. It was being menaced from Saxony by Jerome Bonaparte, with 12,000 Westphalians, and from Poland by Prince Poniatowski, with some 30,000 Poles.

---

[2]I owe this insight to the expert on the battle, Gunther Rothenberg.

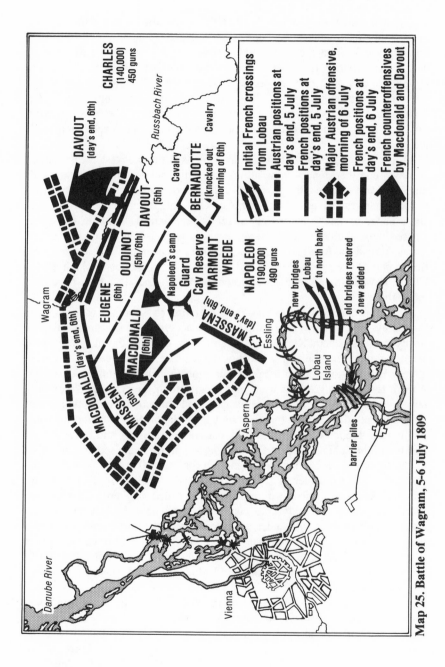

Map 25. Battle of Wagram, 5–6 July 1809

On the night of 4–5 July 1809, Napoleon's army crossed the Danube in the midst of violent thunderstorms and torrential rain and hail, blown by howling winds from the north. "That kind of tempest," wrote Macdonald later, "was extremely favorable to crossing the Danube by bridges . . . shielded by the Isle of Lobau, which was heavily wooded." Doubtless it was also a good night to catch the enemy off guard. The French army initially used the bridges on the east side of Lobau, outflanked the Aspern-Essling-Enzersdorf line, and then, as the defenders began evacuating the line, poured across all the bridges.

The day of 5 July was one of sparring as the armies tested each other. At day's end the French—now all on the north bank—were in contact with the Austrians all along the Russbach. Napoleon, impatient as always, tried to mount an offensive with the corps of Oudinot, Bernadotte, and Davout, spearheaded by the Army of Italy under Eugene and Macdonald, which had crossed the Danube in the afternoon and was fresher than most corps. Macdonald forced the Russbach but was viciously counterattacked, and his men fled in panic. Their path was blocked, however, by grenadiers of the Imperial Guard, bayonets fixed, who forced them back into line. The army rested for the night.

The Archduke Charles observed that French strength was weighted toward his left (the east) and made his plans accordingly. On the morning of 6 July, he sent General Klaus von Klenau's corps crashing through the cavalry screen on the French left, just north of the Danube. Klenau carried the main attack. His mission was to break through the French line, taking down the Aspern-Essling bridges as he went, and sweep into the French rear. Kolowrat's corps was to follow him in a sweep across the French rear, completing a total envelopment. At the same time, Charles kept Napoleon's attention by bombarding the French center with heavy batteries of artillery and, after almost two hours, launching a massive infantry attack in the same sector. The brunt of the blow fell on Bernadotte's Saxon corps of 18,000 men, which broke and fell back in disorder. They were surprised, attacked by overwhelming numbers, and had difficulty in understanding orders in French. Bernadotte, moreover, failed miserably as a commander. Notably, he left his forward division in column, while under heavy cannon fire, for over an hour before the Austrian infantry came at them. Napoleon, finally fed up with him, sent him from the field in disgrace. Masséna, on the Saxons' left, temporarily plugged the gap left by Bernadotte until Macdonald and Eugene could shift left to free him.

Napoleon then sent Masséna to stop Klenau, who in late morning had broken the sole French infantry division (Boudet) near Aspern and seemed to have a clear road to the French rear. Incredibly, Klenau halted when he saw Masséna's divisions in motion and observed that Kolowrat's corps, which had come up slowly on his left rear, was doing nothing. While the Austrians hesitated, Masséna made a sweep across the field such as has seldom been seen in war. Pulling his troops back and edging southward, the marshal allowed enough space for them to organize and then sent them forward in column and line, firing and closing with the bayonet. During Masséna's movement southward, the Austrians were kept in check by incessant French cavalry attacks. The impetuous and colorful General Lasalle was killed in action, and Marshal Bessières was wounded. Masséna stopped Klenau and, as action slowed in mid-afternoon, formed a solid front in Essling and counterattacked, driving Klenau out of Aspern and slowly westward. The archduke's brilliant attack *sur les derrières* of the French had failed.

It was Napoleon's turn to strike back. A mile or more behind the left center of the line was the French emperor's camp, protected on all sides by the Guard (20,000 men and 60 to 70 guns), part of the reserve cavalry (8000), Wrede's Bavarian division (7000), and Marmont's corps of Dalmatians (12,500). As the fighting developed, he sent Marmont up at mid-afternoon to take the pressure off the cavalry and reinforce Masséna. Meanwhile, Napoleon had detached Macdonald's corps from Eugene's army to mount an attack on the Austrian center. It was supported by a battery of 112 guns, pushed as close as possible to the enemy center. After a heavy barrage, Macdonald went forward with eight battalions in line, two abreast, flanked by nine battalions in column on either side. The Austrians gradually gave ground, but their artillery wreaked havoc among the attackers, taking no less than 5000 casualties. The enemy then rallied, partly under pressure of Austrian cavalry, and drove its own infantry forward with the flat of the sword. Macdonald's offensive stalled, but Napoleon reinforced him in the nick of time with Wrede's Bavarian division and a brigade of Guard cavalry. The tide began to turn, and Napoleon gave Macdonald impetus by sending up all the battalions of the Young Guard.

Macdonald succeeded (or at least stabilized his line), and Eugene, on his right, took Wagram. This set the stage for the key action of the battle, although Napoleon never acknowledged it: the attack on the Austrian left by Davout's corps, which had been at work all day. During the early morning hours, Davout had cleared the south bank of the Russbach of Austrian forces, and by about 10:00 AM had his artillery firing from two sides on the village of Markgrafneusiedl, which anchored the Austrian left. About noon, his infantry crossed the river and captured the town, knocking the major pivot from under the Austrian defenses. Davout then turned the enemy flank, widening his front until he was driving west along the river, rolling up Charles's line. By 3:00 PM, fatigue had all but stopped the movement of the corps, but the battle really was over anyway. In mid-afternoon, the French were advancing all along the line. At about 4:00 PM, Charles recognized that the battle was lost, and ordered a phased withdrawal, which continued into the night. He marched his army northward into Moravia.

## The Outcome

Napoleon had not won a clear-cut victory; Charles still had at least 80,000 men who were organized and capable of fighting. But Napoleon insisted that he had scored a triumph, even to Josephine, whom he wrote at 5:00 AM on 7 July that the battle was "decisive and complete." He gave the letter a touch of nonchalance by adding, "I am sunburned."

Charles soon lost heart, however, if he had not at Wagram. His retreat was marked by bitter and bloody rearguard actions. He was ill[3] and not certain that his army, though formidable in appearance, could hold together for another major battle. He was aware that his retreat from Wagram made it more likely that Russia would heat up its war against Austria in Poland, where the czar had already sent a Russian corps to reinforce Poniatowski. (Alexander wanted Austrian Galicia.) Thus Charles asked for a truce on 12 July, and Napoleon happily granted it. The archduke then retired from the army. The Emperor Francis felt compelled to wait until the ill-fated British expedition to Belgium (Walcheren Island) was recalled, but he talked in the meantime and finally made peace in October 1809 in Vienna, at Schönbrunn Palace, where Napoleon had been in residence.

Bonaparte was much relieved, or he would have resumed the war much earlier. He advertised in his bulletins that in the battles of "Enzersdorf and Wagram . . . all the forces of the Austrian monarchy have been destroyed," but he knew he had no triumph comparable to Austerlitz. He was happy to have peace on any reasonable terms, but he compulsively squeezed as much from the Austrian emperor as he could—a fact that Francis would remember bitterly in 1813, when he might have saved Napoleon (then his son-in-law), but instead joined his enemies. Bonaparte took the remaining Austrian territory in the Balkans, gave the czar part of Austrian Galicia and, to the outrage of Alexander, annexed the rest of Galicia to the Duchy of Warsaw; he returned to Bavaria the Tyrolian lands seized in 1805 and ceded to his German allies parts of the heartlands of old Austria.

## Analyzing the Victory

Davout was again the key offensive commander in Napoleon's success. Without the earlier defensive actions of Masséna, however, his efforts could have been in vain. The emperor, as usual, preferred to place the laurels on other brows. He glorified Macdonald in his bulletin and created him a marshal; a few days later he gave Marmont the baton as well; he again praised Eugene. All deserved honors. But at Wagram, as at Jena-Auerstädt and Eylau, it was the steady pounding of Davout's superbly trained corps—always the best in

---

[3]An epileptic, he had been getting worse.

the French army—which guaranteed the victory. Masséna also played a crucial role in scotching the archduke's offensive on 6 July. (The two marshals were made princes in 1810: Davout, Prince of Eckmuhl [Eggmühl], and Masséna, Prince of Essling.) Overall, once more, the factor of good subordinates gave Napoleon an edge.

Beyond that, Napoleon won because of careful planning and superior numbers of men and of guns. He showed signs of having learned to maneuver great masses of men. His direct role in the victory, however, was setting up Macdonald for his victory push, backed by the 112-gun battery, and reinforcing him from the great cluster of units which surrounded the imperial camp. In effect, Napoleon commanded the center, while Davout handled the right and Masséna the left. Curiously, using the great battery of cannon, which seems an obviously Napoleonic innovation, was a lesson he learned from the Austrians on this campaign. Massed Austrian artillery had sealed his fate at Aspern-Essling. He thereafter assigned 60 or more guns to the Imperial Guard artillery as a base for forming batteries. He also discovered that massed artillery was a good substitute for the skirmishers (*voltigeurs* or *tirailleurs*) who usually softened up and disorganized the enemy before major attacks.

And again, Napoleon won because of the mistakes of his enemies and the inferiority of Austrian corps commanders and troops. The Archduke Charles's attack *sur les derrières* of the French on 6 July was brilliant and might have succeeded if Klenau and Kolowrat had been more aggressive. All in all, considering the character of his officers and troops, Charles might have done better to stand on the defensive. When the attack failed, his men came reeling back, spent and demoralized.

Any weaknesses (ignoring Bernadotte) for Napoleon seemed to lie with his foreign troops. Charles's breakthroughs came against the Italians on 5 July and the Saxons on the 6th, yet the troops were veterans and the Germans true professionals. The Italians, on the 5th, were victims of an ill-considered order from Napoleon himself. It seemed wrong to Macdonald in the twilight at the end of an exhausting day, and he told Eugene so and proposed to question Napoleon about it. Eugene snapped nervously, "My God, No, he gave the order to attack, we attack!" In the case of the Saxons, Bernadotte undoubtedly demoralized them by keeping them so long in column under heavy artillery fire.

Generally, foreign troops served Napoleon well in 1809. Macdonald's Italians matched the French in performance before Wagram and on the second day of the battle. The Saxons had a good record before Wagram. Troops of various German states had guarded Napoleon's rear in Germany, and the Bavarians performed prodigies at Abensberg, Eggmühl, and Wagram. Jerome, who had a superb Westphalian army of 25,000 built around regiments of Hessians (famed as mercenaries), left half of it at home and menaced Bohemia with the other. Poniatowski, with the Polish army of about 45,000, had guarded the Duchy of Warsaw, frayed the nerves of the Archduke Ferdinand in Bohemia, and actually invaded Austrian Galicia, which Napoleon confiscated at the peace. Because so many of them seemed unalterably loyal—especially the Germans and Poles—and because he needed them, the French emperor kept adding foreign elements to his army. If the best were mercenaries and professionals who thought of service with the French as the "fat life," it did not matter. In 1812, he would march on Russia with more foreigners than Frenchmen.

# 9

## THE FATTENING
### Compromises with the Old Order
### European Empire, 1809–1812


### Compromises

Napoleon occupied Schönbrunn Palace at Vienna until October 1809, when the Austrians finally signed a treaty of peace. At this time, he was worrying over the future of his dynasty, suspecting that his successor would not be accepted by the hereditary monarchs of Europe. He had no legitimate heir, and although the constitution allowed him to adopt one, such a step had not been heard of since Roman times. He decided that he must remarry and produce a legitimate male heir (in France a female would not do) by a new wife from an established dynasty of a major power. He was convinced he could father a boy, because he had had a son by a former mistress as well as two daughters by others. (Moreover, a child was due in early 1810 by Countess Walewska, his beloved and utterly faithful Polish mistress; he knew it would be a boy, and it was.) Thus at the end of 1809 he divorced Josephine, giving her the château of Malmaison and an empress's income.

Meanwhile, he contracted a marriage with the Archduchess Marie-Louise von Habsburg (of the oldest reigning family in Europe), the daughter of his erstwhile enemy, Francis I of Austria. Napoleon expected this marriage either to make him a member of the "club" of legitimate European monarchs or to produce a son who would be born a member. What he had won by talent and by the sword, therefore, he proposed to preserve by compromising with the Old Regime.

Napoleon, after all, had been born an aristocrat. He remembered his father's great pride in being named a French count after Louis XVI recognized his Italian patent of nobility. He was well aware that, because of the same title, he had gained admission to the king's military schools. Metternich, reminiscing about Napoleon years later, said: "He laid great stress on the nobility of his birth and the antiquity of his family. More than once he went out of his way to show me that envy and calumny alone could have cast any doubt on [the facts]."

In the aftermath of the "whiff of grapeshot" at the Tuileries in 1795, he had met Josephine de Beauharnais, part of whose allure was that, by marriage, she was of the high aristocracy, the widow of a viscount—and a wealthy and well-connected one (not all viscounts were equal). When they were wed, he undoubtedly supposed that he had married "above himself," despite the lady's notorious reputation. After he was named First Consul and ruler of France in 1799, Josephine influenced him to multiply his contacts with the old aristocracy. She took the lead by calling pretty young noble ladies to be her maids of honor. (Some choices she regretted, since they also became Napoleon's "ladies in waiting.") She moderated Bonaparte's love for the large and garish (although she had to allow him his buildings and monuments) and created an aristocratic atmosphere at "court." While he was in Egypt, she had purchased the Malmaison estate where she created a truly royal retreat. She saw to the decoration, staff, and retinue of other palaces later. In 1802, two years before the empire was proclaimed, Miot de Melito wrote: "The Tuileries and Saint-Cloud are no longer the residences of the chief magistrate of the republic, but the court of a sovereign."

The desire to reconcile Frenchmen and to strengthen his government prompted First Consul Bonaparte to recall from exile thousands of aristocrats and, where possible, to restore their property. The same reasons, plus a predisposition to think that there was exceptional talent to be tapped among the old nobility (and there was much talent), motivated him to employ the nobles and their sons in government and the army. Before the return of the *émigrés*, aristocrats who had never left France or who had emigrated briefly had done him good service; there were such as Talleyrand (before the days of treason), Berthier, his chief of staff, Davout, eventually a marshal, Louis de Ségur, a skilled diplomat, and the latter's son Philippe-Paul de Ségur, who became Napoleon's aide-de-camp.

The new emperor created his own nobility in 1804. Thereafter he often explained that the great difference between the old and the new was that his nobles had no legal privileges, but they were given an even greater legal edge by having wealth and property heaped upon them. The most startling fact, however, is that, by 1814, one-half of the new nobles were members of noble families of the Old Regime. Similarly, some three-fifths of the officers commissioned after 1804 were old nobles. For example, the Duke de Fézensac, an aide-de-camp of Berthier, listed other aides he worked with in 1812 (four others of Berthier and five of Napoleon); all were nobles. Of the eight marshals created after 1804, four were nobles of the Old Regime—Marmont, Grouchy, Poniatowski, and Macdonald—while the others were of the upper middle class.[1]

---

[1]There were twenty-six marshals in all: eighteen created in 1804, and eight named after-

**Foreign Nobility and Monarchy**

In Italy and Naples, Napoleon granted liberal constitutions but allowed his local rulers to govern through members of the old ruling class. (Examples in Italy were Francesco Melzi d'Eril, a grand officer of the viceroy and senator, and the Marquis Arborio di Breme, minister of the interior; in Naples, the Prince di Pignatelli-Cerchiara, minister of marine, and the Marquis di Gallo, minister of foreign affairs.) And after much huffing and puffing over the translation and installation of the *Code Napoléon*, he allowed high clerics, all aristocrats, places in government, which all but guaranteed that the Code's secular spirit would not prevail. (In Italy, Archbishop Giovanni Bovara was minister of ecclesiastical affairs; in Naples, Cardinal Ruffo di Scilla was a confidant of King Joseph Bonaparte.) In Holland, Louis Bonaparte governed through the Dutch aristocracy (Izaac Gogel, Twent Van Raaphorst, Dirk Van Hogendorp et al.). In the end, that kingdom was annexed to France, but the Dutch establishment continued to populate the government.

In Germany and Poland, Napoleon gave constitutions and the *Code Napoléon* to the states he controlled directly—Westphalia, Berg, Frankfurt, the Duchy of Warsaw. However, the aristocracy was given the task of enforcing these revolutionary documents. Jerome Bonaparte, in Westphalia, ruled essentially through German nobles (G. A. von Wolffradt, Ludwig von Bülow et al. were ministers, all the prefects were nobles). So did Napoleon in Germany at large. As to Poland, the French emperor was plainer than usual about it: "I want a camp, not a forum." The nobles ran the government (Prince Josef Poniatowski was minister of war, Count Stanislas Potocki was president of the council of ministers); the more liberal ones were tamed by the Church, led by the formidable Cardinal Ignatius Raczynski. In the Confederation of the Rhine and allied states, he encouraged modernization and reform but exerted control solely through the princes and kings.

In Spain, in his lust for power, Napoleon not only drew the nobles into his government (Don Francisco Cabarrus, Don Manuel Romero et al.), but made a bid for the bishops (with no exceptions also nobles) by recognizing the Roman Catholic Church as the sole and established one. This drew a pledge of loyalty even from the Grand Inquisitor, Don Raymondo Ettenhard y Salinas. The results, at first, seemed to be good, but in the end the French emperor had sacrificed revolutionary principle for nothing. Most of the nobles went over to the rebels, and the Church remained the prime factor in keeping the population at "war to the knife" against the French.

Elsewhere, Napoleon's policy of Old Regime discipline and liberal rhetoric seemed to work amazingly well. But that was only as long as he was a winner at war. After the disaster of Russia, his allies among the old rulers

---

ward. Of those given the baton in 1804, eight were nobles of old title; of the eight created after 1804, four were old nobles.

found it easy to take their countries into the enemy camp. With some exceptions they had little or nothing to lose, or so the Allies made it seem. (Saxony was a major exception; the czar wanted to divide the state between Prussia and a Russian-dominated Poland; Bavaria knew it would have to give up the Austrian Tyrol, but survival seemed more important; such was the case with most states with territorial gifts from Napoleon.) Similarly, in France, success had bred acceptance. Louis Bergeron quotes Madame de Boigne: "[After the Austrian marriage], you could easily count the women who would not go to court. The number was so small that, if the Emperor's good fortune had lasted a few months longer, there would have been none." But his good fortune did not last, in part because of the marriage.

## Marriage, Fatherhood, and the Warrior

The story of Napoleon's meeting in March 1810 with the eighteen-year-old Marie-Louise at Compiègne and his premature possession of his bride hardly needs retelling. (Actually, they had been married by proxy in Vienna, which ruins the tale.) Napoleon did everything he could to overcome her hostility to the French and her fear of the forty-year-old "ogre" she had married. Apparently he succeeded, even before their religious wedding on 2 April. The marriage was extraordinarily happy. Napoleon was like a schoolboy, talking with embarrassing frankness about the earthy charms of German girls and in the same breath of his bride's more elevated virtues. "She has the soul of a rose!" He lost any interest in traveling away from Paris unless the new empress went with him. When he found she was pregnant, he was ecstatic and became even more of a homebody.

In March 1810, during the marriage furor, he had packed Marshal Masséna off to Spain to contend with Wellington. Masséna tried to convince Napoleon that he was too old and ill for the job. Moreover, he said, the marshals and corps commanders would obey no one but the emperor himself. "The time is gone when armies . . . had only one will . . . [that of] the commander in chief. Military virtue is not the same. They still fight for glory, but not with the same [spirit of] self-sacrifice of the . . . Republic." Napoleon convinced him that, except for a touch of rheumatism, he was fine and that the climate of Portugal would cure his aches. "Napoleon combined Italian finesse with French grace; he was irresistible in his moments of . . . friendship." Masséna was won over, but the marshal was right about himself and, unfortunately for his master, the French army as well. He went to the Iberian Peninsula but, as he sobered from the imperial hypnotism, very reluctantly. He was unsuccessful against Wellington, as we know.

In 1811, Napoleon again declined to go in person against Wellington but sent Marshal Marmont to replace Masséna. The emperor's expected heir, Napoleon Charles, titled the king of Rome, was born on 20 March 1811, his arrival announced by a 101-gun salute. Napoleon, the doting father, added to his nursemaids a grizzled sergeant of the Imperial Guard, who awkwardly carried the imperial baby about. Meanwhile, Russia threw down the gauntlet by the czar's *ukase* of 31 December 1810, which withdrew that country from the Continental System and thereby severed its alliance with France. In 1811 and early 1812, Napoleon was forced to prepare for war in Russia. In March 1812, as he left Paris for Russia, the emperor restored Joseph to command in Spain, a mistake which doomed the Bonaparte Kingdom of Spain.

Napoleon's behavior is particularly strange in that he recognized very early that a single commander was needed in Spain. He coined a maxim which might have suggested that he was the man: "In war, men are nothing, one man is everything." In fact, he had been too content in Paris to travel to the Peninsula in 1810 or 1811; otherwise, he probably could have concluded the Peninsular War in either year. Since he did not exert himself to go, the empire was much weakened prior to the Russian Campaign.

## A Fat Man in a Fatter Empire

Without great exaggeration, it can be said that the Austrian marriage killed the General Bonaparte who lived within the emperor of the French and thus made a contribution to killing his empire. Perhaps military genius can ill afford happiness. By 1812, the lean, hard-driving, general of 1809 was a fat, middle-aged, sedentary ruler. He was out of shape and out of touch with the army. Except with his family, Napoleon had become short-tempered, impatient of any disagreement, foul of language, and generally tyrannical. This was disturbing even to his friends, especially since he seemed to see no limit to his power. The magic of his reputation would help lead the *Grande Armée* of 1812, but the man Napoleon was not the same, as became all too evident during the rigors of the Russian Campaign.

In 1809–10, moreover, there had been a "fattening" of the Grand Empire. Austrian territories in central Europe went to Napoleon's German allies. Austria's Balkan territories became the Illyrian Provinces, a Slavic extension of France. The Papal States were divided between the Kingdom of Italy and France, which took Rome, the "Second City of the Empire."[2] In addition, Napoleon in 1810 had driven his brother Louis from the throne of Holland and annexed the country to France. He gave most of Spain to military governors and treated King Joseph as if he were trying to force him to abdicate. He allowed Davout, in Westphalia, to defy King Jerome's laws, prompting Jerome to ask Napoleon if he wanted him to abdicate. Murat was accused of crimes and threatened by French troops concentrated at Gaeta. Eugene was

---

[2]For this Pius VII excommunicated Napoleon, who received the news just after his defeat at Aspern-Essling. The pope was seized and imprisoned at Savona in 1809.

given notice that he would lose Italy in twenty years to Napoleon's son. It appeared that the system of satellite kingdoms was doomed, and that Napoleon meant for his son to inherit all their territories, in addition to France itself.

There was more. Napoleon annexed the Hanse cities and large areas of north Germany to France, in order to better enforce the Continental System, under which all Europe was suffering varied degrees of privation. The territories taken included Oldenburg, a possession of Czar Alexander's brother-in-law.

The czar was uncertain whether Napoleon could be stopped, but he decided he had to challenge him anyway. The French emperor had violated his promise of sharing power with Alexander in Europe and the Ottoman Empire. The Continental System was ruining the Russian economy, which depended on the export of grain, timber, and other raw materials to Britain and elsewhere. More alarming, Alexander had begun to think that if he did not renounce the French alliance he was likely to suffer assassination (like his father) by his nobles. Their fortunes also were being ruined by the Continental System, since they owned vast wheatlands and forests. Their pride had suffered constantly since 1807, and they thirsted for revenge. Russia had no allies except Britain, which could send money, weapons, and advisers but no troops. Industry was almost nil. The population was only 31,000,000, or the same as that of France proper, without annexations. To defy Napoleon, who controlled all of Europe, was irrational, but Alexander decided to try the irrational and, in the end, he prevailed.

As we know, the czar issued a *ukase* on 31 December 1810 in which he broke with the Continental System and left the French alliance. He then bid for an alliance with Sweden and peace with Turkey (a war Napoleon had fomented), and by 1812 he had both. Sweden's price was the promise of Norway, a possession of Napoleon's ally, Denmark; Turkey settled for Russian evacuation of Moldavia and Wallachia. This, then, was the situation on the eve of the Russian Campaign in 1812.

# 10

## HEAT, ICE, SNOW, AND DISASTER
### The Russian Campaign, 1812

> The enemy has always been
> beaten and has not taken . . . a
> single Eagle. . . . My losses are
> real . . . but the calamity will end
> when the cold ends.
> —Napoleon after his return
> from Russia

### The Emperor in 1812

A very different Napoleon made his appearance in the Russian Campaign of 1812. He was withdrawn, kept to his command tent, called frequent councils of war but did not listen well, held incessant reviews but seldom checked the condition of his troops in the field, and persisted in an unrealistic view of his enemy. "Why is the Emperor in the rear of the army?" bellowed a frustrated Marshal Ney in the middle of the bloody Battle of Borodino. "If . . . he is no longer a general . . . then he should go back to the Tuileries and let us be generals for him." Napoleon was so changed that some writers have contended that he was already ill with the cancer that would kill him. That seems unlikely, however, since he lived nine years more and fought three campaigns—in 1813, 1814, and 1815—before his exile to St. Helena, where he died in 1821.

Napoleon was, in fact, middle-aged and out of condition from the soft life he had led since 1809. He was fat, which made him slightly effeminate in appearance. He did not stay on top of developments because of fatigue;

his short attention span and lapses of memory may be accounted for similarly. Fatigue and his embarrassment at his appearance kept him from his usual close contact with the troops.

The emperor's style of life in the field had changed as well, so that it resembled that of some Oriental monarch rather than the soldier of the Republic he had once been. His and Berthier's staff and retinues required a whole transport battalion. Napoleon's household alone, without Berthier's, took along 150 saddle horses, 500 other horses and mules, 50 carriages, and a mobile hospital. Mules ridden by liveried servants carried multiple sets of silver tableware marked with the imperial coat of arms. He had chefs, valets, and other servants, in addition to a dozen secretaries, who also had servants. The ministers who accompanied him were equally well served. His headquarters had provisions for 6000 men for 60 days. His and Berthier's tents covered acres when set up, a lengthy process; the emperor's tent alone had two drawing rooms, a study, and a bedroom, and there were seven other tents for his personal staff and retinue. He was guarded on the march by a cavalry squadron of about 100 men given the honor for a day or so, plus two infantry battalions and *gendarmes d'élite* (military police). In camp he usually had these and more. At Borodino the whole Imperial Guard of 30,000 men formed a square around his tents. All this helps to explain why Napoleon took a spirited *Grande Armée* twice the size of any he had ever commanded—an awesome and seemingly unbeatable force—drove it into wreckage in the vast expanses of Russia, and doomed it to a most awful military tragedy: the retreat from Moscow.

## Opposing Forces

Drawing on the lesson of Wagram, Napoleon determined to have masses of troops so great that he would overwhelm the enemy. He even hoped that the *Grande Armée* of 1812 would so intimidate the czar that Alexander would make terms without a fight, or certainly after the first encounters. To amass such numbers, he demanded troops from every country in Europe, even from his most reluctant allies, Prussia and Austria. Two years earlier, for efficiency's sake, in October 1810, Napoleon had created the Army of Germany, under Marshal Davout, comprising Davout's corps and French garrisons already in Germany. The emperor began reinforcing it in February 1811, ordered Davout to put a French corps on the Vistula River in April, and gradually brought German and Polish troops under his command. The marshal found himself overall commander of the buildup in Prussia, Saxony, and Poland. Napoleon redesignated his command the *Grande Armée* in November 1811. Marshal Berthier took over as chief of staff and de facto commander on 1 February 1812; Napoleon arrived in May.

Meanwhile, General Henri Clarke, the minister of war, saw to the establishment of depots in the Rhineland and sent supplies to points designated by Napoleon in Germany on several parallel routes into Poland and East Prussia, from which the campaign would be launched. By June 1812, Napoleon had a field army of 611,000 men with 2000 guns and 250,000 horses. The first wave was 490,000 strong; 121,000 more would follow. Behind them in Germany and the French Rhineland were over 130,000 more, making the total French forces over 740,000.

The *Grande Armée* of 1812 was decidedly not French, but a European army—a testimony to Napoleon's power. There were 300,000 French, but only 200,000 of them were from the territorial France of 1789. The remaining 100,000 were from new departments; that is, they were really Dutch, Belgian, German, Swiss, or Italian. Thus, fewer than one-third of the troops were Frenchmen by birth. The remaining 311,000 comprised 130,000 Germans from the Confederation of the Rhine, 90,000 Poles and Lithuanians, 27,000 Italians and Illyrians, 5000 Neapolitans (the Royal Guard), and 9000 Swiss, plus paltry contingents from the reluctant allies—20,000 Prussians and 30,000 Austrians. Hidden within French corps were regiments of Spanish, Portuguese, and others, and the Imperial Guard was, as always, international. The Guard and reserve cavalry, included in the totals above, numbered 47,000 and 60,000 respectively.

Czar Alexander could not match such numbers. His advisers had promised 600,000 but delivered only 450,000, of which no more than 130,000 were ever massed for battle. His forces would have been even slimmer had he not concluded the alliance with Sweden and made peace with Turkey. The one allowed him to withdraw 30,000 troops from Finland, the other 60,000 men from the Ottoman frontier.

In May 1812, Napoleon, en route to the front and escorted by the spectacular cavalry of the Imperial Guard, made a procession across Germany. People turned out en masse all along his way to see him, even at night by torchlight. More than usual in the past, however, he remained invisible in his coach. Only in the larger towns and cities did he appear astride his little grey Arabian horse, wearing his faded green "good luck" coat, in austere contrast to his gaudy guardsmen. On 16 May, in Dresden, he was met by the Austrian emperor and all the kings and princes of Germany (save the king of Prussia, who arrived the next day). There were twelve days of talks and festivities before he went on to join the army. He wanted a demonstration that his allies were behind him and wanted to impress the Russians with that fact. And personally, no doubt, he needed adulation and reassurance. He was already tired from the journey, and the campaign had not even started.

On 30 May he took command of the army at Posen. En route to Kovno, where he would cross into Russia, Napoleon held reviews for the Guard and selected units almost daily but otherwise was little seen. He did not mingle with the men at all hours as he had in earlier years. Perhaps what he said to

Caulaincourt in November 1812, he should have admitted to himself earlier: "Late hours, hardship, war are not for me at my age. I love my bed, my repose, more than anything; but I must finish my work." Three weeks later the invasion of Russia began.

Napoleon's first wave was deployed in three widely separated armies. The main force, or northern wing, of 250,000 men was commanded by Napoleon himself and was poised to cross into Russia from East Prussia. The south wing of 80,000 men was under King Jerome Bonaparte, whose headquarters initially was in Warsaw. Between were 80,000 troops under Eugene de Beauharnais. The northern flank of the *Grande Armée* was guarded by Macdonald's corps (30,000) and the Prussian contingent (20,000), under Ludwig Yorck von Wartenburg. The south flank was left to the Austrians (30,000), commanded by Prince von Schwarzenberg.

Jerome, at age twenty-eight, was a flagrantly handsome younger version of Napoleon. He had been a hell-raiser and womanizer during his teen years as a French naval officer and had upheld his reputation royally in Westphalia. His German officers respected his military abilities, but he was distrusted in the French army because he had served in only one campaign (1806–07), and in a minor capacity. Eugene, at thirty-one, looked middle-aged because he was balding and wore a heavy moustache, but he was tall, slender, well-muscled, and generally the picture of a professional cavalryman. He had gained acceptance among the marshals because of his outstanding performance in the 1809 campaign.

On the Russian side, directly opposing Napoleon, was Prince Mikhail Barclay de Tolly, with a maximum of 130,000 men, roughly half the numbers of the French. To his south, opposite Jerome, was Prince Bagration, with 50,000 troops. South of the Pripet Marshes, for all practical purposes out of play, were 40,000 men under Tomassov. That was all. Other Russian forces, many just being organized, were far to the rear. Barclay alone had to sustain the initial assault of Napoleon. It seemed almost no contest.

**Kovno-Vilna-Vitebsk**

Napoleon's main force crossed the Niemen River on 24–25 June. The emperor watched for most of the first day from a hilltop on the near side of the river; then, assured that Kovno was taken, he crossed and set up his headquarters in the town. The Russians had gone into retreat. The only enemy the French saw were the Cossacks of the rear guard, colorful fleeting phantoms who struck occasionally at Murat's advance screen of cavalry and then galloped out of gunshot range. On 26 June the army took Vilna, the capital of Lithuania, without a fight. Napoleon ordered work to begin on a major base at Vilna, which could be supplied from Königsberg and Danzig via the Baltic Sea and the Niemen.

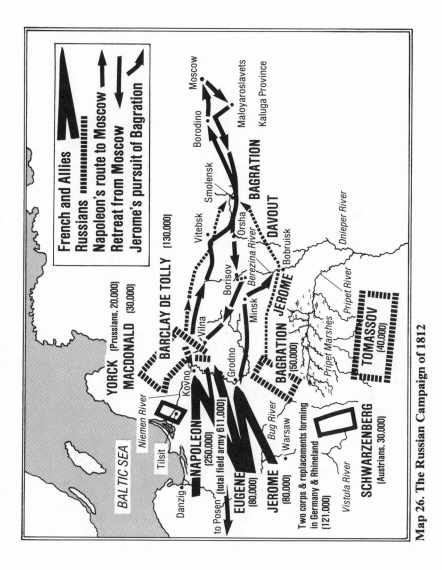

**Map 26. The Russian Campaign of 1812**

The Russians seem to have had no plan to draw Napoleon to the limit of his supply lines and destroy him, as is often said. They had no plan beyond mere survival, which for the moment meant retreat, until they had the numbers and position to give the French a fight. Napoleon was led along, in short, by day-to-day decisions of the Russian generals. Neither did the people (or the army, consistently) follow a scorched-earth policy. This is a myth. The only villages burned were set afire by Cossack bands or, very rarely, by other army units. The line soldier, whatever his province, was a peasant farmer and resisted burning another peasant's crops.

The French emperor spent three weeks in Vilna, largely handling political matters. He considered long whether to restore the Kingdom of Poland to include Lithuania. The local nobles loudly approved and hailed Napoleon as their liberator from Russian tyranny. A *Te Deum* was sung in the cathedral, and balls and dinners were held nightly. In Warsaw, however, the Polish Diet had assembled, and the nobility (no one else counted in Poland) proved divided. In the end the emperor postponed a decision on the kingdom and established a provisional government for Lithuania.

Napoleon might well have been better employed personally directing the hot pursuit of the Russians. His wing of the French army was marching for Vitebsk, following Barclay's army. He did make major decisions, of course, and transmitted his orders through Berthier, but on a day-to-day basis the army simply trailed after Murat, who pressed ahead with the cavalry. For a few days they trudged in "suffocating heat" and then in pouring rain. The temperature dropped, making men and horses ill. Both, by the end of the first week, were suffering from hunger. The plan, as usual, was to live off the land after the first few days (five at most), but this proved impossible. The country was vast and under cultivation. The villages generally had not been burned or demolished by the Russian army, which had taken away most of the horses, but they were at great distances from the march route. The pace, set by Murat's cavalry, was too fast to allow for foraging. By the first days of July, men were falling out from hunger and fatigue, and horses were dying by the score.

Marshal Murat, brave fighter that he was, had never bothered to learn about the care of horses or men, or their limits. His pace was killing his horses and the men who followed him.[1] By letting Murat lead, Napoleon sentenced his army to slow murder by exhaustion. At the time, the losses seemed justified if he could catch and defeat the Russians. In mid-July, having missed all this, Napoleon finally left Vilna to follow the army with his headquarters.

---

[1] Horses have about the same stamina as men over long distances but must be taken along slowly—alternating the walk and trot—and fed well. A horse can be killed by making it canter, or slow gallop, for over four or five miles without rest. At full gallop, a horse cannot go over two or three miles without great risk.

In the meantime, Jerome, to the south, had the mission of preventing Bagration from moving north to reinforce Barclay, but he was not moving fast enough for Napoleon. On 1 July, from Vilna, the French emperor had sent Marshal Davout with a corps of 35,000 to intercept Bagration, presumably fleeing eastward before Jerome (actually he had veered south), and to trap the Russians between their two forces. Davout secured Minsk, but he wrote Napoleon that he did not know Jerome's position and that the king had not contacted him. The news angered Napoleon, who was still at Vilna and assumed Jerome was to blame. On 6 July, he sent Davout orders to take command of Jerome's army when he made contact.[2]

Jerome, after a slow start and impeded by heavy rains and swollen rivers, meanwhile was on the track of Bagration, who had skirted Minsk and gone south, passed through at Mir on 10 July, and was marching to cross the Berezina River at Bobruisk. According to Jerome, he heard that Davout was at Minsk on 14 July and sent a messenger asking him to join in the pursuit; the same messenger returned within hours with a curt note from Davout and Napoleon's orders placing the marshal in command. Davout says he sent Napoleon's orders on the 13th. At any rate, Jerome left the army in a fury and returned to Westphalia. Napoleon covered his desertion with orders. Time thus was lost in joining the forces, and Bagration made good his escape to the north. He eventually joined Barclay near Smolensk. Davout soon united his troops with Napoleon's, as did Eugene (although both supplied garrisons for towns along the route). The French emperor expected Barclay and Bagration to turn and fight at Vitebsk, but they did not. So the pursuit continued in the direction of Smolensk—the road to Moscow.

At Vitebsk, however, Napoleon paused for fifteen days (29 July to 12 August) to organize the provincial government, a useless task since he was in a Russian city (if once Lithuanian), and looting by French troops was alienating the mostly Lithuanian peasantry in the countryside. He also wasted time with reviews, especially of the Guard, who marched before him daily in parade dress. He commanded his military administrators and medical personnel to be present at these reviews and ordered them publicly to improve the food supply and hospital care for the troops. "But," wrote Fezensac, "it is not enough to give orders; the orders must be capable of execution." The country was ravaged; horses needed for transport were dying; and in hospitals, more food would have been the best medicine.

Napoleon, then, was seeing his men almost exclusively at reviews, where their commanders tried to make them look as fine as possible. Therefore

---

[2]One can hardly fault Napoleon for preferring Davout to Jerome as an army commander. The playboy king of Westphalia was out of his league—although brave enough, as he would prove at Waterloo. What is odd is that the emperor did not send him home earlier. Jerome had been brought to Warsaw to be crowned king of Poland; his "cover" was army commander. Napoleon decided to delay a solution for Poland, but there is no doubt why he brought Jerome to Warsaw. See Abel Mansuy, *Jérôme Napoléon et la Pologne* (Paris: Alcan, 1922).

he could ignore the truth that his army was disintegrating, although it had yet to fight a major battle. By the time the French main force reached Vitebsk, about 300 miles into Russia, no less than one-third of the men were missing. They had fallen from hunger, thirst, disease, fatigue, and the pounding of the elements. The weather, first hot, then wet, had turned very hot again, and the army had marched in clouds of stifling dust. Long before Napoleon left Vitebsk, he had ordered the army into pursuit of the Russians and again allowed Murat's cavalry to set the pace.

## Battle of Smolensk

On 16 August, at Smolensk, 400 miles into Russia by the march route, Barclay and Bagration at last seemed ready to stand and fight. As the French approached, they received artillery fire from the ancient city wall, a formidable barrier almost 3 miles long, 25 feet high, 10 feet thick, and protected by a moat. On 17 August the French assailed the walls but breached them only at a few points and at great cost in lives. On the morning of 18 August, they found the walls deserted. With caution and some disbelief, they penetrated through the city, where many buildings were ablaze, to the Dnieper River. There they took cannon fire from the opposite shore. For most of the day, the artillery of the two armies dueled across the river.

Napoleon did not know it, but Bagration, in arrogant disobedience to Barclay (in overall command), had begun withdrawing toward the Moscow road, separating his army from the main force. Barclay was forced to follow during the night of 18–19 August, and the next morning he was marching away briskly, covered by a tough rear guard. On the 19th the Russian armies were still separated and in reach of the French. Murat, Davout, and Ney crossed the river and went into pursuit, but their work was uncoordinated.

Earlier, on the assumption that the Russians still were defending the river line, Napoleon had ordered Junot to take his corps across, southeast of Smolensk, and attack the enemy flank. Junot had arrived only on the 18th, however, and his orders were imprecise. He did cross the river, but when he found himself on the enemy flank, near Lubino, he pulled back and waited for orders. Murat appeared and urged him to attack the Russians, but Junot refused to move. If he had driven eastward, he might have separated the Russian armies and surely would have blocked or disrupted the Russian retreat if he had executed the move smartly, but he did not execute it at all. The enemy thus got away again, cleanly, with effective rear-guard fighting as they went. Their casualties were some 15,000, almost double those of the French (8000 to 10,000), but the French were allowed no prisoners except men on the verge of death.

Napoleon lost an opportunity on 19 August to defeat the two Russian armies separately. Had he been in closer touch with his leading corps—

Davout, Ney, and especially Junot—and with Murat, he might have crushed the Russians as they fled Smolensk. One can blame the French emperor's lack of information on the corps commanders; there is no doubt that Murat did not keep him informed, and the others only reported at intervals. But the Napoleon of old would have been across the river and looking over his front, not sitting at headquarters waiting for reports. In fact, on the 19th, Napoleon knew neither the location of the Russians nor of his own corps, and he was not there to lead, if necessary. He put the blame on Junot, an easy scapegoat, since he had never recovered from the onus of losing Portugal in 1808. If one wants to deal in excuses, then it can be argued that the general was losing his grip on reality in 1812 (Junot went mad in 1813), or he would have attacked. That may be. It is even likely, but it does not excuse Napoleon.

On the 19th the French emperor did arrive toward the end of a hot little battle at Lubino, where Ney defeated the Russian rear guard. He lavished compliments on the marshal and his corps, made promotions, and passed out decorations. But the enemy was gone, and the only result of the encounter had been to double the French casualty figure. Napoleon had started the campaign with the knowledge that, all other factors aside, he had numbers greater than the Russians. More and more, that was not so. He had reached Smolensk with 156,000 men and left with fewer than 148,000. Under his direct command were five corps—Eugene, Davout, Ney, Junot, and Poniatowski—plus Murat's reserve cavalry and the Guard under Bessières. The march had taken a heavy toll on all of them, save the Guard. The emperor had reduced the ranks further by leaving detachments behind in seven towns, including Smolensk, where he ordered another major depot established. Furthermore, he had detached the corps of Oudinot and Saint-Cyr (combined strength only 28,000) to help Macdonald and Yorck guard his northern flank, and Reynier's corps to ensure that Schwarzenberg kept Tomassov south of the Pripet Marshes. On his south flank (but included in the 148,000 under his direct command), Napoleon had a whole cavalry corps under Latour-Maubourg and, detached from Poniatowski, a Polish division of 6000 men under Dombrowski.

Napoleon put the army, led by Murat's cavalry, on the road for Moscow. He and the Guard remained in Smolensk for another week and then joined the rear of the column. Hardly had he arrived when Murat and Davout appeared before him, Murat complaining that Davout's infantry was slowing his advance, and Davout accusing Murat of setting a killing pace. They almost drew swords before the emperor intervened and promised Davout that his men would not be pressed so hard.

In private, though, Napoleon ordered Murat to drive ahead as fast as he could. The killing pace resumed, with devastating effect on the ranks. Moreover, the seemingly limitless spaces along the high road to Moscow had a terrifying influence on the minds of men bred among the ordered, small plots of western Europe. They contributed to the general malaise of an army growing weaker from hunger, thirst, oppressive heat and dust alternating with pouring rain, and increasingly cold nights. Every mile saw more men and horses fall by the wayside. The morale of those who marched on grew ever worse. If haphazardly, the Russian army had stripped the country of food and burned villages in the French path. French foragers, half-mad with hunger, brutally handled any peasants who seemed to be concealing food. Napoleon himself was short-tempered from the frustration of a continual pursuit without battle. At Vyazma, 95 miles from Moscow, he entered a still-burning village to find some of his men looting a vodka and wine shop. He jumped from his carriage and awkwardly ran at them, cursing in French and Italian and flailing at them with his riding crop. They fled in disbelief.

Meanwhile, Marshal Kutuzov had taken command of the Russian army, a force of 120,000 men who were hungry and ragged but in better condition than the French. Czar Alexander had decided to entrust the fate of the Russian empire to the man whose advice he had ignored at Austerlitz (and who had stoically accepted blame for the czar's defeat). Kutuzov was sixty-seven years old, ill, and so fat it took several men to get him on horseback. He was, withal, the best respected of all the Russian generals. The czar had exiled him to a command against the Ottoman Turks, whom he had fought since 1807, but he had turned the assignment to advantage and made a reputation as a consistent winner. He and the czar had agreed that Moscow should be defended. Kutuzov chose to stand at the crossroads village of Borodino, 75 miles west of the ancient capital.

On 1 September, at Gzhatsk, Napoleon's mood suddenly turned joyous. Scouts brought word that the Russian army was preparing battle positions only a few miles away, near Borodino, on the Kalatsha River. Napoleon halted the march of the army for three days. He first had his officers count heads (after the furious 150-mile march from Smolensk, he had only a general idea of his numbers, which decreased by 18,000 between Smolensk and Borodino), then allowed time for the ammunition trains to arrive, and finally made his plans. On 4 September he gave the order to advance again, and the *Grande Armée* drove in the enemy's scouts. On 5 September the army took the Russians' delaying positions, centered on a redoubt about a mile in front of the enemy line.

On 6 September the *Grande Armée* faced the enemy. Napoleon established his headquarters behind the village of Valuyeva, some two miles from the enemy lines. The Guard infantry—30,000 men present—was drawn up around his tents in a huge square and bivouacked for the night in that position. The emperor ordered all regiments to put on parade uniforms, to make the Guard more imposing than ever; most of the men rested while the light cavalry reconnoitered the enemy positions. Even then, Napoleon did not go among the troops. He did make three short forays to the front while deciding on his orders for the next day, but otherwise he kept to his headquarters, evaluating reports from his scouts.

That same day, Napoleon issued orders to the army to attack at dawn on the next, 7 September. He detailed heavy artillery barrages to prepare the assault; half the order was directed to artillery commanders, including Sorbier, of the Guard. (The French had 587 guns, the Russians 640.) During the cannonade, Poniatowski was to break through the Russian positions astride the old Smolensk road and turn the Russian left (south) flank. When Eugene saw the French right go forward, he was to take Borodino and then attack the Great Redoubt, the central fortification on the Russian line. That was all. No mission was given to Davout's and Ney's corps, or to Murat's cavalry, between them and Poniatowski. By their placement, Davout and Ney, supported by Murat, were set to attack the *flèches* (lesser fortifications) on the Russian left (south center); Junot's corps and the Guard were in reserve. "Once the combat is joined," the order ran, "orders will be given according to the dispositions of the enemy." That sounded like the Napoleon of old, but his orders would come very slowly.

**Battle of Borodino**

On 7 September at 2:00 AM the French army mustered for battle. Commanders read a proclamation from Napoleon to the troops: "This is the battle you have longed for! Now the victory depends on you: you need it. It will give you abundance, good winter quarters, and an early return home." The soldiers cheered; they still could hope it was all true. The marshals and key generals, meanwhile, were with Napoleon at Valuyeva. "Behold, the sun of Austerlitz!" he declaimed as the dawn broke. The commanders nodded agreeably; some aides cheered; all went forward to their posts. They did not yet despair of victory, but they certainly expected no Austerlitz. The emperor displaced his headquarters forward to the redoubt captured on the 5th, over a mile behind the front. It was on a rise, but from there he could not see Borodino, or much of the center and right of his army. It did not matter to him, apparently; he had convinced himself that, if the Russians would fight, he would win.

The day began with unusual blundering, though not of Napoleon's making. At 5:00 AM Poniatowski ordered his corps forward, but it was literally trapped by the forest, brush, briars, and brambles along the old Smolensk road. It was 8:00 AM before he reached the line of battle, and Napoleon long since had launched Davout at the Russian left. Meanwhile, at 6:00 AM more than 100 guns had begun the preparation for an assault on the enemy center and left, but the balls fell short. Atmospheric conditions had reduced the normal range of the guns, and a half-hour or more was wasted by moving them forward. Finally, they delivered their fire with some effect, and Davout prepared to attack the Russian left; at the same time Ney's guns prepared the way for his advance on the Russian center, and Eugene bombarded Borodino.

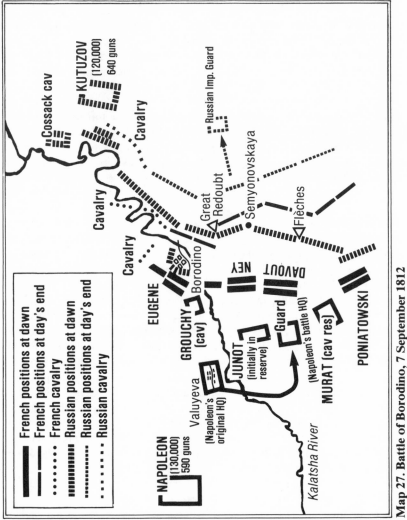

**Map 27. Battle of Borodino, 7 September 1812**

Napoleon stayed at his headquarters, as he would for most of the day. In fairness to him, we should say forcibly that he was quite ill. The day before, as if presaging things to come, the temperature had dropped radically and a prolonged thunderstorm swept across the area. Napoleon had contracted a violent cold, accompanied by a high fever, which weakened him and helps account for his unusual inactivity during the Battle of Borodino, even compared to other battles on this campaign. He seldom had been ill in his whole life and, as is often the case with such fortunate people, sickness hit him hard when it came. Says Philippe de Ségur, one of his aides-de-camp: "We saw him sitting or walking slowly in front or a little to the left of the redoubt . . . far from the battle. [In similar situations] . . . we had seen him act calmly, but here, it [was] a dull [detached, vacant] calm, a feeble *douceur.*" The emperor failed even to make use of the Guard artillery, his favorite sport in battle, only sending it forward occasionally, as if on whim.

At about 7:30 AM, Davout led his corps forward, although Poniatowski had not come up and he was short two divisions. It captured the south *flèche* but was dislodged by a Russian counterattack supported by the Russian Imperial Guard cavalry and seemingly innumerable guns. Davout's horse was blown out from under him by an artillery ball; the marshal was momentarily dazed and severely bruised but not seriously wounded. Though in some pain, he mounted a new horse and got on with the battle.

At about 8:00 AM, on Napoleon's belated order, Ney came up on Davout's left, with Murat close behind, and they began a concerted attack on the Russian center and left. Ney assailed the north *flèches.* He took and lost them several times in brutal fighting, finally securing them with the help of Murat's reserve cavalry (Latour-Maubourg's corps). At about 9:00 Junot's corps moved into line between Davout and Ney, and by 10:00 all the *flèches* were taken and Ney's infantry occupied most of the Semyonovskaya Ridge. At 11:00, however, Bagration unexpectedly counterattacked and retook the *flèches.* (He was killed in action.) Poniatowski, meanwhile, had straightened the line on Davout's right, and they all went forward once again, together.

Before noon the *flèches* again were taken by the French, and the Russian center and left fell back. Murat charged repeatedly at the head of one or another corps of cavalry, pushing the enemy eastward, but they would not break. Accordingly, Murat and Ney both rode to Napoleon's camp and demanded that the Guard be committed, the Gascon, in the frenzy of battle which often took control of him, spewing expletives in the *patois* of his youth. The battle could be won with one heavy final assault, they both said, but they needed the Guard. Their men and horses were exhausted. Napoleon then displayed "a hesitation never known before." He made everyone wait until Marshal Bessières, commanding the Guard, made a reconnaissance, a matter of a half hour, and then said no to an attack by the Guard. Instead, he ordered one division of the Young Guard forward to be used in case of a Russian counterattack. "If I have a battle tomorrow [and the Guard is gone]," Napoleon asked, "how will I save it?" It was barely 1:00 PM.

The marshals went away angry. They (and Ségur and others) always believed that the battle could have been won at mid-day. It is impossible to say if they were right, but it is certain that Napoleon's hesitation gave the Russians a chance to reorganize, to dig in on a second line of hills to the east, and to fight on. On the French right (the Russian left and center), where Napoleon had planned to win the battle, there was little but artillery action for the rest of the afternoon.

Meanwhile, on the French left, Eugene had taken the city of Borodino by 9:00 AM and crossed the Kalatsha to attack the Great Redoubt. The fighting was vicious and often hand-to-hand; he captured and then lost the redoubt. At about 11:00 AM, Murat reinforced him with the cavalry corps of General Montbrun, who was killed in action, but Eugene retook the redoubt. He was forced to give it up, however, in order to reinforce his north flank, which was assailed by Russian cavalry (Platoff's Cossacks and Uvarov's cavalry corps). The Russian attack was repulsed, essentially by Grouchy's cavalry corps, but time was lost. At about 2:00 PM Eugene again concentrated on the redoubt, reinforced by the same cavalry corps, now led by Auguste de Caulaincourt. Eugene took the redoubt, but General de Caulaincourt was killed in the assault. The Russians gave ground; Grouchy's cavalry pursued them for almost two miles but was stopped by Russian Imperial Guard cavalry. When Napoleon heard of the deaths of Montbrun and Caulaincourt, he was much affected; Montbrun had been an old comrade, and Caulaincourt's brother Armand served at his headquarters as grand equerry. (He was later Napoleon's foreign minister.) But there were more; in all, sixteen French generals were killed and thirty-one wounded.

About 4:00 PM, Napoleon sensed that a time of decision had come in the battle. He mounted his horse "with effort," rode to the heights of Semyon-ovskaya, and for the first and last time that day looked over the Russian positions. He returned to his headquarters to find a clutch of commanders, including Ney and Murat, again demanding that he commit the Guard. He consulted Berthier, who suggested that, if an attack were to be made, it should involve all available troops, not just the Guard; and, he said, it was late in the day. Berthier then fell silent. Bessières was more blunt: "Europe lies between [Your Majesty] and France. You are 800 leagues from Paris."[3]

Napoleon again refused to commit the Guard. Instead, he ordered artillery preparations for the next day. But the battle was over. There would be no next day. Dawn on 8 September revealed that the Russians had marched away, apparently in some confusion and disarray. Kutuzov even had left his sick and wounded behind, a very unusual act for the Russians except when

---

[3]Eight hundred French leagues were about 1900 miles.

routed. Murat was sent in pursuit, and the *Grande Armée*, or what was left of it, followed along the highway to Moscow.

**Aftermath**

Russian casualties were at least 45,000. French casualties were 28,000 to 31,000, including the 47 generals. Napoleon was appalled. He moved his headquarters a bit eastward, to Mojaisk, but for several days he returned to the battlefield to walk in obvious grief among the thousands of torn and contorted dead bodies, as if hoping that the nightmare somehow would disappear. Wrote Ségur: "The losses were immense and out of proportion to result. Everyone . . . wept for some dead friend. . . . What mourning in Paris; what a triumph for the enemy; what a dangerous subject for thought in Germany." The men sensed that the victory was empty. At the campfires there was no singing, or laughter, and little talk. The officers were morose and fearful.

Napoleon, naturally, proclaimed a victory anyway. The Russians had left the field of battle; *ergo*, he had won. He exaggerated Russian casualties and understated his own, playing up the glory of the "triumph." Privately, he was deeply depressed, puzzled, and frustrated. "I have beaten them. I have beaten them. It means nothing?" he said over and over, in various forms, to Caulaincourt and others in the months to come. But Kutuzov also claimed victory, and with some justice. He had not lost, and the French were no closer to final victory than before. He had reduced French forces by 30,000 men, or by one quarter, and he had made an orderly, strategic withdrawal. The Russian commander could reinforce his army with relative ease and even was building an auxiliary by arming selected peasant villages. He had supplies in plenty.

Napoleon would have to draw reinforcements from units detached on other missions, or depots set up en route, or they would have to march 700 to 1000 miles from Germany or the Rhineland. The supply line to Kovno, where Napoleon had crossed the Niemen, was 650 miles long, and convoys had to be guarded all the way—especially east of Smolensk, where standing orders required an escort of at least 1500 infantry and cavalry with some artillery.

**Moscow**

On 14 September 1812, Napoleon entered Moscow with 95,000 men. The French army had marched the seventy-five miles from Borodino to Moscow without resistance and found the city undefended and almost deserted. Kutuzov had marched south, followed by most of the populace. The only inhabitants seemed to be madmen and prisoners released by Count Feodor Rostopchin, the governor of Moscow, prior to departing. It soon appeared that there was a considerable French community of merchants, businessmen, and others in hiding, and that some Russians had elected to remain behind. Initially, the French were pleased to see these people, but they soon found that they only created problems.

Napoleon installed himself and his staff, retinue, and the Imperial Guard in the Kremlin. On the night of the emperor's entry, the city began to burn, probably set afire by the released prisoners acting under orders from the governor. The fires spread quickly, since the structures were mostly of wood, and for the next five days the *Grande Armée* fought nothing more glorious than fires. On 20 September, therefore, Napoleon wrote to Czar Alexander:

> The beautiful . . . superb city of Moscow no longer exists. Rostopchin had it burned. Four hundred incendiaries . . . have been shot. . . . Such conduct is atrocious and without reason. . . . I have made war on your Majesty without animosity: a note from him before or after the last battle would have stopped my march. I might even have been able to sacrifice . . . the advantage of entering Moscow. If Your Majesty still has any of his old sentiments for me, he will take this letter in the best spirit.

Napoleon obviously expected the czar to propose terms. He thought that to make peace was the only rational move Alexander could make. But the czar did not; he did not even reply. What had he to gain? The winter would soon force the French to retreat west to winter quarters. Kutuzov made Alexander's silence even more maddening by occasionally sending Napoleon notes which raised his hopes. These messages may have prolonged the French stay in Moscow, but no one will ever know whether Kutuzov planned that or foresaw the consequences of a few days' delay. At any rate mid-October came, and still Napoleon waited and agonized over what to do.

While the czar delayed, Napoleon considered that, within reason, he must hold Moscow until Alexander came to terms. If he withdrew to the west, it would signal weakness and make his bargaining position worse. Winter was too near for a march on the capital, St. Petersburg, where the czar resided. And it was too late to renew the pursuit of Kutuzov. Moreover, if he withdrew, his European allies might defect—especially Austria and Prussia. His whole alliance system might collapse. His enemies had been cheered too much already by the news from Spain, where Wellington had taken Madrid.

Napoleon also feared the reaction at home to a setback. There was always the danger of a coup in Paris while he was away. His withdrawal would make one more likely. Furthermore, he did not want to have to supply his huge army throughout the winter. If the czar would not make terms, then

Napoleon could withdraw to Smolensk, or perhaps even Vilna. In either case, supplying the army would be very difficult and costly. In sum, Napoleon had planned for a short campaign. All his actions had been predicated on the assumption that he could dispense with Russia in 1812. His last chance to do that was by holding Moscow as long as possible and bringing the czar to terms.

In Moscow, says Fézensac, the French found furs and diamonds, but no shoes; plenty of vodka, liqueur, wine, jams, jellies, and sugar, but no bread and meat. Actually, initially there were considerable stores of grain and flour within the city, mostly in cellars, and meat on the hoof and fresh cabbages in the nearby countryside. But the French supply personnel did not move quickly to collect, sort, and guard the food. Thus there was plenty for a few weeks, but the troops soon were suffering from malnutrition and, with much of the city destroyed, from exposure. The weather turned colder by the day, with rain, fog, and generally miserable conditions. Replacements arrived, but they only took the places of unfortunates who had died. The countryside was empty of provisions; the peasants would not supply the French no matter how much money they offered, and sometimes they killed foraging parties. Supplies coming from the west included little food. Men lost the will and energy to search and sat silently, staring vacantly at their fires. Occasionally one quietly would slump over, dead.

On the other hand, Kutuzov established his army near Kaluga, to the south, where the land had not been stripped of food and forage. He drew in reinforcements, organized and armed selected bands of peasants, detailed his Cossacks to interdict French supply routes, but put little direct pressure on Moscow. What was the point? To Napoleon, then, the only Russian threat was from the south, along the Nara River. Kutuzov's Cossacks were on the south bank; Murat outposted the north bank. Within a few days an informal truce was effected, and the French and Russians even met, talked, and traded a little. Murat, to his delight, found he was the idol of the Cossacks. Platoff admired his dash and had given orders that "the King of Naples, with the high plume," was to be captured, if possible, but not killed. This went to the Gascon's head; he even talked of winning the Cossacks to the French side, an idea slyly encouraged by canny Russian officers.

In Moscow, meanwhile, the French army was dying from varying degrees of exposure to the cold, wet weather, and from malnutrition and disease. The hospitals could not begin to treat the sick. The horses also were dying, for lack of forage, by the hundreds every day, and without them there was no transport, no movable artillery, and no cavalry. Perhaps 20,000 horses perished during the month in Moscow. Even Murat's cavalry was slaughtering horses in order to have something to eat.

Napoleon himself mostly stayed within the Kremlin walls, where he reviewed the Guard daily, emerging with fanfare to hand out medals and make promotions. He sent out strange orders from the Kremlin; for example, one was for the local purchase of 10,000 horses, a total impossibility. (More realistically, he sent orders to Hugues Bernard Maret, his foreign minister, in Vilna, to procure 14,000 in Germany and Poland, authorizing 4,000,000 francs for the purchase. But there was not time for the horses to arrive before the snows.) Napoleon also decreed that the markets be opened and that peasants who brought foodstuffs to sell be protected absolutely. He gave orders to find materials and make clothes and shoes. None of this could be done.

Napoleon, working as always, busied his secretaries, dictating assessments of the situation and alternate plans of action, sending orders to strengthen his lines of communication, stopping the movement of more artillery to Moscow, ordering cadres back to France to train new regiments for 1813—even placing the Comédie Française under his protection. Still, he had time to kill, so he played *vingt-et-un* (blackjack) with Eugene and others. He read novels, memoirs, and histories from his traveling library and new ones ordered on the march from his bookseller in Paris, M. Barbier, whom he chastised from Moscow for not sending him the latest works. Finally, however, the French emperor no longer could ignore the approach of winter and the deterioration of his army.

## The March to Smolensk

Napoleon opted for a strategic withdrawal to Smolensk, where he judged adequate supplies for winter were available. On 17 October he ordered preparations for departure. The plan was to go south, via Kaluga and Elnya, then east to Smolensk, to avoid the route taken to Moscow and to march through country where food and forage might be found. On 18 October, as if signaled, the Russians attacked Murat viciously across the Nara River. He was surrounded and almost captured, but he cut his way out with most of his men and joined Napoleon in Moscow.

Preparations went forward, still for taking the southern route. Since Smolensk was only a ten- to fourteen-day march away, Napoleon hoped to evacuate every single man in his army, including the wounded and sick, and the members of the French community of Moscow as well, if they cared to go. He ordered Berthier to provide transportation for every soldier who could not walk. Every available vehicle was to be used—carriages, wagons, caissons, carts. Had the weather been normal, he might have pulled off the evacuation neatly. On 19 October, then, the *Grande Armée* marched southward and for five days met little opposition. On 24 October, however, at Maloyaroslavets, the Russians stood in force behind the Luzha River. Eugene's corps took the brunt of the battle, capturing and losing the village ten times before nightfall. He sealed a victory by committing an Italian division (under Domenico Pino) and his Royal Guard, 5000 strong. The Italians made heroes of themselves, but the units were destroyed.

In the evening Napoleon held a council of war. The question was whether the army should continue on the Kaluga route, or turn back to the Borodino road and return the way they had come. Murat wanted to cut a way out for the emperor along the planned route. Napoleon soberly thanked him but said that saving the army was the major consideration. Davout then suggested an alternate route via Medyn to Smolensk, which avoided Borodino and went through relatively untouched country. Murat shouted that Davout's plan was stupid—that he was proposing to march across Kutuzov's left flank. The two seemed about to draw swords, but Napoleon silenced them. The marshals and emperor then agreed to withdraw via Borodino to Smolensk, on the assumption that Kutuzov meant to contest every foot of the Kaluga route. (But the famed British observer with the Russians, General Sir Robert Wilson, assures us that Kutuzov was about to run.)

On the next day, 25 October, the army marched northward, after a confused start during which Cossacks almost captured Napoleon. His carriage was surrounded; he, Berthier, and Caulaincourt jumped out and drew their swords to defend themselves. Fortunately, the thunder of the Guard cavalry moving up startled the Cossacks, who disappeared like startled deer. The army moved onward, on the third day passing the somber and depressing battleground of Borodino, still littered with corpses and the debris of the armies. The withdrawal was proceeding as planned despite harassing attacks by Cossacks, Russian cavalry, and occasional peasant militia bands. All was going well, except that some of the men had had to jettison their loot to keep up and much of the French community turned back, unable to stand the rigors. At the same time, Kutuzov was content to march parallel at a distance in the south.

On 4 November the first snow fell in earnest. By 6 November there was perpetual ice and snow to contend with, and the withdrawal turned into a disaster. Temperatures dropped to 16 degrees below freezing. Men died by the thousands from exposure and starvation, the more quickly if they found wine or vodka to drink. The horses, who pulled their loads on wheels through the heavy snow, also dropped by the wayside—perhaps 15,000 in the next five days. By the time the army reached Smolensk (9–13 November in an elongated column), half of the cavalry was on foot. The Guard cavalry and artillery had priority on surviving horses. Much artillery had been abandoned, and most all vehicles. Such food as the men carried from Moscow—in theory, each man had left with four days' rations—long since had been exhausted. Horse flesh became the major sustenance, and there were grisly scenes where starving men carved up freezing horses before they were dead.

It was 13 November by the time the entire army straggled into Smolensk. Only 50,000 remained of the almost 100,000 men who had left Moscow. The army had disintegrated astoundingly in just nine days. Napoleon was not far wrong in the 29th Bulletin: "Until 6 November the weather was perfect, and the army executed its movement [withdrawal] very well." But then came the snows, and by the time of their arrival at Smolensk, the army was in shambles and reduced by half, of whom only 30,000 were capable of fighting. Moreover, discipline had broken down. The army looted the depots of the city, and it became apparent instantly to Napoleon that he could not winter there. He ordered the march to continue to Vilna, and he and the lead elements departed on 13 November.

The rear guard, 6000 men under Marshal Ney—3000 of his III Corps (of 37,000 in June) and 3000 replacements—left on 18 November. At Krasnii, they found their way blocked by 30,000 Russians under General Miloradovich. Summoned to surrender, Ney replied by attacking and held out until nightfall. In the evening, Ney was approached by an officer of his staff, who asked:

> "What are we going to do?"
> "Cross the Dnieper," said Ney.
> "Where is the road?"
> "We will find it."
> "And if it isn't passable?"
> "It will be."

Leaving campfires to deceive the enemy, Ney did get his corps across the Dnieper on the ice, thus eluding the mass of Russian regular troops. The next morning found Ney on foot among his men, fighting in deep woods, but fortunately for him mostly against Cossacks and irregulars. Eugene returned to reinforce him, and the two marched to join the main column. Ney had saved his corps, after a fashion. It numbered only about 900 men.

On 19 November Napoleon wrote to Maret in Paris that he had lost virtually all his horses, 30,000 in less than a week. A little earlier, he had summed up that problem: "Horses, horses, and horses, for the *cuirassiers*, for the dragoons, for the light cavalry, for the artillery and military transport. That is the greatest of our needs." The loss of the horses greatly increased the human casualty rate, since all but the Guard cavalry were now on foot. There was virtually no artillery or transport except in the Guard, either. The number of Napoleon's effectives dropped by the day. The organized units were followed by a horde of stragglers who were lucky if they were captured by coolheaded Russian troops; the very luckiest, and they were few, were taken in by kindhearted peasants.

## To the Berezina

At Orsha, Napoleon directed the army on Borisov by way of a more southerly route to Vilna, although it meant crossing the Berezina River. The reason was the threat from the north of the Russian army of Wittgenstein (30,000 men), which was opposed by the reduced corps of Victor (12,500) and Oudinot

(11,000). Kutuzov, with 80,000 men, was two days' march to the southeast, and Tshetshakov, with 35,000, was behind the Berezina at Borisov. Napoleon's main army, in short, was in danger of being boxed in. With its numbers dwindling by the day, it could only escape total destruction or capture if it could cross the Berezina and make it to Vilna. When Napoleon made his decision, the Berezina was frozen over, as was usual in November, but again the weather turned against the French. A premature thaw turned the river into a formidable obstacle.

As the emperor approached Borisov on 24 November, he could count on fewer than 25,000 men to fight, although there were almost as many stragglers. He had only a dozen or so guns; the rest had been abandoned for lack of horses. It was the same with ue cavalry. From the reserve and Guard he managed to organize a "Sacred Squadron" of four companies of 150 men each; General Grouchy commanded in Murat's name; generals served as captains, colonels as lieutenants. Fortunately, Napoleon was reinforced at Borisov by first Oudinot and then Victor, whose corps were half-sized but in fair condition and well-equipped. Their arrival brought French effectives to perhaps 48,000. Still, the combined forces of Wittgenstein and Tshetshakov outnumbered them; moreover, they were in much better condition and had an oversupply of artillery.

Probably Napoleon's reputation alone saved the *Grande Armée* from total destruction before it reached the Berezina. The Russian generals were loath to attack him. Furthermore, they could not be sure, with visibility reduced by snow and fog, just how many fighting men were in the French column, which stretched for miles. All the Russians were cautious; Wittgenstein was especially tentative in his approach. Kutuzov slowed his march, either from prudence or under the assumption that Wittgenstein and Tshetshakov could dispatch Napoleon.

As the army reached the vicinity of Borisov on 25 November, Napoleon suddenly came alive and took charge. The river was deep and wide and full of ice floes; on the opposite bank was a Russian army of 35,000. But he had learned of a ford eight miles north, at Studenka—just discovered by cavalry Colonel J.-B. Jubenal Courbineau. Napoleon also learned that General Jean-Baptiste Eblé had not totally destroyed his bridge train at Orsha, as ordered, but had retained necessary forges and tools; timbers for bridges could be taken from the buildings of Studenka.

A plan—simple, as of old, but likely to succeed—had formed in Napoleon's mind. He would feint at Tshetshakov, opposite Borisov, and pin him down while bridges across the Berezina were built at Studenka and a bridgehead established on the opposite bank; the army then would dash across at Studenka. On 26 November the French noisily went through the motions of attacking Tshetshakov from Borisov. Meanwhile, upstream, Polish cavalrymen rode across the river, carrying infantrymen behind them who, with the support of artillery from the opposite bank, established a bridgehead. General

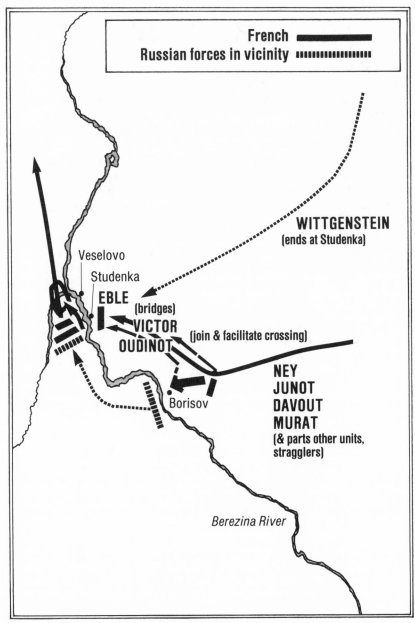

**Map 28. The Crossing of the Berezina, 26-29 November 1812**

Eblé, meanwhile, began construction of two bridges, each over 100 yards long, one for foot traffic and one for vehicles. They were finished by 2:00 PM, and Oudinot's corps was across by dark. On 27 November the remnants of the corps of Ney, Davout, Junot, and Eugene, with the reserve and Guard, went across.

On the 27th, Tshetshakov finally divined what the French were doing and attacked northward. Oudinot blocked him, while the other corps organized on the west bank to march away. In the afternoon, the French faced crises. First, the larger bridge broke, dropping vehicles, horses, and men into the icy waters. It was soon repaired, but meanwhile men rushed the other bridge and in the crush many were pushed off into the water. Then Oudinot was wounded; his men lost heart and began to fall back, causing even some of the Young Guard to give ground. For a half-hour or so it appeared the western bridgehead would be lost. Marshal Ney, however, seized command; the sight of the fiery redhead galloping to the front rallied the men, and the French lines were reformed. Wrote Fézensac: "That famous warrior, who had saved the Third Corps at Krasnii, now saved the entire army and the emperor himself on the banks of the Berezina."

On 28 November, Victor stood off Wittgenstein and guarded the eastern approaches to the bridges while thousands of stragglers went across. Snow and dropping temperatures hampered the French effort, but it succeeded. During the night, Victor withdrew his corps to the west bank, leaving the bridges to Eblé and a small rear guard. Wittgenstein meanwhile closed in, and on the morning of the 29th his artillery was firing on the bridges. Eblé held as long as possible, all while urging stragglers to move across. At 9:00 AM, however, Wittgenstein's forces were almost upon him, and he withdrew his last men and burned the bridges behind him. A few hundred stragglers were caught on the bridges and perished; perhaps 10,000 were left behind to become prisoners or victims of the Cossacks.

Napoleon escaped the Russians with 100,000 men—fewer than 50,000 effectives, the rest stragglers. Due credit must be given to Colonel Courbineau, General Eblé, and Victor, Oudinot, and Ney. But the French emperor had "awakened," and it made a difference. The Berezina crossing, if made in retreat, was still a victory. The road to Vilna, where wintering was possible, thus was opened to the remnants of the *Grande Armée*.

With his army free to march westward, Napoleon decided he was needed more in Paris. A new army had to be raised. Also, there had been an attempted coup against his government in October, the Malet conspiracy. For a few hours, the half-mad ex-General Claude François de Malet seized ministerial offices after convincing some regiments of the Paris garrison that Napoleon had died in Russia. On 5 December, therefore, at Smorgoni, Napoleon turned the *Grande Armée* over to Murat and departed for Paris. He traveled incognito, with Caulaincourt as his companion, first by sledge and then carriage. Before dawn on 19 December he was in the Tuileries.

The 29th Bulletin of the *Grande Armée* (3 December 1812) had been printed in the *Moniteur* three days before the emperor arrived. It admitted that the army had suffered a "calamity," from which marauding Cossacks, especially, had tried to profit, but it gave the impression that the Russians had been thoroughly bloodied by Eugene and others. With some justice, Napoleon blamed the catastrophe on the weather, emphasizing the unusual cold, even for Russia, and illustrating it with the statistic that 30,000 horses had died in a "few days" in mid-November. He gave no casualty figures for the army, however, nor did he hint at the hideous condition of the men. Instead, he praised the "*bonne humeur*" and "*gaieté*" of the soldiers under trying conditions. Most of the bulletin concerned the crossing of the Berezina, pointing out the acts of heroism and sloughing over the suffering and death. He gave exaggerated figures on the number of Russian prisoners taken in that action. At the end he again stated that the cavalry was almost entirely on foot and mentioned his "Sacred Squadron" under Grouchy and Murat. But the impression conveyed was that, although the army had suffered, it could recover with rest and some resupply. The bulletin ended with the notorious words: "The health of the Emperor has never been better."

### Murat and Eugene Take Command

Napoleon probably left Murat in command because he was the ranking officer, and because he thought Murat's follow-me type of leadership was appropriate to the situation, where skill at strategy and tactics were useless. Also, he did not want Murat to return to the Kingdom of Naples, lest he defect, either of his own volition or that of his spider queen, Caroline Bonaparte. (There was as yet no Allied coalition, but if Naples declared neutrality, it would damage the empire.) The Gascon had led the way to Moscow with exuberance and there maintained his optimism, but during the retreat he had become increasingly morose. He had let slip doubts about Napoleon's future and was obsessed with getting back to Naples, mostly because he feared Caroline might seize control. After Napoleon's departure for Paris, he began contemplating treason or, as he preferred to call it, independent action as a sovereign king.

On 8 December, Murat led the army into Vilna, where he might have wintered; there were 4,000,000 rations of biscuit and meat in the warehouses. But discipline was nil, and again the depots were looted. Murat also became overanxious about Russian pursuers. "I will not be trapped in this *pot de chambre!*" On 9 December he ordered the army to march on to Kovno, abandoning 20,000 men in hospital and his own rear units, which were still straggling into town. He might have moved in a more leisurely fashion: Kutuzov reached Kovno long after Murat had passed on into East Prussia, and the Russian marshal had only 35,000 men. His army had dwindled, also.

Murat ultimately led the remnants of the *Grande Armée* to Posen, 400 miles to the west. There, in mid-January 1813, he could count 40,000 organized, if demoralized, troops (including some from garrisons along the way) and perhaps 20,000 stragglers—many pitiful scarecrows, some stark mad from their experiences. It was too much for Murat, who bolted the army for Naples within days, leaving the command to Eugene.

The precise extent of Napoleon's losses on the Russian campaign is beyond calculation. The French records show that 210,000 Frenchmen alone were killed, captured, or disappeared in 1812. Records for other nationalities in the *Grande Armée* are spotty. However, the figure must have been above 500,000 men, roughly the difference between the number who entered Russia and those who returned (counting the Prussians and Austrians). Russian records show that over 170,000 men were captured between Moscow and the Vistula. Ignoring the fact that some Frenchmen were captured earlier, deaths in combat or by disease or exposure then must have been at least 330,000.[4]

Napoleon's performance in Russia disillusioned his marshals and generals—some almost totally. The officer corps and noncommissioned officers at large also were more skeptical than ever before. By contrast, the French population continued staunchly loyal to the Bonapartist government and produced enthusiastic recruits and draftees for the campaigns of 1813–14. The image of Napoleon as invincible, which he had carefully cultivated since 1796, was forever damaged. He still struck fear into the hearts of his enemies, but he could never lead quite as before.

At Posen, when Murat decided that he had had enough, he wrote orders for Eugene on 17 January 1813 to take command and, without waiting to see him, departed for Naples. The viceroy took over the army and began a masterly withdrawal to the Elbe, where in March he formed positions hinged on Magdeburg to await the return of Napoleon. Along the way he gathered in other survivors of the campaign. The first was Macdonald's corps of 12,000, reduced by Yorck's Prussians who had gone over to the Russians on 30 December. Poniatowski's corps, which had retreated through Poland, added another 8,000. The corps of Reynier, Augereau, and Grenier, barely engaged in the campaign, netted still another 30,000 troops.

Frederick William of Prussia sympathized with the defection of General Yorck to the Russians, but he was wary. Finally, on 28 February, after Russian troops had crossed the Oder River, he signed a treaty of alliance with the czar. On 17 March, after Eugene had evacuated Berlin, he issued his famous appeals to "my people" and his army and declared war on France. Meanwhile Bernadotte, acting for the king of Sweden, had made a treaty with Britain on 3 March, which gave him a healthy subsidy to remain among the Allies.

---

[4]Chandler, in *Campaigns*, 853, says that the dead and captured totaled 570,000. Col. John Elting, co-author of West Point's *A Military History and Atlas of the Napoleonic Wars*, in a letter to this author, sets the number at "not much above 400,000."

On 27 March the Russians occupied Dresden, and the king of Saxony, erstwhile ruler of the Duchy of Warsaw, fled to Bavaria. He averred that his alliance with France remained solid, but he wavered, as did the king of Bavaria and other rulers of the Confederation of the Rhine.

Finally, Austria, after enlarging its army, refused Napoleon's request (20 April) to put it at his disposal. Instead, Metternich informed the French emperor that his country would act as an "armed mediator" for the time being. Ultimately, where Austria would stand would depend on French military fortunes in the coming months of 1813. The same applied to the states of the *Rheinbund*.

# 11

## THE KILL
### From Lützen to Elba, 1813–14

### Never So Many Before

By August 1813, Napoleon would find himself pitted against the armies of all Europe. He had never been in that position before. In fact, because of his enemies' mistakes, or other factors, he had fought essentially one great power at a time in each of his earlier campaigns. In 1796–97, he had commanded one of several French armies fighting Austria. (Egypt, 1798–99, needs no comment.) In 1800 he again had fought only the Austrians in Italy. In 1805 he had met first the Austrians at Ulm, and then largely Russians at Austerlitz. In 1806–07, he had fought first the Prussians at Jena-Auerstädt, and then mostly Russians at Eylau and Friedland. In 1808–09, he had gone against Spanish armies only, leaving Soult to pursue the small British contingent. In 1809 he had faced only the Austrians, finishing them at Wagram. In 1812 he had fought the Russians with all Europe (save Sweden) officially on his side.

In 1813, however, Napoleon eventually had to face the combined armies of all the major European powers, with field forces twice the size of any he could bring into battle. In 1814, it was the same, except that the odds were worse. His enemies had multiplied, while he had lost all his allies except Eugene's Kingdom of Italy. He had to meet armies invading France from Germany, Switzerland, and the Netherlands, while in the south Soult fended off Wellington, who had invaded France from Spain. Especially during the Campaign of France of 1814, Napoleon proved himself still capable of brilliant scrambling. But he had neither the resources, trained manpower, nor commanders to stand for long against the weight of enemy numbers. He fought magnificently, but it served only to enhance his already legendary stature as a commander.

On 30 April 1813, Napoleon returned to Naumburg from Paris to take command of a reborn *Grande Armée*. Eugene's Army of the Elbe, initially 50,000 survivors of the Russian disaster, was the nucleus. New troops were conscripts and National Guardsmen from France and troops levied by Napoleon's allies. Through March 1813, in France, the emperor had transferred

180,000 troops from the National Guard, called up 250,000 conscripts of the class of 1814, 137,000 from the class of 1813, and 100,000 from the classes of 1809–1812. During the next twelve months, 635,000 more would be called.[1] Not more than 350,000 of them were ever sent to Germany. However, Napoleon's German allies furnished some 40,000 troops, despite losses of 90 to 95 percent sustained in Russia. (Westphalia, for example, sent 22,000 to Russia; 760 stood muster at Küstrin in January, and perhaps 700 others returned.) Poniatowski and 10,000 faithful Poles were present for duty. Napoleon shortly sent Eugene back to Italy, and in June 1813, the viceroy sent 38,000 Italians to the *Grande Armée* in exchange for 50,000 French for his Army of Italy.

The whole *Grande Armée* in Germany numbered 300,000 when Napoleon arrived (at its peak, in August 1813, over 400,000), including 50,000 (later 88,000) in foreign contingents. It had 40,000 cavalry and 1250 guns. The new cavalry was far inferior to that lost in Russia; the mounts also were inferior, and many of the men rode poorly. The infantry comprised mostly green soldiers, often (at least among the French) well motivated and enthusiastic, but neither tough nor well trained. The mass was leavened with jaded veterans of the Russian disaster and commanded by uninspired (at best) marshals and generals. The army was big, but not comparable in strength or quality to any *Grande Armée* of the past.

### Battles of Lützen and Bautzen

Initially, Napoleon had 120,000 men under his direct command. He was faced by a force of about 110,000 Russians and Prussians, with Wittgenstein commanding largely Russians and Blücher largely Prussians. Kutuzov had been acknowledged as supreme commander, but he died in April, and Czar Alexander had not appointed a successor. As usual, the Allies were surprised by Napoleon's early appearance in Germany.

The French emperor was unaware of his advantages or the precise location of the enemy. Nevertheless, on 1 May, the day after his arrival, he ordered his army across the Saale River and marched on Leipzig. The Allies fell back before him, opposing his advance only at scattered locations. At one of these, near Weissenfels, Marshal Bessières was killed by a cannonball. His death affected Napoleon deeply. The marshal was one of his oldest comrades; he had first served him in 1796, in Italy, as a captain of cavalry in his Guides, predecessor of the Imperial Guard. He was only the second marshal to die in all of the wars and campaigns. His death from the "first volley of the enemy," as Berthier wrote, seemed a sad omen. Napoleon gave

---

[1]The last order, however, in March 1814, for 160,000, could not be executed before Napoleon's abdication and was renewed in 1815.

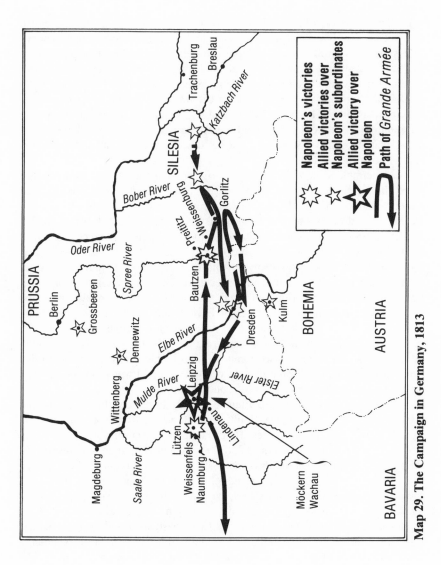

**Map 29. The Campaign in Germany, 1813**

him an epitaph worthy of a Gascon: "Bessières lived like Bayard; he died like Turenne."

On 2 May, at Lützen, Napoleon won a victory over the Allies, but it was not an easy one. Wittgenstein and Blücher, with three-quarters of their forces massed (73,000), caught Napoleon with his corps widely separated. It was mid-afternoon before he assembled enough troops to stem the Allied advance. It was getting dark before he had them outnumbered (he began with 45,000 and finished with 110,000), and it was dark before he forced them back by committing both the Young and Old Guards. The fighting went on for some hours in the darkness, but the Allies were well-bloodied and withdrew. Napoleon had his victory, but his cavalry arm was so undependable that he could not follow up on it.

Nevertheless, he was overjoyed. His proclamation to the troops compared the victory to those of Austerlitz, Jena, Friedland, and Borodino. His bulletin claimed that the French had destroyed the Royal Guard of the king of Prussia and badly hurt the Guards of the Russian czar. "I am again the master of Europe," he exulted to Duroc. Napoleon estimated French casualties at 10,000, the Allies' at 25,000 to 30,000 (in fact, 20,000 each was nearer right), and pulled the heart strings of the French with: "The ambulances on the field of battle offered a touching spectacle: the young soldiers, seeing the Emperor, hid their suffering and cried '*Vive l'Empereur!*' For twenty years . . . I have commanded the armies of France, and I have never seen such bravery and devotion." He wrote letters reassuring his German allies of certain victory. In all of this he also was reassuring himself. He was fully aware that he had to make a comeback as a general, and he had exerted himself to the limit during the battle. Furthermore, says Marmont, "It was probably the day when, in his whole career, he most courted danger."

Napoleon then dispatched Eugene to Italy to protect the kingdom and raise more troops, and he gave Soult, recalled earlier from Spain, command of the Guard, replacing Bessières. He brought up further reinforcements from France, increasing his numbers to 250,000. Responding to an obsession with taking Berlin—to punish the Prussians—he gave Ney command of a separate army of four corps, with orders to march on Berlin. Napoleon then followed the retreat of the Allies at all speed, which, by his earlier standards, was a snail's pace. On 16 May, Macdonald's cavalry finally found the enemy near the fortified town of Bautzen, 100 miles to the east; spies and meager cavalry reports put the enemy at 150,000 (the actual number was 96,000). Napoleon ordered Oudinot to move up south of the town. Ney was ordered to divide his army, attack the Allies at Bautzen from the north with two corps (his own and Lauriston), and allow Reynier and Victor to continue the march on Berlin. Ney misunderstood and directed all his corps southward, which turned out to be fortuitous.

On 19 May at 10:00 AM Napoleon was before Bautzen. By the end of the day, he had 115,000 men in position, and Ney was approaching from the north with 85,000 more, a total of 200,000. The enemy, 96,000 under Wittgenstein, was behind the Spree River, their positions anchored on the town, in the south center, but with a second line on hills a mile to the rear and the reserve another mile behind it. However, there were only scouting and probing actions on the 19th.

Napoleon's plan for the 20th was to pin the enemy along the Spree with the Guard and four corps—Oudinot, Macdonald, Bertrand, and Marmont—while Ney hit the enemy's north flank and swept through his rear. Unhappily, Ney was still miles away, so that only his advance guard figured in the actions of the day. On 20 May, then, the French began the battle at noon with an intense bombardment of the enemy center. At 3:00 PM the infantry attacked across the Spree with the engineers, under fire, throwing up bridges. By 6:00 PM, the French, by sheer force of numbers, carried Bautzen and the first Allied line. Thereafter, action fell off as both sides reorganized for the next day. Ney was approaching with his corps; Lauriston's and Reynier's were near the battlefield. The plan for the 21st was for Oudinot to attack in the south and draw as much of the Allied reserve that way as possible. Ney now was in position and would attack south into the enemy rear, as previously planned. At the right moment Soult, with Bertrand's corps, the cavalry corps of Latour-Maubourg, and the Guard (if Napoleon so ordered), would crack the enemy center on a plateau, as at Austerlitz, and seal a total victory.

On the morning of 21 May the battle resumed in all sectors. However, the Allies launched a major offensive against Oudinot on the south flank, which had the marshal calling for help by mid-morning. Napoleon sent him nothing and ordered him to hold until other planned attacks were launched. By about 11:30 AM Marmont and Macdonald had made forward progress, and Ney was pressing in from the north. At about noon, Napoleon ordered Soult forward, and by 2:00 PM he had pushed Blücher's corps back a mile. But then the attack stalled, since Ney had not been able to drive south of Preititz (which he should have bypassed). Also, Lauriston was moving too slowly, and Reynier had not arrived. The battle turned into a bloody slugging match, with the French sustaining heavy losses but making progress.

At dusk, Napoleon threw the Guard into the center, and it drove Blücher's corps steadily back. But Ney and Lauriston had not cut the Weissenburg and Görlitz roads, the enemy lines of retreat, and the enemy easily made a fighting withdrawal. At 10:00 PM a violent rainstorm ended the battle. In the morning, the Allied army was gone; the French were too exhausted and short of cavalry to pursue. Each side had suffered about 20,000 casualties. Napoleon had another victory, but with twice the numbers of his enemy, he had scored only a limited victory—and he had been forced to commit his precious Guard to achieve that.

The czar had interfered with Wittgenstein's operations, thus helping Napoleon. Principally, however, the French emperor had suffered from inferior troops, a lack of cavalry, and especially a lack of good commanders, such as those who had won or saved his battles in the past. Davout could have been there, but had been sent against Hamburg, which was not yet of real importance in the war. Lannes was dead; Masséna was in *de facto* retirement, as was Augereau; Murat was in Naples, up to no good; and so it went.

The French marched on to take Dresden, which, in theory, put Saxony back in Napoleon's camp. Davout indeed took Hamburg, thus securing the lower Elbe. The French emperor seemed to be regaining his suzerainty in Germany. But he had problems. The cavalry still was not combat ready. Cossacks were roaming freely in the French rear, destroying convoys and small detachments. The French had some 90,000 sick and stragglers, in addition to 40,000 casualties from the two victories. Moreover, the emperor's green troops were flagging. It was symptomatic that some were cutting off their trigger fingers or shooting themselves in the hand or foot, hoping to be sent home. Napoleon countered this "epidemic" by ordering that two such from each corps be shot by firing squad before the whole corps.

When, on 2 June, the Allies asked for a suspension of hostilities to talk truce, Napoleon agreed. On 4 June an armistice was signed which was to last until 20 July (later extended to 16 August). Napoleon's official reasons for halting the war were his lack of cavalry and Austria's hostile posture. In fact, he needed time to rest, reorganize, discipline, reinforce, and resupply his army. The Allies needed the same, and they also hoped to bring Austria into the war on their side.

**Austria Swings the Balance**

On 14 June, therefore, the czar proposed a congress at Prague to discuss means to a general peace. He had been inspired by Metternich, who committed Austria to attend and then went to Dresden to interview Napoleon on 26 June. Napoleon offered to pay a "ransom" if Austria remained neutral, but Metternich merely urged him to participate in the Prague conference; he finally agreed to send Caulaincourt. However, Napoleon had no doubt that Austria intended to side with the Allies. "I will beat you," he shot at Metternich. "But I have seen your troops," the handsome and arrogant minister replied, "they are boys and old men."

On the same evening, 26 June, all of Austria's doubts about joining the Allies were erased. News arrived of the disastrous defeat on 21 June of Joseph Bonaparte by Wellington at Vitoria, marking the *de facto* end of the Bonaparte Kingdom of Spain and making it all but certain that Wellington soon would invade France from the south.

On 19 July Austria agreed, by the Reichenbach Convention, to join the Allies if Napoleon did not accept the peace terms offered by the Prague

Congress. He was asked to cede the Duchy of Warsaw to Russia and Illyria to Austria, to restore Prussia to its size in 1805, and to dissolve the Confederation of the Rhine. He refused, since he considered the demands outrageous. The powers considered them reasonable, in view of Napoleon's disadvantages. Wellington's victory aside, Austria already had raised 300,000 troops and was calling up more; Russia and Prussia had strengthened their armies, and Bernadotte was moving into the field, encouraged by British subsidies and the promise that Norway would go from Denmark to Sweden at the peace. In Naples, Murat and Caroline were negotiating terms of treason with Austrian envoys. In Germany, Napoleon's allies were almost certain to defect to the Allies at his first reverse. On 12 August, Austria joined the Allies. Blücher resumed the war the next day, four days early.

Thus in August 1813, Napoleon found himself against all the major European powers, who were fighting with armies partially financed by the British and had the British Navy at their service. Soon arrayed against him were four great armies, the strength of which would grow, not diminish, as the campaign progressed: the Army of Bohemia (240,000), under Austrian Prince von Schwarzenberg; the Army of the North (120,000), under Swedish Crown Prince Bernadotte; the Army of Silesia (95,000), under Prussian Prince Blücher; and the Army of Poland (60,000), under Russian Marshal Bennigsen. These totaled 515,000 but soon would exceed 600,000.

Napoleon's forces had expanded also, but we know the nature of the reinforcements—green French troops and uncertain allied and foreign contingents. He formed three armies and placed two marshals and himself in command: Oudinot (120,000, including Davout's 35,000 at Hamburg), Ney (85,000), and Napoleon (165,000), for a total field army of 370,000. Another 60,000 men comprised detachments and fortress garrisons. In fact, Napoleon commanded both his army and Ney's, drawing on Oudinot at will. Nevertheless, his main army never numbered over 250,000, and it shrank with every battle he fought.

When fighting began again, Napoleon was minus Soult, whom he had sent to command the Army of Spain, soon fighting in southern France against Wellington's army. He had added Murat to his roster of marshals, however. He had ordered the king to the army because he needed him—and to get him away from Naples. The emperor suspected rightly that Murat was in contact with the enemy. Murat came because Napoleon was winning (or had won at Lützen and Bautzen) when he left Naples, which made him very nervous about talking with Metternich's representatives. The Gascon also came because his heart was still with Napoleon. Queen Caroline was less emotional.

Napoleon first had considered concentrating his forces and awaiting the next Allied move, or rather placing the corps close enough together so that they could be quickly concentrated for battle. This would have been in line with his professed practice and probably would have been the best plan for

1813. He thereby could have preserved the strength of his men and waited for the enemy to make mistakes before striking, thus carrying another of his usual battlefield tactics to the strategic level.

He abandoned concentration, however, for a plan under which his three armies would operate separately, and one (Oudinot) beyond the effective range of support of the others. Oudinot was to march for Berlin with the mission of taking the Prussian capital and destroying Bernadotte's army. Again, Napoleon was driven by the obsession with punishing the "traitors" Frederick William of Prussia and Bernadotte; he dispersed and wasted strength in the process. Ney's army was to advance into Silesia against Blücher. Napoleon would go after Schwarzenberg in Bohemia.

On these plans Napoleon consulted his marshals—a practice to which he had become increasingly prone. None made objection except Marmont, who expressed a preference for concentration, to take better advantage of enemy moves, and on the flattering (if nonetheless real) ground that separating the armies would deprive two armies of the advantage of the presence of His Imperial Majesty on the battlefield. Since the three-army plan prevailed, the choice of Oudinot over Davout to command the second largest one seems inexplicable. Davout had proved his ability for independent command at Auerstädt in 1806, and his corps, usually called in at the last minute, had decided battle after battle. It is conceivable that, if Davout had commanded against Bernadotte, the outcome of the whole campaign might have been different.

The French army was not very optimistic. Wrote Marbot, commenting on the early and moody celebration of Napoleon's birthday before the truce ended: "The least clairvoyant of officers sensed that we were on the eve of great catastrophes." Murat, who unwillingly had reported in from Naples, was not spreading cheer. "[Napoleon] will sacrifice France and the army and kill you all," he told Belliard.

The Allies agreed to the Trachenburg Plan, under which they were to avoid battle when Napoleon was present and try to isolate and destroy his subordinates. An army commander was to retreat if attacked in force by Napoleon, while the others closed in on his flanks. This plan worked very well until Allied numbers made such caution unnecessary. If Napoleon had kept the *Grande Armée* massed from the start, the Trachenburg Plan would not have been effective.

**Battle of Dresden**

On 21 August, Napoleon launched his army toward Blücher in Silesia, leaving Saint-Cyr's corps to guard Dresden. Saint-Cyr, however, soon found himself under attack by Schwarzenberg's Army of Bohemia and signaled Napoleon for help. Blücher was in retreat, so Napoleon turned back with the Guard, giving Macdonald command of the improvised Army of the Bober [River]. With Napoleon gone, on 26 August Blücher suddenly turned to fight, on the Katzbach River. He demolished Macdonald's force of two infantry and two cavalry corps and captured 15,000 men and 100 guns.

On the same day, Napoleon was preparing to meet Schwarzenberg at Dresden. Saint-Cyr had fortified the city, which allowed the French emperor to build his forces from 35,000 to 70,000 on the 26th while fighting off Allied probing attacks. Schwarzenberg, meanwhile, had to endure the presence of the emperor of Austria and the king of Prussia (and shortly the czar). Francis wanted to retreat because Napoleon was there, although his force was neither massive nor attacking. Frederick William, a bolder man than in 1806, insisted on fighting and got his way. Schwarzenberg limited himself to exploratory attacks while bringing up reinforcements and amassing 150,000 men and 400 guns.

On 27 August, Napoleon's army had grown to 120,000 and 250 guns, Schwarzenberg's to 170,000 with still 400 guns. Napoleon took the offensive. Murat, with the corps of Victor and cavalry of Latour-Maubourg, assailed the Austrian left flank, while Ney, commanding Mortier's corps and Nansouty's cavalry, attacked the Austrian right. The corps of Saint-Cyr and Marmont, backed by the Guard, held the French center. Success would have meant double envelopment of the enemy. Despite hard fighting, that was not achieved. However, the Allies sustained 38,000 casualties to 10,000 for the French. Moreover, their army was divided by a tributary of the Elbe; several days of rain had swollen the river and made the battlefield a sea of mud. The artillery was bogged down, negating the Austrian firepower advantage.

On the night of 27–28 August, the Allies reverted to the Trachenburg Plan and retreated away from Napoleon. On the morning of the 28th, the French found the enemy gone except for light rear guards. Therefore, Dresden was a victory for Napoleon but an indecisive one, made empty by defeats of his subordinates elsewhere. It would be his last victory in Germany. Napoleon put his army into pursuit, but since he still lacked adequate cavalry, his grasp of the location of the retreating columns was poor.

In the north, meanwhile, Oudinot had moved on Berlin. He came up against Bülow's Prussians of Bernadotte's army, and on 23 August he was defeated at Grossbeeren and driven southward. Enraged by Oudinot's defeat, Napoleon dispatched Ney northward to take over the army facing Bernadotte while he again went eastward after Blücher. Even accident seemed to favor the Allies.

Napoleon ordered General Dominique Vandamme, operating south of Dresden, to cut across the enemy route of retreat and destroy the Austrian trains. On 29 August, an Austrian corps under Ostermann blocked his path at Kulm, but he had superior numbers and prepared to crush it. On 30 August, however, Kleist's Austrian corps, retreating from Dresden, blundered into Vandamme's rear, and suddenly the French were outnumbered 54,000 to

30,000. Vandamme's corps fought gamely, but only half of it escaped, and Vandamme himself was captured.

Ney, in the meantime, took over Oudinot's command and resumed the offensive against Bernadotte. On 6 September he was abruptly stopped and badly defeated at Dennewitz, only 70 miles north of Dresden. Again, Bernadotte had been spearheaded by his Prussian corps under Bülow and Tauenzien, the latter one of the few "rocks" of Jena in 1806, and happy for revenge. Napoleon had advanced against Blücher again, picking up and reorganizing Macdonald's corps as he went. Blücher retreated before him and notified Schwarzenberg, who again went for Dresden. When Napoleon returned to Dresden, Schwarzenberg withdrew, by which time Blücher was edging toward Macdonald. On 22 September, Napoleon ordered Macdonald against Blücher once more, intending to follow, but he was threatened from the north and called off the offensive.

The French emperor, still not aware of the Trachenburg Plan, saw that Allied armies were closing in on him from the north, east, and south and might soon cut his communications with France, if nothing worse. Platoff's Cossacks were already wreaking havoc on the roads west. The weather steadily was getting worse, with cold rain and the hint of ice and snow to come. Muddy roads made maneuvers ever more difficult, especially with artillery. To top everything off, Berthier, Napoleon's right arm, was sick. "It is a horrible time," the emperor wrote Marie-Louise.

On 24 September he ordered a withdrawal behind the line of the Elbe, considering Wittenberg and Magdeburg—both fortresses in French hands— his line of retreat in any extremity. In early October, Napoleon moved west, sending Marmont via Leipzig to reinforce Ney against Bernadotte, whom he dearly wanted to smash. Instead, Bernadotte, reinforced by Blücher, forced Ney steadily southward. Blücher (Yorck's corps), then Bernadotte, crossed the Elbe, threatened Napoleon's rear, and denied his retreat via Wittenberg and Magdeburg. Saint-Cyr, meanwhile, was left to defend Dresden. Murat, commanding three corps plus cavalry south of Dresden, was pushed toward Leipzig by Schwarzenberg's army, while Bennigsen's Army of Poland, soon to reinforce him, had paused to blockade Dresden (finally surrendered by Saint-Cyr on 11 November).

## Battle of Leipzig

By 15 October all mobile elements of Napoleon's main army were being driven toward Leipzig. There occurred the great Battle of the Nations, which raged for four days, 16–19 October. On the 16th, Napoleon had 177,000 men and 700 guns in the Leipzig area. The Allies had in contact 200,000+ under Schwarzenberg in the south and 54,000 under Blücher in the northwest. On the 18th, Napoleon had 195,000 and 700 guns, but the Allies had added Bernadotte and Bennigsen for a total of 410,000 men and 1500 guns. The numbers go far toward telling the story.

On 16 October, then, Napoleon massed six corps, plus cavalry and the Guard, supported by a battery of over 100 guns under Antoine Drouot, and attacked Schwarzenberg at Wachau, south of Leipzig. French infantry made bold advances from mid-day onward but was never properly supported, although the cavalry did its best. Latour-Maubourg, hero of many battles, was gravely wounded. Every advance was followed by a withdrawal behind the cover of Drouot's guns. On the same day, Marmont was attacked by Blücher at Möckern, north of Leipzig, and at sunset was forced to retreat toward Leipzig. On the 16th, Napoleon gained nothing; the Allies gained time.

On the 17th Napoleon made a feeble attempt, without results, to negotiate with the Allies. Reynier's corps (18,000 + ) reinforced the French. The Allies, however, welcomed Bennigsen (70,000) and, by the next morning, Bernadotte (85,000). There was only light action, but Napoleon decided that he must withdraw to the west.

In the early hours of 18 October Napoleon drew his army into a tight circle around Leipzig and secured his line of retreat over the Elster and Luppe Rivers and through Lindenau. The Allies attacked the French in all quarters, and the battle raged until dark. The French held, despite the defection of their Saxon, and some other German, allies to the enemy, and after dark the withdrawal began in earnest.

On 19 October the Allies stormed Leipzig as the defenders thinned out, but the French rear guards held, in orderly succession, while the various corps, if in some disorder and disoriented by close-up fire by former German allies, proceeded over the Elster bridge and Leipzig-Lindenau causeway. Until 1:00 PM everything went well; it appeared that Napoleon would make good his escape. But it was not to be. About 1:00 PM, in a panic and unable to find his superiors, a corporal put a match to explosives and blew up the bridge. The corps of Macdonald, Poniatowski, Lauriston, and Reynier were trapped. They fought desperately but were driven into the river. Macdonald swam to safety; Poniatowski, already twice wounded, tried to swim the river on his horse and drowned. (He had been made a marshal only three days before.) Lauriston and Reynier were captured. Some men of all corps swam out. However, 30,000 French were captured, some 38,000 had been killed or wounded, bringing total casualties to about 68,000. The Allies had about 54,000 casualties.

After the Battle of Leipzig, Napoleon granted Murat's oft-repeated request to return to Naples. The emperor was afraid that, if he kept him longer, Caroline would take Naples into the Allied camp (in fact, she already had, tentatively, on 17 October). He counted on Murat's guilt, if not loyalty, to delay the process of treason. They parted at Dresden with a public embrace.

Napoleon was finished in Germany. He made for the Rhine and, as he did, his remaining allies joined the victors, and the Napoleonic states of Germany reverted to their old rulers. King Maximilian Joseph of Bavaria, who owed his royal title to Napoleon, had deserted to the Allies on 8 October, before Leipzig. Saxony had been occupied by the Russians, and its troops went over to the Allies during the Battle of Leipzig, as noted above (in 1815, Prussia got half of Saxony; the king kept what was left). Württemberg joined the Allies after Napoleon passed through in late October 1813. Jerome Bonaparte fled when Westphalia fell on 26 October, and the Dukes of Hanover (King George III of England), Brunswick, Hesse-Cassel, and other minor rulers recovered their lands. Prussia took over its former possessions in Westphalia (Magdeburg, etc.), the Rhineland, and Switzerland (Neuchâtel) in November. Prussia also got the Grand Duchy of Berg, composed of the former territories of Prussia, Bavaria, Nassau, and the city of Münster. The Grand Duchy of Frankfurt reverted to its parts—the imperial cities of Frankfurt and Wetzlar and the principalities of Hanau and Fulda, pending disposition by the Congress of Vienna. The disposition of the claims of some 300 princelings whose lands had been incorporated into larger states had to await settlement by the Congress of Vienna in 1814–15.

Napoleon left the army for Paris on 7 November. By the end of November 1813, what remained of the *Grande Armée* of 1813 was across the Rhine, except for troops left in strongholds in Germany. Davout still held Hamburg (and would until after Napoleon abdicated in 1814); Lemarois, Magdeburg; Lapoype, Wittenberg; and there were garrisons in a dozen lesser places.[2]

Meanwhile, on 8 November, the Allies offered Napoleon rule over France with its natural boundaries—the Alps and the Rhine—in return for peace. Austria and most of the German states would have been satisfied just to have France relinquish control over Germany and Italy. The destruction of Napoleonic France might mean Russian domination of central Europe, a change from bad to worse. The czar already had established a Russian-dominated Kingdom of Poland, which, it was clear, he would fight to keep. He also was the champion of Prussia, to whose king he had promised all of Saxony, and he obviously was determined to have a say in the disposition of all the German states. Moreover, he had a candidate for king of France— Bernadotte—whom he hoped to control. However, any ruler of France except Napoleon would make Russian involvement in European affairs easier, since he would be chosen (or restored if he were a Bourbon) by the Allies and thus lack clout in international affairs. Napoleon refused the offer, apparently in the belief that he somehow was being hoodwinked. The Allies then mutually pledged to invade France (1 December 1813).

---

[2]Glogau, Magdeburg, Erfurt, Würzburg, Wesel, and Mainz also held out.

## Campaign of France

Napoleon embarked on the defense of France with a field army of not over 120,000, comprising survivors of the German campaign, new conscripts, and National Guardsmen. In addition, he had the 100,000-man Army of Spain, under Soult, which battled Wellington in the south of France. Eugene had 50,000 Frenchmen in the Army of Italy, but he was fighting his own war for his own kingdom.

On 29 December, Blücher (110,000) began crossing the Rhine, while Schwarzenberg led the main Allied army (210,000) through Switzerland. Bernadotte's army (100,000) was approaching through the Netherlands, but only parts of it came into play against Napoleon, and very late. Blücher and Schwarzenberg planned a juncture on the Langres Plateau, between the Marne and Seine rivers, and a combined march on Paris. Napoleon's plan was to prevent their juncture by getting between them and attacking their most exposed units—or the army most off balance—demoralizing and disorganizing them, driving them apart, and eventually destroying each separately. In getting between the Allied armies, Napoleon risked being crushed between them. And considering the quality of his troops, it was a grave risk indeed.

In January 1814, Blücher advanced into Champagne with his corps widely separated and in close control of only about 53,000 men. On 29 January, Napoleon, with 30,000 troops, surprised and defeated him at Brienne. Schwarzenberg was exasperated at Blücher's "infantine rage to march on Paris" which had made him run into Brienne "like a fool." Napoleon's most inveterate enemy was nearing seventy-two. The old Prussian, however, was able to reorganize only five miles to the southeast, at La Rothière, where Schwarzenberg, now in a cooler temper, reinforced him to 110,000. By 1 February, Napoleon also had been reinforced (to 40,000) and attacked Blücher at La Rothière. This time Napoleon was surprised by Blücher's strength and driven back. Already, Allied numbers were beginning to tell. The Allies decided that Blücher would move down the Marne valley toward Paris while Schwarzenberg followed the valley of the Seine, to the south. But Blücher continued to move carelessly, with his corps dispersed.

During 10–14 February, with only 31,000 troops, Napoleon wreaked havoc on Blücher's army, bloodying and beating his corps in four successive battles. The scrambler had revived. On 10 February, he hit Olssufief's corps at Champaubert and literally destroyed it. On the next day, he hit Sacken's corps at Montmirail, 12 miles to the west, drove it westward in disarray, attacked Yorck, who was moving south to reinforce Sacken, late in the day, and drove him back as well. On the 12th, the French forced Sacken and Yorck to cross the Marne at Château-Thierry and retreat northward. Napoleon, meanwhile, went after Blücher, who directly commanded only two corps and some cavalry (32,000). Marmont found the Prussian near Champaubert, and

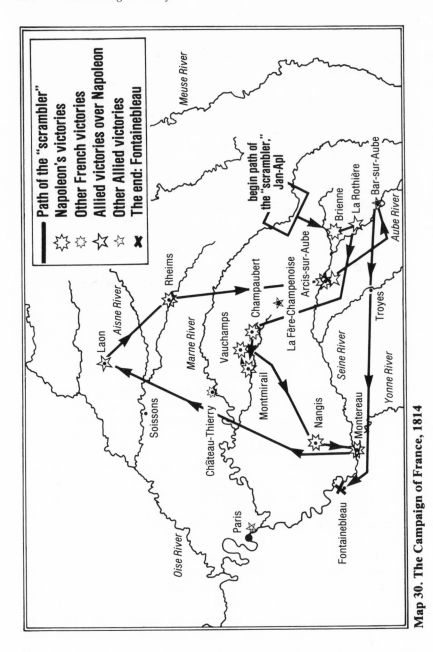

**Map 30. The Campaign of France, 1814**

Napoleon ordered him to decoy Blücher westward while he drew in all available forces (still, with Marmont, only about 31,000). He trapped and destroyed Blücher's advance guard at Vauchamps on 14 February. Blücher tried to retreat, but the maneuver became very disorganized. Grouchy's cavalry got around him and barred his path, taking a fearful toll of lives. He finally broke' free, but with the loss of 7000 men.

Napoleon, exhilarated by his four victories, turned south to strike at Schwarzenberg. For the first time, French villagers turned out to cheer with real enthusiasm. In the beginning, numb from years of war and bad news, they had been largely neutral. Their patrotism had been enhanced, however, by the looting of Allied troops; the Cossacks, especially, robbed and burned with gusto and were given to drunken binges during which they considered rape and murder as sports. The French were shocked enough to form bands of volunteer partisans and strike at the enemy. They also came forward with badly needed food for Napoleon's men, food they had hidden earlier from both friend and foe.

The emperor left the corps of Mortier and Marmont to guard the approaches to Paris. Each marshal had about 6000 men; their corps were at division strength. Napoleon himself moved south with 70,000 men against Schwarzenberg, who had his army more concentrated than Blücher but was still vulnerable to attack in detail. On 17 February, at Nangis, he surprised the corps of Wittgenstein and sent it flying into Wrede's Bavarians, who were saved only by nightfall. On the 18th he found the Prince of Württemberg who had been ordered to hold Montereau, on the north bank of the Seine, and drove him into the river. Schwarzenberg, thoroughly shaken, began withdrawing southward by stages.

At this juncture the Congress of Châtillon, where Caulaincourt was representing Napoleon, offered the French emperor France with the boundaries of 1792 in return for peace. Napoleon, against the advice of his foreign minister, refused. He was exultant over his victories, still distrustful of Allied offers, and he thought he could win. In fact, Napoleon's forces were thinning and getting ever more weary. He ignored that, in every major encounter, he had been forced to commit the Guard either to win or to escape with his skin. His ultimate reserve had become a corps of regular shock troops. Moreover, the Guard was a shadow of its former self. Old Guard regiments were down in strength to a few hundred. Most of the guardsmen now were Young Guard, often veterans only of the campaign of 1813, if that. Some were merely imposing draftees. When Napoleon wrote on 11 March, "The Young Guard melts away like snow," he was referring to casualties prior to the Battle of Laon, but also to desertions, almost unknown before in those ranks.

After Napoleon's victory at Montereau, Blücher could have joined with Schwarzenberg, but instead he marched on Paris. Napoleon left Macdonald, with 40,000 men, to follow Schwarzenberg and went after Blücher with

30,000. It was a mistake. On 27 February, Schwarzenberg turned on Macdonald's force (with Oudinot in the lead) at Bar-sur-Aube and defeated the French. To the north, meanwhile, Blücher was joined by Winzengerode and Bülow from Bernadotte's Army of the North, bringing his numbers to 85,000. Napoleon fought Blücher at Laon on 9–10 March and lost. His maximum strength, counting all available local reinforcements, was 37,000. Marmont, who came near Laon with 9000 men, never made contact and was driven away separately. Napoleon retreated to Soissons and assigned Marmont and Mortier to cover Paris.

Indefatigable, Napoleon still hoped to kill the Allied giants closing on him. Hearing of an isolated Prussian corps at Rheims, he marched across Blücher's front, destroyed it, and then raced south to strike at Schwarzenberg. On 20 March, at Arcis-sur-Aube, he met the Austrian on almost even terms, 21,000 to 20,000, and came off the winner. But Schwarzenberg was stronger than he thought. On 18 March, after hearing of Napoleon's descent on Rheims, he had ordered a general concentration between Troyes and Arcis-sur-Aube. Thus, on 21 March, when Napoleon ordered his army south, he ran into a solid mass of 90,000 troops. Macdonald (30,000) had withdrawn toward Paris and was 40 miles away. With no help in sight, Napoleon withdrew eastward.

The Allies, after some days of uncertainty, began marching on Paris again. Napoleon, meanwhile, concocted a new strategy: he would cut across the Allied rear, ruining their communications and disconcerting their plans. With this in mind he directed his army and Macdonald's to a line east of Vitry. He then ordered Marmont and Mortier to join him. They obeyed, but thereby were put in Schwarzenberg's path. On 25 March, at La Fère-Champenoise, they were badly mauled and driven back to Paris.

When Napoleon heard of this on the 27th, he made for Paris with his army via Bar-sur-Aube, Troyes, and Fontainebleau. On the 30th, at Troyes, he found the army exhausted and, leaving it to Berthier, rode ahead with a small escort to Fontainebleau and then, with only five companions, to within eleven miles of Paris. Early on 31 March, at Essonnes, he found that Paris had been surrendered by Marmont and Mortier only hours before.

## Abdication and Exile

Napoleon returned to Fontainebleau, where he eventually assembled 60,000 troops. He proposed to march on Paris, and his troops cheered, but while he prepared, Talleyrand formed a provisional government in the capital and persuaded the French Senate to depose the emperor. On the following day, 4 April, Napoleon was confronted by his marshals, who refused to march. "The army will obey me!" he shouted. "The army will obey its chiefs," Ney replied sadly. Oudinot, Macdonald, Moncey, and Lefebvre, all the marshals present, were of the same mind. Napoleon could not oppose all his old comrades-in-arms, so on the same day he abdicated in favor of his three-year-old son, Napoleon Charles. When this proved unacceptable to the Allies, he abdicated unconditionally two days later (6 April 1814).

Empress Marie-Louise and Napoleon Charles had been evacuated from Paris on 29 March by Joseph Bonaparte. Their flight ended at Blois, where Marie-Louise, quite literally, awaited Napoleon's orders to join him. He sent none, perversely waiting to see if she would come to him, now that he had fallen. Probably, she wanted to go and, until about 10 April, she could have made the journey. But then, Allied troops appeared, and she and the boy were delivered to her father, the emperor of Austria. Napoleon never saw them again.

Meanwhile, Murat, who had left the *Grande Armée* on 25 October 1813, was back in Naples on 5 November. On 8 November he told the Austrian ambassador that he was ready to help Austria expel the French from Italy—in return for the Papal States, Tuscany, and Sicily. In December, however, influenced by Caroline, coldly determined to remain a queen, he decided to settle for Naples, and on 11 January 1814 he formally allied with Austria. He soon found himself facing Eugene and his Italian-French army. Murat was given command of his own Neapolitans (30,000) and an Austrian corps under General Count Laval von Nugent. He reinforced the army of Field Marshal Bellegarde, already trying to conquer the Kingdom of Italy.

Eugene had refused the entreaties of his father-in-law, the king of Bavaria, to defect to the Allies. If he had done so in the fall of 1813, the Allies might have made him king of Italy, a promotion from Napoleon's gift of the title of viceroy. His wife, Augusta, asked him to think of the future of their children. But Eugene thought it his duty to fight for Napoleon, and he never wavered.

Murat, conscience-stricken, tried to avoid committing his troops against Eugene. Nugent, catching on to Murat's game, drew some Neapolitans in, but the king extricated them as soon as possible. It was 14 April—after Napoleon's abdication, although he did not know it—before Murat ordered his Neapolitans to attack, and only after repeated demands from Bellegarde and threats from Lord Bentinck, the British representative.

In February, Eugene had shortened his lines to fronts along the Mincio and the Po, hinged on Piacenza, Mantua, and Peschiera. On 16 April, when the news reached him of Napoleon's abdication, he still held these positions and was conducting limited attacks on the Allies. With Napoleon down, he still accepted only a truce with Bellegarde. If popular elections had been possible, he might have kept the throne of Italy, but such was not the case. The Austrians were determined to recover control over northern Italy. They blocked Eugene's attempts to appeal to the Congress of Vienna, subverted his government, and fomented riots in Milan and elsewhere. He was forced to choose between abdication and causing a civil war (between his supporters and those of, or supported by, the Austrians). He abdicated and went into exile in Bavaria, a permanent guest of his father-in-law, the king, who furnished him with a lavish retirement.

Murat was in despair over what he had done. "Never doubt my heart," he wrote Napoleon after the abdication, "it is worth more than my head!" His agitation was increased by the scorn of the Allies. The Austrian generals were angry that he had not prosecuted the war against Eugene; the British evidently hated a traitor, even from the enemy camp, and resented his behavior. He did not consider his kingdom safe, and in fact it was not.

From their point of view, the Allies provided well for the Bonaparte dynasty. Napoleon was granted sovereignty over the island of Elba, between Corsica and the Italian mainland; Marie-Louise became Duchess of Parma. All the members of the family retained their property and wealth; even Josephine was left undisturbed at Malmaison, where she died suddenly in May 1814. But to Napoleon, the world had come to an end. On the night of 12–13 April, he tried to commit suicide. He used a capsule he had carried in Russia, however, and it only made him sick. Accepting that his fate was to live on, he recovered quickly and, on 20 April, said his famous farewell to the Old Guard, drawn up in the White Horse Court of the château of Fontainebleau:

> "*Adieu, mes enfants!* Would that I could press you all to my heart; at least I can embrace your banner!"
>
> General Petit, seizing the Eagle, came forward. Napoleon . . . kissed the flag. The silence . . . was broken only by the sobs of soldiers.

Napoleon, repressing tears of his own, was helped into his carriage and whisked away. On 4 May he was in Elba. But France and Europe had not seen the last of him.

# 12

# THE GLORIOUS IRRELEVANCE

*The Waterloo Campaign, 1815*

## The Irrelevance of Waterloo

The campaign of Waterloo was unsurpassed for drama and left both sides bathed in glory. It let Napoleon make his public exit from the world stage to the thunder of cannon and made Wellington a British legend. Waterloo was irrelevant otherwise, however; it is almost impossible to argue that this mini-war had any historical significance. It did not change the world, although, to many nineteenth-century Europeans (and surely the British), it seemed to have saved it. It would have made little difference if the Allies had lost. To argue that it would have, we must assume that the Allies would have quit if Wellington and Blücher had lost. And that was about as likely as Napoleon's bodily ascending to Heaven, considering the Allies' enormous advantages.

Napoleon's chance for ultimate victory in June 1815 was even slimmer than in 1814. Even if he had been the general he was in 1796, it probably would not have mattered. Because his political supporters (as opposed to the common people) would not stand for a long war, he had to go all-out for a quick victory. Thus, his strategic and tactical abilities were of limited use. His marshals were old and tired, and most were either unwilling or physically unable to serve him; some who offered (e.g., Murat) he turned down (for reasons explained below). His one new marshal, Grouchy, was a walking mistake, later often blamed for Napoleon's defeat. His corps and division commanders were second-rate, with notable exceptions, such as Generals Honoré Reille and François Kellermann (the younger). After twenty years of war and the death of so many valiant young generals, men capable of high command were scarce. Napoleon's regiments were a mixture of veterans and greenhorns, more enthusiastic than in 1814, but not markedly better as fighting men. Even the Imperial Guard, although it brought together the best surviving veterans, had half-strength battalions and thus was something of a facade—an illusion of a Guard.

The Allies had been reunited by Napoleon's return. They had confident commanders fresh from victories: Wellington, Blücher, and many exceptional younger men. They were under no pressure to win quickly but could maneuver and fight on their own terms. Finally, Allied superiority in numbers was greater than in 1814. Napoleon was outnumbered 2 to 1 at the start, and within weeks the odds would rise to 4 to 1, and eventually 5 or 6 to 1.

Napoleon lost at Waterloo because his attack was hurried and unsophisticated, because he let his subordinates control the tempo of the battle, because he was badly outnumbered late in the day, and maybe because Wellington was a better general, at least on 18 June 1815. However, even if Napoleon had won, it is difficult to believe that this could have led to anything more than a replay—probably a shorter one—of the Campaign of France. No matter how well Napoleon fought, he probably would have been ruined by a combination of Allied numbers and rebellion or undercutting by his government in Paris.

### Flight from Elba

The emperor of Elba spent his first few months reorganizing the government, reviewing and re-equipping 700 volunteers from the Old Guard (his army), refurbishing his two châteaux, putting up buildings, repaving roads, and the like. He was hurt because Marie-Louise did not write and angered that his son was being brought up in Vienna as the Duke von Reichstadt. He was comforted by visits by his mother, his sister Pauline, and (in open secrecy) by Maria Walewska and their five-year-old son, Count Alexander Walewski. Napoleon soon became bored, however, and he also was going broke, since Louis XVIII failed to send his promised yearly stipend of 2,000,000 francs.

The news from France was that King Louis was unpopular and growing more so. He was an uninspiring figure; no one believed that his constitution would be enforced; the Church behaved as if it were reestablished; and the noble exiles who had returned with the monarch were fat, rich, demanding, and haughty. Napoleon's marshals and prefects, whom Louis had retained, selectively, to control the army and government, were well-paid but snubbed at court.[1] Moreover, Louis had been forced to raise taxes. He had demobilized most of the army, so France swarmed with malcontent veterans on half pay.

All this encouraged Napoleon to return. When he heard that the powers at Vienna were squabbling bitterly over the reorganization of Europe, he began making his plans. After dark on 25 February 1815, Napoleon blithely sailed for France on the brig *Inconstant* and landed on 1 March between Antibes and Cannes. He immediately marched with his Guard for Paris,

---

[1]The marshals included Berthier, Ney, Marmont, Jourdan, Augereau, Brune, Mortier, Victor, Macdonald, Oudinot, Suchet, and Gouvion-Saint-Cyr.

avoiding the royalist Rhône valley, with French troops joining him as he marched.

The most incredible scene occurred on 7 March, near Grenoble, where the way was barred by the 5th Regiment of the Line. Napoleon, with his gambler's instinct and flair for the dramatic, pushed through the Guard into the open. A young captain cried, "There he is . . . FIRE!" There was dead silence. Napoleon opened his coat and shouted: "Soldiers of the Fifth! I am your Emperor. If there is one among you who would fire on his Emperor, here I am!" Again there was silence. Then suddenly cries of *"Vive l'Empereur!"* rang out, as the men rushed to reinforce Napoleon's growing army.

At Auxerre, Marshal Ney, who had promised King Louis he would bring Bonaparte back in an iron cage, fell into Napoleon's arms. On 29 March, the emperor was in Paris, where he was carried on the shoulders of a cheering crowd into the Tuileries. The rotund and puffing Louis XVIII long since had fled into exile.

## Choices

Napoleon knew that the quickest way to take power was through the existing establishment: the politicians, or so-called *notables*. Most of them owed their careers to Napoleon, but they either were quietly hostile to him or (in the majority) tentative in their support. Among them were former ministers, such as Fouché, Jean-Antoine Chaptal, and Joseph Defermon; former generals-politicians, such as Régis-Barthélemy Mouton-Duvernet and the prefect Jacques-Claude Beugnot; entrepreneurs, such as Augustin and Alphonse Perier; Napoleon's new nobles, from the marshal-princes, such as Berthier, to his surgeon, Larrey; nobles of the Old Regime, such as the Marquis de Lafayette, whose fortunes he had saved; and even the intelligentsia, such as Benjamin Constant and Chateaubriand. The emperor knew that, to gain the *notables'* backing, he would have to share power with them. In addition, he would have to win acceptance by the European powers—and quickly—either by diplomacy or war. In short, he could get the *notables'* support with minor concessions, and they even could be expected to finance a short war, but not a long one.

Napoleon's alternative was to appeal directly to the people, who overwhelmingly supported him. He represented French glory, and the emotional attachment to him was enormous. More practically, however, the people remembered the Napoleonic years as prosperous: farmers had been paid top prices for their products, unemployment had been almost unknown, and wages were good. There also had been law and order, but under Louis XVIII, the roads were becoming unsafe again as desperate, unemployed people and burned-out ex-soldiers turned to banditry.

Napoleon announced early on, however, that he did not want to "become king of a Jacquerie." It would require formation of a new leadership group, and perhaps something like the Terror, to get rid of the old. He preferred to take his chances with the *notables*. The emperor granted a new constitution, the Additional Acts, and under it appointed a Senate and had elected a Chamber of Deputies. He hoped that this would please French liberals such as Lafayette, a new deputy, and certify his peaceful intentions to the Allied powers. In the end, it did neither, but a government—one which the *notables* accepted, if temporarily—quickly began to function.

To the European monarchs, whose representatives were at the Congress of Vienna, he pledged to keep the peace and rule France within its existing boundaries. But on 13 March, even before he had reached Paris, they had declared him an outlaw: "an enemy and disturber of the tranquillity of the world." On 25 March, Austria, Prussia, Russia, and Britain pledged to keep 150,000 troops each in the field until Napoleon was defeated, a total of 600,000. Minor powers in Germany alone would furnish another 100,000. War, then, became Napoleon's only hope of survival as emperor.

## Murat Reallies with His Emperor

To Murat, still king of Naples by virtue of his betrayal of Napoleon in 1814, the emperor's return was a golden opportunity to salve his conscience. Queen Caroline Bonaparte thought they were safer with the Allies: "I know him [Napoleon]; he will kill us!" Nevertheless, on 19 March, Murat marched to attack the Austrians in northern Italy with his Neapolitan army (100,000 men, on paper). When Napoleon heard, he was outraged; he still had some hope for negotiations with the Allies, but Murat had confirmed their worst fears.

Napoleon knew, moreover, that Murat was not really fighting for him; he was out to become ruler of all of Italy. Murat's kingdom was in jeopardy because he had made a great show of joining the Allies in 1814 but had fought hardly at all; the powers at Vienna might dethrone him even if he kept the peace. Italian unification would give him greater power and would be easy, according to his ministers (notably Antonio Maghella and Francesco Ricciardi), who were predominantly members of the Carbonari, Freemasons, and other pan-Italian societies. They had told him all Italy would rise and furnish him with 150,000 troops or more. On 30 March, expecting a great flood of volunteers, he proclaimed Italian independence at Rimini. There were veritably none. Obviously the Italian intelligentsia had grossly overestimated the interest of the common man in Italian unity—much less his willingness to die for it. As in Germany, pan-nationalism was a generation or more away.

Murat marched forward with his Neapolitans anyway; he had the Austrians outnumbered 2 to 1. At first the enemy retreated, but then, in chance encounters, it found that Murat's army was a paper tiger. For whatever reason, the men were not motivated to fight for Italy, or Naples, or the king, or anything else. The Austrians went on the offensive, and within a week Murat's army was in disorganized retreat to the south. On 3 May, he managed to pull a sizable force together at Tolentino and commanded it with great valor, leading infantry into line and heading cavalry charges. Nonetheless, he was defeated and his army scattered to the winds.

The king escaped to Naples, where he faced a startled Queen Caroline in the palace. "You seem surprised to see me, Madame; I assure you I have done my best to die." So he had. Caroline, however, was merely embarrassed. She already had surrendered Naples to the British, under Lord Robert Campbell, whose fleet was anchored in the harbor. Murat disguised himself and fled, eventually to Marseilles, from whence he wrote Napoleon, offering his services.

The emperor ignored him. After some weeks, Murat went to Corsica, recruited 300 men, and returned to Naples, landing near Pizzo in October 1815. He purported to believe that "his people" would restore him to the throne. Probably, he was committing suicide. At any rate, he was captured by Bourbon troops, tried by a court-martial which included some of his own former generals, and shot by a firing squad. Brave and vain to the end, he gave the order to fire after admonishing the soldiers to "aim for the heart. Spare the face." It was a sad end for the First Horseman of Europe, whom Napoleon could have used at Waterloo. But the Gascon probably would have died of boredom amid the wars of words of the nineteenth century.

## Napoleon's Plans and the Army

Napoleon considered it mandatory that he strike first. He put together an army of 300,000 regulars and mobilized 170,000 National Guardsmen for interior duty. However, his field army numbered only 125,000. Napoleon had to allot troops to defend the frontiers and hold down rebels in the perennially royalist Vendée and Rhône areas. The Allies had 400,000 men under arms and a potential of 700,000. The French emperor's only hope was to take the enemy armies one at a time.

Napoleon determined to attack the two nearest armies, in Belgium: Wellington at Brussels, with an Anglo-Dutch army of 110,000; and Blücher at Liège, with 120,000 Prussians: first Wellington, then Blücher. Wellington was closer, and Napoleon was possessed of the idea that if he hit *les Anglais* hard, Wellington would run for the British fleet at Ostend. Perhaps he had been overly impressed by Sir John Moore's retreat to Coruña in 1809; at any rate, it cheered Napoleon to think that this was standard British behavior. Once Wellington was dispensed with, he planned to deal with Blücher. He hoped that the Allies would then bid for peace.

As far as his own forces were concerned, most of the still-fit marshals either had gone into exile (e.g., Marmont and Victor) or had declined to rally to him (Macdonald, Gouvion-Saint-Cyr). To Napoleon's extreme chagrin, Berthier, the chief of staff in all his campaigns, had fled with his German wife to her father in Bavaria.[2] He was really irreplaceable. Napoleon declined the services of Murat, as we know, and also of Oudinot. In practical terms, this was a mistake; Murat, surely, would have been useful on the Waterloo campaign.

Present and accepted for combat duty were Marshals Davout, Soult, Ney, and Mortier. Napoleon's assignments of them were predictable but perhaps not in his best interest. Davout, unquestionably the best independent commander available, was made minister of war. (Did Napoleon still fear a rival reputation, even in the extreme circumstances of 1815?) Marshal Soult, also an outstanding troop commander, was made chief of staff, although generals were available whom Berthier had trained: for example, Jacques Pelet. The emperor made Marshal Ney, in effect, his deputy commander, and that famous firebrand was destined to be the battlefield commander at Waterloo. Mortier was given command of the Imperial Guard, but he became ill and was succeeded by General Antoine Drouot. Napoleon created one new marshal, Grouchy, a marquis of the Old Regime who had repeatedly distinguished himself as a cavalryman. He was designated to command the cavalry reserve, but he was given a more critical assignment in the field.

As for corps commanders, Jerome Bonaparte was denied command of a corps and given a division, which was unjust, if not a grave mistake, considering his performance at Waterloo. The corps commanders were either of the second line or unknown quantities. Reille had served mostly in Spain. Lobau had led the Guard with exceptional valor at Aspern-Essling, but he had been a staff officer in Russia and was captured in 1813. Vandamme was valiant but more famous as a looter; he had gotten corps command initially by default, when Augereau had fallen ill at Wagram. Jean-Baptiste Drouet, Comte d'Erlon, had risen to corps command in the Army of Spain where, significantly, his fellow generals called him "the count." Gérard had been a corps commander for only a few months in 1813–14. The cavalry corps commanders were somewhat better: Kellermann had been a hero as early as Marengo, while Exelmans, Milhaud, and Pajol had long service. All had the mandatory flaw of the cavalryman, excessive impetuousness.

Of the five regular corps, four were at about normal strength, 18,000 to 25,000 men; Lobau's corps, however, had only 10,000. The cavalry corps also were thin; the largest corps at Waterloo (Kellermann) numbered 3400, or slightly over brigade strength. The Imperial Guard had 13,000 infantry in 23 battalions, or an average of 565 men per battalion (normal strength 840).

---

[2]Berthier died on 1 June 1815 in Bamberg. He fell from a window, possibly a suicide.

The Guard cavalry numbered 4100 men in 5 regiments and 1 squadron; the regiments were a little over half-strength.

The Imperial Guard comprised 8 Old Guard battalions and 15 of the Young Guard. The Middle Guard, recruited in 1806–1809, had disappeared into the Old, or served in cadres for new Young Guard regiments. The Young Guard comprised survivors from 1813–14, plus officers and men selected from line regiments, plus volunteers and some draftees—all chosen for imposing appearance, height, and spirit. Even the Old Guard had received 2 officers and 20 men from each line regiment to fill out its ranks.

It was hardly the *Grande Armée* of old. It was officially the Army of the North or, in Napoleon's orders, just "the Army."

## Advance into Belgium: Ligny

On 15 June 1815, Napoleon crossed the Sambre River at Charleroi and marched into Belgium. He put Ney on the Brussels road with 45,000 men, but he held back the other 80,000 while he evaluated news that Blücher was approaching fast from the northeast. When he confirmed the fact, he shifted his 80,000 troops toward Ligny and, by noon on 16 June, was fully engaged with Blücher and 85,000 Prussians. Ney, on the same morning, encountered the enemy at Quatre Bras and cautiously joined battle, unsure whether he was facing the whole army of Wellington.

Blücher had marched too precipitously, and Wellington was almost too casual about "Boney's" approach. The duke, in Brussels, was attending a ball given by the Duchess of Richmond on the evening of the 15th (as is almost too well-known). Just after midnight, in the early hours of the 16th, a messenger arrived to tell him Napoleon was at Charleroi. He quietly gave orders for his army to concentrate on Quatre Bras, 10 miles north of Charleroi. He then continued calmly to dance. After the ball, Wellington had supper, then returned to his quarters around 2:00 AM and went to bed.

At 4:30 AM he was awakened by an agitated general who reported that the French had taken Charleroi. "I dare say they have," said the duke. "Well, I have done all a man can do." And he went back to sleep. Actually, he had done all he could, since his army was west of Brussels, and it would require fifteen to eighteen hours to move all units to Quatre Bras. He was lucky that the Prince of Orange was close enough to hold the place until he arrived.

Wellington reached the battlefield at Quatre Bras about 11:00 AM on 16 June. He found the Prince of Orange, with 8000 men, holding at bay an obviously larger French force. He began reinforcing Orange as fast as possible and by day's end had 36,000 men. Meanwhile, he heard from Blücher at Ligny, only five miles away, and even rode over to confer with him and his chief of staff, Gneisenau. He learned that Napoleon and the bulk of his army

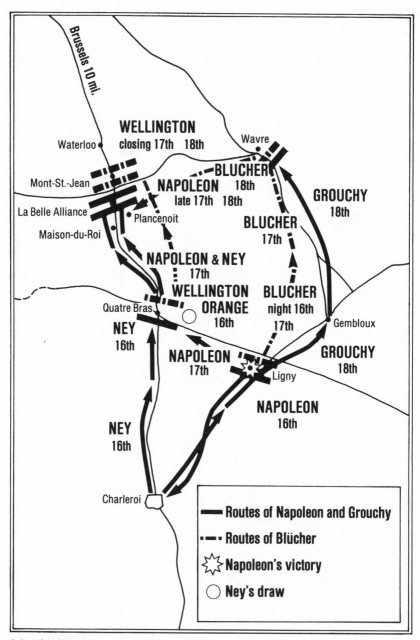

**Map 31. The Waterloo Campaign: Ligny and Quatre Bras, 16-18 June 1815**

were at Ligny, but he was unable to reinforce Blücher because of the risk that Ney would break through at Quatre Bras and disperse his army before it was assembled.

Blücher, *"Alter Vorwärts"* (Old Forward), now seventy-three years old, rushed his army into battle, or most of it; if he had waited a day, Bülow's corps, marching from Liège, would have brought his numbers to 116,000. Always a cavalryman at heart, the square, muscular, mustachioed old Prussian rode with several aides, one of whom was detailed to keep his pipe filled and brandy bottle ready. Blücher was a legend in the Prussian army, typically leading the way forward, shouting, cursing, or joking with his *kinder*, but sometimes driving them along with the flat of his sword. His great dream was to capture Napoleon and have him shot. The 85,000 men he commanded at Ligny were in some disorder. Many regiments were dragged out from long marches, and most were full of green recruits and volunteers. Still, they fought like tigers.

Napoleon launched his major attack about 2:00 PM with two corps and the reserve cavalry, which went at the Prussian left. In reserve were Lobau's corps and the Guard. Sensing victory, he ordered d'Erlon's corps from Ney's army to march east and hit Blücher's right flank. An aide carried the order to d'Erlon, who complied, but no one told Ney. On hearing that d'Erlon was marching away, the marshal angrily ordered him back. Almost to Ligny, d'Erlon turned back for Quatre Bras. The result was that he participated in neither battle. His failure to arrive on Napoleon's left probably deprived the emperor of a decisive victory, although he beat the Prussians anyway.

The French drove the Prussians back through Ligny and neighboring villages by bloody hand-to-hand fighting. At about 8:00 PM, with night closing in, Napoleon committed the Old Guard, followed by Milhaud's cavalry, and broke the Prussian center. Blücher tried to restore his line by leading a cavalry charge in person, but his horse was shot out from under him, and he was ridden over several times and lost from sight. Gneisenau, thinking Blücher was probably dead, ordered a retreat on Wavre, which went off in good order, so that on the 17th and 18th the Prussians were no more than 10 miles from Wellington's force. Blücher found a horse and galloped after his army, joining the headquarters after midnight.

Meanwhile, at Quatre Bras, the normally impetuous Ney was behaving with exaggerated caution. If he had attacked early in the day, he probably would have broken the 8000 men under the Prince of Orange and rolled up Wellington's army, which was strung out all the way back to Brussels. But Ney was all too familiar with Wellington's tactics from service in the Peninsula and feared that there might be hordes of redcoats on the reverse slopes of hills before him. Thus he had Reille's corps (20,000 men) work slowly through the woods and farms, pressing the Allies back on the crossroads. By about 4:00 PM, however, the enemy had 20,000 men present and stopped Reille short of Quatre Bras. Ney called for d'Erlon (20,000) and prepared to attack, but he learned that the count was marching toward Ligny. Ney ordered him back but attacked without waiting for him.

The incident apparently threw Ney from anger into the fury of battle for which he was famous. Suddenly everywhere, he ordered Kellermann's cavalry on Quatre Bras at the charge and goaded Reille ahead. Kellermann took Quatre Bras but was driven out by Allied artillery. At about 6:30 Wellington, now at 36,000 men and perhaps 100 guns, counterattacked. Ney fell back, awaiting d'Erlon, who was nearing the field. Night fell, and the battle died. On 16 June, Napoleon had won an indecisive victory at Ligny, and that only by committing the Guard. Ney, at best, had a draw. Nevertheless, Napoleon believed he now could keep Blücher at bay while he went after Wellington. Rain began as the battles ended on the 16th and poured down all the next day.

Wellington had planned, if Blücher won, to combine their armies and attack Napoleon at once. At dawn on 17 June, however, he got the report that the Prussians were in retreat on Wavre and ordered his army to retreat on Mont-Saint-Jean, 10 miles to the north and 10 miles west of Wavre. He sent a message to Blücher that, if the Prussian could reinforce him with "even one corps," he would stand at Mont-Saint-Jean. (Wellington's rear-echelon headquarters was at Waterloo, 2 miles to the north.) Blücher promised to be there with two corps or more. The Allied armies slogged northward on muddy roads in driving rain, the men soaked to the skin but not cold (it was June, after all). Their wagons, caissons, and wheeled artillery rutted the roads, making the going even harder for the French, who shortly followed.

Napoleon rose late and acted sluggishly on the 17th. He ordered Grouchy to pursue Blücher with 33,000 men—2 corps (Vandamme and Gérard) plus 2 cavalry corps (Exelmans and Pajol). The emperor and Grouchy both assumed that Blücher was retreating eastward toward Liège or Namur, and not northward. Thus, although cavalry patrols moved out at dawn to find the Prussians, they went in the wrong direction. Grouchy also went east, because he thought he was on the right track; he spent the night of the 17th at Gembloux and only on the 18th moved toward Wavre. He was destined not to arrive at Waterloo.

All morning on the 17th, Ney pressed Soult for orders, but the chief of staff could give him none. Finally, at about 11:00 AM, Napoleon ordered Ney (now reinforced by d'Erlon) to attack Quatre Bras, while he marched from Ligny to take Wellington on the flank. Before Napoleon could march, however, he got word from Ney that the Allies had evacuated Quatre Bras. The emperor thus simply joined Ney about 2:00 PM, and they followed Wellington's army north.

The French marched in mud, sometimes knee-deep; the infantry had to help push and drag the artillery along; heavy rain continued to fall, making ponds of depressions and rivulets of every rut. To add to the natural miseries, they had to suffer bombardment by the horse artillery of Wellington's rear guard under Henry Paget, Lord Uxbridge. He had been the most celebrated hero of Moore's retreat to Coruña (Spain, 1809), commanding the cavalry of the rear guard, and he was a master at choosing positions from which his artillery could blast the French column and scurry away, leaving dead and wounded and splintered vehicles behind. It took the French until midnight to cover the ten miles between Quatre Bras and the battlefield Wellington had chosen south of Waterloo and Mont-Saint-Jean. They were stopped by fire in the blackest of nights from Wellington's outposts; his lines were already generally in position for the battle he anticipated on the 18th.

## Positions at Waterloo

Wellington placed his army on a ridge across the north end of a dished plateau which ran south from Mont-Saint-Jean to Maison-du-Roi. Napoleon arrayed the French on a similar ridge about a mile to the south, centered on La Belle Alliance. Wellington intended to begin battle on the defensive and had picked his position accordingly. The forward slope, facing the French, was steeper than the reverse slope, which was gentle but ideal for putting troops in defilade, shielded from artillery fire, moving them in cover, and concealing their positions and numbers. To the west, the ridge hooked gently south, which made the Allied front concave. The total Anglo-Dutch force at Waterloo was 68,000 with 157 guns. By evening, Blücher would arrive, and the numbers would rise to nearly 140,000 against Napoleon's 72,000.

The core of Wellington's army comprised a small, seasoned British force of 20,000 infantry and 8000 cavalry, including 5000 infantry and 2000 cavalry of the King's German Legion (KGL); the remainder of the 68,000 consisted of Dutch (16,000) and German troops from Hanover (13,000), Brunswick (5000), and Nassau (6000). The British units were heavy on Scots regiments and Royal Guards. A majority of the senior officers and half the men had served under Wellington in the Peninsula, as had most of the officers and men of the KGL. The Peninsular veterans infected the whole army with an overweening confidence in Wellington. Moreover, the French faced British units with traditions older by far than that of the Imperial Guard—units of men of fierce pride, whom Napoleon would have to kill to make them give way. And they would not be easy to kill; whereas the French indulged in area fire by the infantry (shooting at a general target), the British and KGL were trained shooters, if not all marksmen, and mostly veterans, whose fire would be devastating and delivered precisely on order.

The Allied left, which Wellington expected Blücher to reinforce, was the thinner, but it had the steadiest units. Among these were Kempt's brigade of Peninsular veterans; Pack's brigade, which included the Royal Scots, Royal Highland (Black Watch), and Gordon Highlander regiments, and behind them

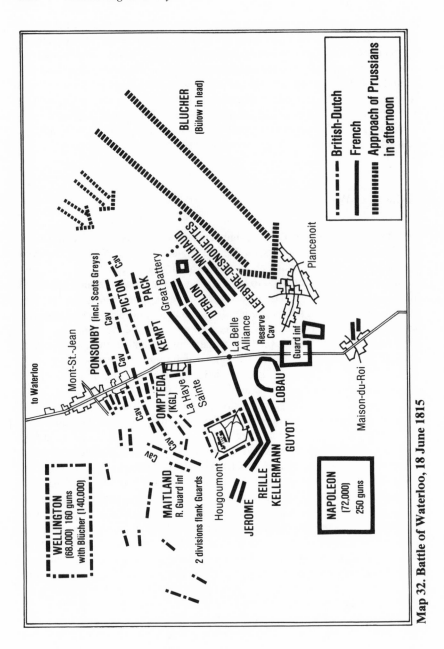

**Map 32. Battle of Waterloo, 18 June 1815**

Picton's division, with the Cameron Highlanders and eight Peninsular battalions. Behind Picton was Ponsonby's cavalry brigade, including the Scots Greys (Royal North British Dragoons). Across the highway from Kempt, further anchoring the center, was the KGL brigade of Ompteda. In the brigades on the right of the highway (and army) were the Coldstream Guards, 73d Highlanders, 71st Highlanders, and Royal Inniskillings, an Irish regiment. Destined to play a major role was the brigade of Royal Guard infantry under Major General Maitland, which was in the first line.[3]

The Allied line had two advance posts. On the right was the château of Hougoumont commanded by the giant Colonel James Macdonnell, a Peninsular veteran, and defended by companies of the Coldstream and 3d Guards and by Hanoverian and Nassau light infantry. On the left was the farmhouse of La Haye Sainte, manned by five companies of the KGL and one battalion of the 95th Rifles. There were questions, particularly about the wisdom of holding Hougoumont, to which Wellington replied laconically, "I have put Macdonnell in charge."

Because of Napoleon's corps organization, his dispositions are easier to describe. His army at Waterloo numbered 72,000 with about 250 guns. On the French left was Reille's corps, including Jerome's division; behind it was Kellermann's cavalry corps and, behind that, a division of Guard cavalry. On the right was the corps of d'Erlon, backed by Milhaud's cavalry corps, who were backed in turn by a division of Guard cavalry. Lobau's corps was in reserve, as were all the Guard infantry and two divisions of cavalry. Small batteries of artillery were ranged in front of Reille's corps. A battery of 80 guns was placed 500 yards in front of d'Erlon's corps. If Grouchy had arrived, Napoleon would have had over 100,000 troops and greatly outnumbered Wellington. This was not to be. Instead, Blücher would reinforce Wellington.

One could say that at Waterloo two defenders faced each other. Strategically, Napoleon always had been the aggressor, but tactically, he had habitually defended by offense; that is, while he had often begun battles, he always held back the heaviest possible reserve and waited for the enemy to make a mistake—and then pounced. "The whole art of war consists of a well-reasoned defense, extremely circumspect, and a bold and rapid offense." Austerlitz is perhaps the best example. Wellington was an almost compulsive defender of selected positions; he only attacked when he was absolutely certain that all the odds were in his favor. His were habits developed in the Peninsula, where until 1813 his forces were always outnumbered. Wellington behaved

---

[3]Ten miles to the west, at Hal and Tubize, Wellington stationed 17,000 troops under Prince Frederick of the Netherlands. They were mostly Belgians, with one British brigade and two regiments of Hanoverian cavalry. They took no part in the Battle of Waterloo. Wellington may have put them there to cover a possible retreat. Probably, he did not trust the Belgian troops since the Belgian citizenry, in vast majority, had been happy under Napoleon's rule but resented serving the Dutch king, whom the Allies had placed over them in 1814.

absolutely typically on the day of Waterloo. Napoleon began typically but ended with all-out frontal attacks because he had no other choice.

Napoleon was under the pressure of time, while Wellington was not. Napoleon had to win, and win on 18 June, or Blücher was sure to join Wellington and he would be outnumbered, even if Grouchy reinforced him. As Wellington later said: "Napoleon did not maneuvre at all. He just moved forward in the old style, and was driven off in the old style."

Both commanders radiated confidence before the battle. Wellington, riding his lines on his chestnut thoroughbred, Copenhagen, said to Müffling, "Now Bonaparte will see how a general of Sepoys can defend a position." Napoleon had repeatedly called Wellington the "Sepoy General" because of his early service in India. On the morning of Waterloo he turned on Soult: "Because he beat you in Spain you think he is a great general. I tell you he is a bad general, and the English are bad troops, and this is going to be a picnic."

**Battle of Waterloo**

On 18 June 1815, the day dawned bright and clear. The ground was soaked, however, and in the early morning hours artillery and wheeled vehicles had to be dragged through a sea of mud. It was 11:00 AM, therefore, before the French were in position.

Shortly afterwards the French artillery, including the great battery, started firing all across the line. At about 11:30, Reille began the battle with an assault on Hougoumont. It began well, with Jerome's infantry driving in the German infantry outside the walls of the château. For long hours they battered at the walls, pushing against the main gate, which was held shut at one point by the huge Macdonnell, almost alone, with his back against the inside. At 1:30 PM the French broke through the gate, but Wellington reinforced the garrison with four companies of Coldstream Guards, and the attackers were driven out again. The château was destined to stand throughout the battle. Late in the day, Napoleon ordered it bypassed, but it was too late. Jerome Bonaparte fought there all day and left the field a hero.

At about 1:30 also, the 80-gun battery began firing again. Neither time had it done much damage, since most of Wellington's formations were beyond the crest of the hill. At about 2:00 PM d'Erlon's corps attacked, marching straight at the Allied center. The vanguard came up against Picton's veterans, lying behind a hedge, and were stopped cold (although Picton was killed). At this juncture, Uxbridge launched his cavalry into their flank. The Scots Greys and Household Cavalry cut through the French and were joined by infantry of the 92nd Highland Regiment, who went to the bayonet, while their pipe major played "Hey, Johnny Cope, Are Ye Waulkin' Yet." The Greys galloped on, attacking the great battery and taking an awful toll on the gun crews. But they went too far; they were hit on the flank and were all but annihilated by French lancers. D'Erlon, nevertheless, was thrown back with heavy losses. At about 4:00 PM d'Erlon's corps, led into position by Ney, again attacked the British center but was thrown back, again sustaining heavy casualties. Twice they had been forced to bypass the farm of La Haye Sainte.

Meanwhile, just after 1:00 PM, the French had sighted a mass of troops approaching from the northeast. For a while, even Napoleon thought it was Grouchy. He sent his aide-de-camp, Bernard, to find out; he was quick returning. "What news?" asked the emperor. "Bad, Sire." "They are Prussians, *non?*" "Yes, Sire." It was Bülow's corps, as was confirmed shortly by a prisoner.

Earlier, at about 10:00 AM, Napoleon had received a message from Grouchy that he was following the Prussians toward Wavre. At 1:00 PM the emperor dictated an order for Grouchy, written by Soult, which said, "March on Wavre and drive out the Prussians." After the approach of Bülow and the Prussians was confirmed, Napoleon added a postscript, which informed Grouchy of the fact and ended, "Thus you should maneuver to join with our right." Grouchy received Napoleon's order probably around 4:00 PM, by which time he was attacking the Prussian rear guard at Wavre. Although he could hear the cannon at Waterloo, he chose to continue the attack on Wavre. In fact, Napoleon's orders were contradictory, but Grouchy's common sense, if not his courage, surely comes into question. He never marched for Waterloo, so Napoleon was deprived of almost one-third of his army.

On the French right, Bülow's Prussians reached Plancenoit. Napoleon ordered Lobau to defend the village and turned his attention in that direction. He now had no reserve, save the Guard. About 4:00 PM, with Napoleon's attention on the Prussians, Ney became battlefield commander. The marshal watched while Wellington's center fell back in what he took to be retreat; actually, they were moving behind the crest for better protection from artillery fire. He decided to go in for the kill and, waving his sword, ordered Milhaud to follow him; by accident or by Milhaud's request, the Guard cavalry of Lefebvre-Desnouettes followed also. Thus, 2800 *cuirassiers*, breastplates shining, went forward, their heavy horses making the ground tremble, followed by 2000 lancers and *chasseurs*—almost 5000 men and horses. Trotting, trotting, in seemingly unending lines, plumes flying, sabers drawn, they awaited the order to charge. Finally, Ney raised his sword high and went into the gallop; the mass followed in magnificent array.

Over the crest of the ridge they went, only to be met by direct fire from British artillery at point-blank range and then to come up against British squares, the men formed three deep, delivering devastating fire. (Wellington had pulled his line back 100 yards and then, when he saw the cavalry coming, ordered the squares formed.) The British infantry, unlike the French, were trained marksmen. The cavalry charged and veered around the squares; hardly any penetrated the enemy formations. If the men were brave, the horses were not, and they balked before the British volleys. The squadrons withdrew, decimated and in disorder.

Ney, in a frenzy, reorganized the survivors, ordered in Kellermann's cavalry corps of 3400 heavy and light cavalry, plus the Guard cavalry (also mixed) of Guyot, and led forward another attack, this time of perhaps 8000 horsemen. Again the attack met the artillery fire and then the squares, and again it failed. Ney, furious, reorganized the mass again and led it forward; he had lost his plumed hat, but his red hair was visible to the men. Yet again the attack failed. Finally, at about 6:00 PM, Ney let the exhausted cavalry rest.

Ney remained convinced, with each charge, that the Allied line would shatter. He resolved to attack once more with infantry and cavalry. Within a few minutes, Ney had called additional infantry from Reille's corps, alerted d'Erlon's survivors, and brought back much of the cavalry for another charge. Just one more solid blow! On he went, and the men followed. This time he did take the farm house of La Haye Sainte, where the KGL and the 95th Rifles had run out of ammunition, but he accomplished nothing more.

After Ney's cavalry attacks, Napoleon had no whole units but the Guard infantry—15 battalions of Old Guard and 8 of Young Guard. Lobau's corps, in Plancenoit, had quickly run into trouble against Bülow's Prussians and other corps following him, goaded on by *Alter Vorwärts*, Blücher himself. By 5:00 PM Lobau had lost Plancenoit to the Prussians. Napoleon sent in four battalions of the Young Guard, then the other four, who retook the village, only to be driven out again. The emperor then committed two battalions of his precious Old Guard, which took and held Plancenoit.

He realized that he must break Wellington's center soon or see the Prussians come smashing through his rear. At about 6:30 PM, Napoleon personally led twelve battalions of the Old Guard down the slope into attack position. The band played "*La Marche des Bonnets à Poil*," and at the sight of the emperor's silhouette and the tall grenadiers and *chasseurs à pied* of the Guard, the men of the shattered front divisions raised the cry, "*Vive l'Empereur!*" The wounded rose or sat up to cheer, and deserters ran back toward their units.

Napoleon, not unaware that he could lose, had left a battalion behind at Maison-du-Roi. He detached another at the front and stationed it at La Haye Sainte to form a base. He then turned eleven battalions over to Ney and went off to check on the action at Plancenoit. Ney had had four horses shot out from under him that day and was on his fifth. He still had no hat and had broken his sword, but he was unconscious of either; he still was possessed by the madness of battle.

Marshal Ney assumed that he was to lead the Guard into battle, and he did. Sometime after 7:00 PM (the accounts differ), the drums of the Guard sounded the *pas accéléré* and Ney led six battalions forward, followed at an interval by five more, all in battalion column, sixty men abreast. Between the battalions were pairs of horse artillery. All were very vulnerable to artillery and well-aimed musket fire. Forward they went in awesome legion, tall fur shakos bobbing, bayonets gleaming. The battered troops of d'Erlon and Reille were urged forward in support of the Guard by officers shouting that Grouchy had arrived to save the day—a deliberate falsehood ordered spread by Napoleon.

At around 8:00 the drummers beat the charge as the Guard neared the crest, but their pace remained deliberate, almost sinister, as if they were the agents of death, which so often they had been. On the march, they had somehow veered to the left and came up against Wellington's freshest infantry, protected all day by Hougoumont, but it was obscured—lying down in tall grain and invisible to the Guard. Suddenly, not 30 yards from the front ranks, the Guard saw appear redcoats without number, as if by magic. It was Maitland's brigade of Royal Guards. Wellington had shouted, "Now, Maitland, now's your time!" The general had ordered, "Stand up!" and "Fire!" The first volley took down the officers and 400 men of the leading battalion of Imperial Guards. They hesitated, then moved forward, only to be hit by another volley, and still another. The ranks stopped and milled about, with officers and noncommissioned officers shouting orders. Over 1200 Guards and 60 officers lay dead. The others went into retreat.

"*La Garde recule!*" went the cry all across the French line, and "*Sauve qui peut!*"—every man for himself! The French army broke and ran in disorder, swirling about the square of the Guard battalion near La Haye Sainte, which made an heroic stand, and running past other units, mostly Guards, who were still fighting both on Wellington's front and around Plancenoit. Ney tried to rally the center, shouting "Come see how a Marshal of France dies!" but he ended up inside the square of Guards in the valley along with Soult, stray Guards and officers by the hundreds—and the emperor. At about 9:00 Wellington, waving his hat, galloped forward and motioned his army into a general advance that carried all before it.

At about the same time, Napoleon, on his little Arabian mare, Marengo, rode rapidly from the protection of the slowly disintegrating Guard battalion at La Haye Sainte, and under cavalry and grenadier escort made it to his carriage within the square of Guards at Maison-du-Roi. Thence he went by carriage to Genappe, half-way to the French border, where he mounted a horse and, accompanied by Ney, Soult, and others, rode for Paris. Behind him, at La Belle Alliance, Wellington and Blücher met and, to the duke's astonishment, although both were on horseback, Blücher embraced him, exclaiming "*Kamerad!*" and "*Quelle affaire!*" At the end, Napoleon had been outnumbered 2 to 1. He was beaten for the last time. His military career was over; his political career had only four days to run.

# EPILOGUE

Napoleon returned to Paris to find that Joseph Fouché had, in effect, seized the government, with the support of the Chamber of Deputies, led by the Marquis de Lafayette. But crowds swarmed about the Tuileries, urging the emperor to fight on. The Parisians had prospered and been proud under Napoleon; he was their only defense against the return of the Old Regime, which they identified with tyranny, hunger, unemployment, high taxes, and general hopelessness. Napoleon could not help marveling over the loyalty of the people, when many of the high and mighty of his own regime had abandoned him. He said to Benjamin Constant, who was watching the crowds with him:

> Do you see them there! They are not the ones I loaded with honors and gorged with money. What do they owe me? I found them poor and I left them poor. But . . . the voice of the nation speaks through them. If I wish, in an hour, the Chamber [of Deputies] will not exist. . . . [But it is not worth the price.] I did not return from Elba so that Paris would be inundated with blood.

The people trusted that Napoleon could fight on, under any circumstances. In fact, he could have continued the war, since Davout had an army of 120,000 near Paris which could be reinforced by Grouchy's corps (then withdrawing from Belgium), the survivors of Waterloo, the National Guard, and frontier forces. But Napoleon saw the futility of continuing. Even if he forcefully dissolved the Chamber of Deputies by turning the Paris mob on it, reasserted himself as chief executive, and levied his own taxes, there was not time to pull an army together. At Waterloo, he had not only lost but also had seen the Guard destroyed; France could not supply another. He decided to settle, if he could, for securing the French throne to his dynasty.

On 22 June 1815, he abdicated in favor of his son by Marie-Louise of Austria. "I offer myself in sacrifice to the hate of the enemies of France." Through his brother Lucien, he tried to get the Senate to accept his son as

Napoleon II, and for a few days he seemed to have succeeded. But then the Senate and Chamber of Deputies both came out in favor of the return of Louis XVIII. For Lafayette and his kind, it was right to support the hereditary monarch; for the majority, it was merely the safest solution.

Napoleon, meanwhile, had left Paris for Malmaison as the Allied armies approached. There he said farewells to his family, and most surely to the memory of Josephine. He then went on to Rochefort, where his brother Joseph had chartered a ship for New York. It was Joseph's plan to impersonate the ex-emperor while he made his escape, but Napoleon declined his offer. Rather than risk being caught sneaking away like a criminal, he surrendered himself to Captain Maitland of the British warship HMS *Bellerophon* and wrote the prince regent of England, asking for asylum:

> Royal Highness, exposed to factions which divide my country and the enmity of the powers of Europe, I have terminated my political career, and I come, like Themistocles, to settle by the hearth of the British people. I place myself under the protection of their laws, which I beseech of Your Royal Highness, as the most powerful, the most constant, and most generous of my enemies.

The British cabinet, of course, rejected his request and declared him a prisoner. At the request of the Allies that he be exiled to a place remote from Europe, they sent him to St. Helena, in the South Atlantic, 1300 miles from the nearest point of Africa and 2400 from Brazil. There he lived out his life— "General Bonaparte," per orders, to his humorless "jailor," Sir Hudson Lowe, and "His Majesty the Emperor" to his faithful retainers, volunteers all. He died of stomach cancer on 5 May 1821, a day officially commemorated in France every year, even in the late twentieth century. In December 1840, at the request of King Louis Philippe, the ex-emperor's remains were returned to Paris and interred in Les Invalides, where they now rest. Lord Rosebery described the scene unforgettably:

> On a bitter December morning the King of the French, surrounded by the princes and ministers and splendours of France, sate in silent state under the dome of the Invalides. . . . Suddenly a Chamberlain appearing at the door announced in a clear and resonant voice, *"L'Empereur,"* as if [the corpse] were a living sovereign: and the vast and illustrious assembly rose with a common emotion as the body was borne slowly in. The spectators could not restrain their tears.

### The Myth and the Mythmaker

Napoleon spent much time in his dying years writing the history of his time. He dictated to Emmanuel de Las Cases for the famous *Mémorial de Sainte-Hélène*. He talked constantly to persons who duly recorded every word:

Generals Gourgaud, Montholon, and Bertrand, whose writings comprise the so-called *Mémoires* of Napoleon; the Irish surgeon O'Meara, whose *Napoleon in Exile* was an instant best-seller; and there are dozens more. In all of this, however, the fallen emperor made no concerted attempt to enhance his military reputation, although he was guilty of some petty, and sometimes reprehensible, alterations of facts. For example, he told Las Cases that at Marengo, he, Napoleon, had drawn out the Austrian army so that Desaix, with the reserve, could finish it off.

The myth he allegedly created was almost purely political. He presented himself as an emperor who governed for the people in France and whose only desire for Europe was to give the nationalities the benefits of the French Revolution. He denied any plan to dominate Europe; instead, he said he had planned a "Federation of Free Peoples." He insisted that he would be remembered for the *Code Napoléon*, and that Waterloo would "eclipse" the memory of all his victories. By easy inference, he was saying that the benefits he planned were more than worth the cost in blood, but that is the only constant message regarding the military.

Napoleon, on St. Helena, also said many things about the "art of war," some of which are contradictory. For example, he said to Bertrand, "The art of war is a simple art . . . it is all common sense; nothing about it is theoretical"; but also, "The art of war has invariable principles." Variations (though not the above) may be blamed in part on the diversity of scribes who took down his words. During the five and one-half years of his exile, however, "*On s'engage, et alors on voit*" [You engage, and then you wait and see] appears repeatedly, in different words and varying prolixity. However he put it, it rings true.

He expanded on his basic rule in discussions of the qualities of a great general with Las Cases:

> [The rarest quality is] the courage of the improviser [*improviste*], who, despite the most unexpected events, retains his force of mind, of judgment, and of decision.
>
> The outcome of a battle . . . is the result of one instant, one thought: one approaches with various combinations, one mixes it up [*on se mêle*], one fights for a while, the decisive moment presents itself, a mental spark [*une étincelle morale*] tells one so; the smallest reserve [wins the battle].
>
> War is composed altogether of accidents. . . . A [great] commander never loses sight of what he can do to profit by these accidents.

These statements confirm that the greatest general of his time had no tactical doctrine; he was an improviser who profited from his enemies' mistakes. His advice on strategy was also simple: to keep corps close enough together so as to be able to concentrate them quickly, not to divide forces in the presence of the enemy, and to maneuver to have greater numbers on the field of battle than the enemy.

NAPOLEON'S
MILITARY PHILOSOPHY

Napoleon had violated his own maxims time and again and gotten away with it. Often he had blundered, but he had always scrambled to victory, until the masses of his enemies overwhelmed him. The truest things he said concerned great commanders, among whom he immodestly, but rightly, included himself. Among these, two rather dull maxims seem to give away Napoleon's major secrets of success: "True wisdom, for a general, is in energetic determination." And "Military genius is a gift of God, but the essential quality of a general-in-chief is strong character and the determination to win at all costs."

Napoleon was probably the greatest commander of all time, but his genius lay in scrambling, not in carrying out a preconceived plan.

# BIBLIOGRAPHY

## Bibliographies and References

Chandler, David G. *Dictionary of the Napoleonic Wars*. New York, 1979.
Connelly, Owen, ed. *Historical Dictionary of Napoleonic France*. Westport, CT, 1985.
Godechot, Jacques. *L'Europe et l'Amérique à l'époque napoléonienne*. Vol. 37, *Nouvelle Clio*. Paris, 1967.
Horward, Donald D. *Napoleonic Military History: A Bibliography*. New York, 1986.
Meyer, Jack A. *An Annotated Bibliography of the Napoleonic Era: Recent Publications, 1945–1985*. Westport, CT, 1987.
Ross, Steven T. *European Diplomatic History, 1789–1815: France Against Europe*. Garden City, NY, 1969.
Tulard, Jean. *Bibliographie critique des mémoires sur le Consulat et l'Empire*. Geneva, 1971.
Villat, Jean. *La Révolution et l'Empire, 1789–1815*. 2 vols. Paris, 1947.

## Printed Primary Sources

Napoléon I. *Correspondance de Napoléon Ier, publiée par ordre de l'Empereur Napoléon III*. 32 vols. Paris, 1858–1870. *Supplément*. Ed. by A. du Casse. Paris, 1887.
———. *Correspondance inédite de Napoléon Ier, conservée aux Archives de la Guerre*. 5 vols. Ed. by E. Picard and L. Tuetey, Paris, 1912–1925.
———. *Dernières lettres de Napoléon*. 2 vols. Ed. by Léonce de Brotonne. Paris, 1903.
———. *Lettres de Napoléon à Joséphine*. 2 vols. Ed. by Mme de Faverolles. Paris, 1933.
———. *Lettres de Napoléon à Joséphine et . . . de Joséphine à Napóléon*. Paris, 1959.
———. *Lettres de Napoléon à Marie-Louise écrits de 1810 à 1814*. Paris, 1960.
———. *Lettres, décisions et actes de Napoléon à Pont-de-Briques et au camp de Boulogne, An VI (1798)—An XII (1804)*. Ed. by Fernand Beaucour. Levallois, 1979.

————. *Lettres inédites de Napoléon.* 2 vols. Ed. by L. Lecestre. Paris, 1897.

————. *Lettres inédites de Napoléon.* Ed. by Léonce de Brotonne. Paris, 1898.

————. *L'Oeuvre et l'histoire.* 13 vols. Paris, 1969.

————. *Mémoires pour servir à l'histoire de France sous Napoléon, écrits à Sainte Hélène, sous la dictée de l'Empereur, par les généraux qui ont partagé sa captivité.* . . . 9 vols. Paris, 1823–1825.

————. *Memoirs.* Reprint of Translation. 4 vols. New York, 1985.

————. *My Dearest Louise: Marie Louise and Napoleon, 1813–1814: Unpublished Letters from the Empress with Previously Published Replies from Napoleon.* Ed. by C. F. Palmstierna. Trans. by E. M. Wilkinson. London, 1958.

————. *Oeuvres littéraires et écrits militaires.* 3 vols. Ed. by Jean Tulard. Paris, 1969.

————. *Ordres et apostilles.* 4 vols. Ed. by A. Chuquet. Paris, 1911–12.

————. *Proclamations, ordres du jour et bulletins de la Grande Armée.* Ed. by Jean Tulard. Paris, 1964.

Beauharnais, Eugène de. *Mémoires et correspondance.* 10 vols. Ed. by A. du Casse. Paris, 1858–1860.

Bigarré, Auguste J., Baron. *Mémoires.* Paris, 1899.

Bonaparte, Jérôme. *Mémoires et correspondance du roi Jérôme et de la reine Catherine.* 7 vols. Paris, 1861–1866.

Bonaparte, Joseph. *Mémoires et correspondance.* 10 vols. Ed. by A. du Casse. Paris, 1851–1854.

Bourrienne, Louis-Antoine Fauvelet de. *Mémoires.* 10 vols. Paris, 1829.

Carnot, Lazare. *Mémoires* . . . *rédigés d'après ses manuscrits* . . . *par P.-F. Tissot.* Paris, 1824.

Caulaincourt, Armand A. L., Marquis de. *Mémoires.* 3 vols. Ed. by Jean Hanoteau. Paris, 1933.

————. *With Napoleon in Russia.* Trans. by G. Libaire. New York, 1935.

Constant, Louis (Wairy). *Mémoires intimes de Napoléon I.* Paris, 1967. Original in 6 vols. Paris, 1830–31.

Davout, Louis-Nicolas, Marshal. *Correspondance.* 4 vols. Paris, 1885.

Dumas, Mathieu, Comte. *Souvenirs.* 3 vols. Paris, 1839.

Fézensac, R.-A.-P.-J., Duc de. *Souvenirs militaires.* Paris, 1863.

————. *The Russian Campaign, 1812.* Trans. by Lee Kennett. Athens, GA, 1970.

Grouchy, Emmanuel de, Marshal. *Mémoires.* 5 vols. Paris, 1873–74.

Las Cases, Emmanuel, Comte de. *Mémorial de Sainte-Hélène.* 8 vols. Paris, 1823. Ed. by André Fugier. Paris, 1961.

Macdonald, Jacques-E.-J.-Alexandre, Marshal. *Souvenirs.* Paris, 1892.

Marchand, Louis. *Mémoires.* 2 vols. Ed. by J. Bourguignon and H. Lachouque. Paris, 1952–1955.

Marmont, Auguste-F.-L. Viesse de, Marshal. *Mémoires.* 9 vols. Paris, 1857.

Masséna, André, Marshal. *Mémoires.* 7 vols. Paris, 1849–50. New Ed. 1966.

Murat, Joachim, Marshal. *Lettres et documents, 1787–1815*. 8 vols. Ed. by Paul Le Brethon. Paris, 1908–1914.
Ney, Michel, Marshal. *Mémoires*. 2 vols. Paris, 1833. [Fragmentary.]
Roederer, Pierre-Louis. *Autour de Bonaparte: Journal*. Paris, 1909.
Savary, A.-J.-M.-René, Duc de Rovigo. *Mémoires*. 8 vols. in 4. Paris, 1828.
Ségur, Philippe-Paul, Comte de. *Histoire et mémoires*. 7 vols. Paris, 1873.
————. *Histoire de Napoléon et de la Grande Armée de 1812*. Paris, 1824.
Soult, Jean de Dieu, Marshal. *Mémoires*. 3 vols. Paris, 1854.
————. *Mémoires . . . Espagne et Portugal*. Paris, 1955.
Staël, Anne Louise Germaine Necker, Baronne de. *Mémoires: Dix ans d'exil*. Ed. by the Duc de Broglie and the Baron de Staël. Paris, 1821.
Wellington, Arthur Wellesley, Duke of. *Dispatches*. 12 vols. Ed. by Lt. Col. Gurwood. London, 1834–1838.


**Interpretive Works**


Camon, Hubert. *Génie et métier chez Napoléon*. Paris, 1929.
————. *La Guerre napoléonienne: Les systèmes d'opérations*. Paris, 1907.
————. *Quand et comment Napoléon a conçu son système de manoeuvre et Quand et comment Napoléon a conçu son système de bataille*. Paris, 1931–1933.
Clausewitz, Carl von. *On War*. Trans. by Peter Paret and M. Howard. Princeton, 1976. First English trans., 1873; from *Vom Krieg*, in Clausewitz's *Hinterlassene Werke über Krieg und Kriegsfürung*. 10 vols. Berlin, 1832–1837.
Elting, John R. *The Superstrategists*. New York, 1982.
Halweg, Werner, ed. *Klassiker der Kriegskunst*. Darmstadt, 1960.
Liddell-Hart, B. H. *The Ghost of Napoleon*. London, 1933.
Marshall-Cornwall, James. *Napoleon as Military Commander*. London, 1968.
Oman, C. W. C. *Studies in the Napoleonic Wars*. London, 1930.
Paret, Peter. "Napoleon and the Revolution in War," in *The Makers of Modern Strategy*. Ed. by Peter Paret, with Gordon Craig and Felix Gilbert. Princeton, 1986.
Van Creveld, Martin. *Command in War*. Cambridge, MA, 1985.
Yorck von Wartenburg, M. *Napoleon as a General*. 2 vols. London, 1902.


**General Histories of the Revolutionary and Napoleonic Wars**


Camon, Hubert. *La Guerre napoléonienne: Précis des campagnes*. 2 vols. Paris, 1925.
Chandler, David G. *The Campaigns of Napoleon*. New York, 1966.
Chuquet, Arthur M. *Guerres de la Révolution*. 11 vols. Paris, 1914.

Dodge, T. A. *Napoleon: A History of the Art of War.* 4 vols. New York, 1904–1907.

Dumas, Mathieu, Comte. *Précis des événements militaires ou Essais historiques sur les campagnes de 1799 à 1815.* 27 vols. Paris, 1817.

Elting, John R., and Vincent J. Esposito. *A Military History and Atlas of the Napoleonic Wars.* New York, 1964.

Jomini, Antoine-Henri de, Baron. *Vie politique et militaire de Napoléon.* 4 vols. Paris, 1827.

Lachouque, Henry. *Napoleon: 20 Ans de campagnes.* Paris, 1964.

———. *Napoleon's Battles: A History of His Campaigns.* Trans. by Roy Monckorn. New York, 1967.

## Biography: Life and Times of Napoleon

Bergeron, Louis. *L'Episode napoléonien: Aspects intérieurs.* Paris, 1972.

Chandler, David. *Napoleon.* New York, 1974.

Chuquet, A. *La Jeunesse de Napoléon.* 3 vols. Paris, 1897–1899.

Colin, Jean. *L'Education militaire de Napoléon.* Paris, 1900.

Connelly, Owen. *The Epoch of Napoleon.* New York, 1972/1978.

———. *Napoleon's Satellite Kingdoms.* New York, 1965/1969.

Herold, J. Christopher. *The Age of Napoleon.* Reprint. New York, 1984.

Lovie, Jacques, and André Palluel. *L'Episode napoléonien: Aspects extérieurs.* Paris, 1972.

Manfred, Albert. *Napoléon Bonaparte.* French Ed. Trans. from the Russian by Patricia Champe. Moscow, 1980.

Markham, Felix. *Napoleon.* New York, 1963.

Mistler, Jean. *Napoléon et l'Empire.* 2 vols. Paris, 1969.

Ravignant, Patrick. *Napoléon.* Paris, 1985.

Roux, Georges. *Monsieur de Buonaparte.* Paris, 1964.

Sorokine, Dimitri. *La Jeunesse de Bonaparte.* Paris, 1967.

Tulard, Jean. *Napoléon ou le mythe du sauveur.* Paris, 1977.

———. *Grand empire, 1804–1815.* Paris, 1982.

Weidhorn, Manfred. *Napoleon.* New York, 1986.

Zaghi, Carlo. *Napoleone e l'Europa.* Naples, 1969.

## Biography: The Marshals et al.

Adelbert, Prince von Bayern. *Eugen Beauharnais, der Stiefsohn Napoleons.* Munich, 1940.

Chardigny, Louis. *Les Maréchaux de Napoléon.* Paris, 1977.

Delderfield, R. F. *The March of the Twenty-Six: Napoleon's Marshals.* London, 1962.

Dunn-Pattison, R. P. *Napoleon's Marshals*. London, 1912.
Macdonell, A. G. *Napoleon and his Marshals*. London, 1934.
Young, Peter. *Napoleon's Marshals*. London, 1974.

Ainval, Christiane d'. *Gouvion Saint-Cyr: Soldat de l'An II, maréchal de l'Empire*. Paris, 1981.
Bernhardy, Françoise de. *Eugène de Beauharnais*. Paris, 1973.
Christophe, R. *Le Maréchal Marmont*. Paris, 1968.
Dupont, Marcel. *Murat, cavalier, maréchal de France, prince et roi*. Paris, 1980.
Foster, John T. *Napoleon's Marshal: The Life of Michel Ney*. New York, 1968.
Gallaher, John G. *The Iron Marshal: A Biography of Louis N. Davout*. Carbondale, IL, 1976.
Garnier, J. P. *Murat, roi de Naples*. Paris, 1959.
Hourtoulle, H. F. G. L. *Davout le terrible*. Paris, 1975.
Marshall-Cornwall, J. *Marshal Massena* [*sic*]. London, 1965.
Morton, John B. *Marshal Ney*. New York, 1958.
Oman, Carola. *Napoleon's Viceroy*. London, 1966.
Tulard, Jean. *Murat*. Paris, 1985.
Watson, Sydney J. *By Command of the Emperor: A Life of Marshal Berthier*. London, 1957.
Willette, L. *Le Maréchal Lannes: Un d'Artagnan sous l'Empire*. Paris, 1979.

**Armies: Old Regime, Republic, *Grande Armée*, and Opposing Armies**

Androlenko, General D. *Histoire de l'armée russe*. Paris, 1967.
Angeli, M. von. *Erherzog Karl als Feldherr und Heeresorganisator*. 6 vols. Vienna, 1895–1897.
Bescrovny, L. G. *Russkaia armiia i flot v XIX veke*. Moscow, 1973.
Blond, Georges. *La Grande Armée, 1804–1815*. Paris, 1979.
Bucquoy, Eugène L. *La Garde impériale*. 2 vols. Paris, 1977.
Bukhari, Emir. *Napoleon's Cavalry*. San Francisco, 1979.
Choury, Maurice. *Les Grognards de Napoléon*. Paris, 1968.
Corvisier, André. *Armies and Societies in Europe, 1494–1789*. Trans. by Abigail Siddall. Bloomington, IN, 1979.
Davies, G. *Wellington and His Army*. London, 1954.
Elting, John R. *The Grande Armée of Napoleon*. New York, 1987.
Glover, Richard. *Peninsular Preparation: The Reform of the British Army, 1795–1809*. Cambridge, 1963.
Jany, C. *Geschichte der königlich-preussischen armee*. 4 vols. Berlin, 1933.
Johnson, David. *Napoleon's Cavalry and Its Leaders*. New York, 1978.

Lachouque, Henry. *Napoléon et la garde impériale*. Paris, 1957. Trans. as *The Anatomy of Glory: Napoleon and His Guard* by Anne S. K. Brown. London and New York, 1961.
Lynn, John A. *The Bayonets of the Republic: Motivation and Tactics of the Army of Revolutionary France, 1791–94*. Chicago, 1984.
Paret, Peter. *Yorck and the Era of Prussian Reform, 1807–1814*. Princeton, 1966.
Phipps, Ramsey W. *The Armies of the First Republic and the Rise of Napoleon's Marshals*. 5 vols. London, 1926–1929. Reprint. 1985.
Pivka, Otto von. *Napoleon's German Allies*. London, 1978.
Quimby, Robert S. *The Background of Napoleonic Warfare*. New York, 1957.
Rogers, Hugh C. B. *Napoleon's Army*. London, 1974.
———. *Wellington's Army*. London, 1979.
Ross, Steven T. *From Flintlock to Rifle Infantry: Tactics, 1740–1866*. Rutherford, NJ, and London, 1979.
Rothenberg, Gunther E. *The Art of Warfare in the Age of Napoleon*. Bloomington, IN, and London, 1978.
———. *Napoleon's Great Adversaries: The Archduke Charles and the Austrian Army, 1792–1814*. Bloomington, IN, 1982.
Scott, Samuel F. *The Response of the Royal Army to the French Revolution*. New York, 1978.
Shanahan, William O. *Prussian Military Reforms, 1786–1813*. New York, 1954.
Tranie, J. *Les Polonais de Napoléon*. Paris, 1982.
Ward, S. G. P. *Wellington's Headquarters, 1809–1814*. London, 1957.
Wetzler, Peter. *War and Subsistence: The Sambre and Meuse Army in 1794*. New York, 1985.
Woloch, Isser. *The French Veteran from the Revolution to the Restoration*. Chapel Hill, NC, 1979.

## Italian Campaigns, 1796–97, 1800

Burton, R. G. *Napoleon's Campaigns in Italy*. London and New York, 1912.
Clausewitz, Carl von. *La Campagne de 1796 en Italie*. Paris, 1899.
Cugnac, G. J. M. R. *La Campagne de l'armée de réserve en 1800*. 2 vols. Paris, 1900–01.
Fabry, Gabriel. *Histoire de l'armée d'Italie, 1796–1797*. 3 vols. Paris, 1901.
Ferrero, Guglielmo. *The Gamble: Bonaparte in Italy, 1796–1797*. London, 1961.
Jackson, William. *Attack in the West: Napoleon's First Campaign Re-read Today*. London, 1953.
Rodger, A. B. *The War of the Second Coalition, 1798 to 1801*. New York, 1961.

Ross, Steven T. *Quest for Victory: French Military Strategy, 1792–1799.* Cranbury, NJ, 1973.
Thiry, Jean. *Bonaparte en Italie.* Paris, 1974.


**Egyptian Campaign, 1798–99**


Barthorp, Michael. *Napoleon's Egyptian Campaigns, 1798–1799.* London, 1978.
Benoist-Mechin, J. G. P. M. *Bonaparte en Egypte.* Lausanne, 1966.
Herold, J. Christopher. *Napoleon in Egypt.* London and New York, 1961.
Lloyd, Christopher. *The Nile Campaign.* New York, 1973.
Marcus, G. J. *The Royal Navy in the Age of Nelson, 1793–1815.* New York, 1971.
Thiry, Jean. *Bonaparte en Egypte.* Paris, 1973.
Warner, Oliver. *The Battle of the Nile.* London, 1960.


**Campaigns of 1805–1807**


Bonnal, H. *La Manoeuvre de Jena, 1806.* Paris, 1904.
Burton, R. G. *From Boulogne to Austerlitz: Napoleon's Campaign of 1805.* London, 1912.
Duffy, C. J. *Austerlitz, 1805.* London, 1977.
Ellis, Geoffrey. *Napoleon's Continental Blockade.* London and New York, 1981.
Glover, Richard. *Britain at Bay: Defence Against Bonaparte, 1803–1814.* London, 1973.
Henderson, E. F. *Blücher and the Uprising of Prussia Against Napoleon, 1806–1815.* London, 1911.
Lachouque, Henry. *Napoléon à Austerlitz.* Paris, 1960.
———. *Jena.* Paris, 1961.
Lettow-Vorbeck, C. von. *Der Krieg von 1806–1807.* Berlin, 1892.
Maine, René. *Trafalgar.* New York, 1960.
Maude, F. N. *The Ulm Campaign, 1805.* New York and London, 1912.
———. *The Jena Campaign, 1806.* London and New York, 1909.
Parker, H. T. *Three Napoleonic Battles.* New Ed. Durham, NC, 1983.
Petre, F. L. *Napoleon's Campaign in Poland, 1806–1807.* London and New York, 1901.
———. *Napoleon's Conquest of Prussia, 1806.* London, 1907. Reprint. 1972.
Thiry, Jean. *Ulm, Trafalgar, Austerlitz.* Paris, 1962.
Tranie, Jean, and Jean-Carlos Carmigniani, eds. *Napoléon et l'Allemagne: La Prusse, 1806.* Paris, 1984.

————. *Napoléon et la Russie: Les années victorieuses, 1805–1807*. Paris, 1984.

## Peninsular War, 1807–1814

Alexander, Don W. *Rod of Iron: French Counterinsurgency Policy in Aragon during the Peninsular War*. Wilmington, DE, 1985.
Arteche y Moro, José Gomez de. *Guerra de la independencia: Historia militar de España de 1808 a 1814*. 14 vols. Madrid, 1886–1903.
Artola Gallego, Miguel. *La España de Fernando VII*. Madrid, 1968.
Aymes, J. R. *La Guerre d'independance espagnole*. Paris, 1973.
Chastenet, J. *Godoy: Master of Spain, 1792–1808*. London, 1953.
Connelly, Owen. *The Gentle Bonaparte: A Biography of Joseph*. New York, 1968.
Davies, D. W. *Sir John Moore's Peninsular Campaign*. The Hague, 1974.
Foy, Maximilien S. *Histoire des guerres de la Péninsule sous Napoléon*. 4 vols. Paris, 1827.
Gates, David. *The Spanish Ulcer: A History of the Peninsular War*. London and New York, 1986.
Girod de l'Ain, Gabriel. *Joseph Bonaparte*. Paris, 1970.
Glover, M. *The Peninsular War, 1807–1814*. Hamden, 1974.
Grandmaison, Geoffrey de. *L'Espagne et Napoléon, 1804–1814*. 3 vols. Paris, 1908.
Hibbert, Christopher. *The Battle of Corunna*. New York, 1961.
Horward, Donald D. *Napoleon and Iberia: The Twin Sieges of Ciudad Rodrigo and Almeida, 1810*. Tallahassee, FL, 1984.
Lachouque, H., and J. Tranie, J. C. Carmigniani. *Napoleon's War in Spain*. Trans. by Janet Mallender and J. R. Clements. London, 1982.
Lovett, Gabriel. *Napoleon and the Birth of Modern Spain*. New York, 1965.
Marti Gilabert, F. *Motin de Aranjuez*. Pamplona, 1972.
Mercader Riba, D. Juan. *José Bonaparte, rey de España*. Madrid, 1972.
Napier, Sir William F. P. *History of the War in the Peninsula and in the South of France from the year 1807 to the year 1814*. 6 vols. London, 1886.
Oman, Sir Charles. *A History of the Peninsular War*. 7 vols. 1902–1930.
Pelet, J. J. *The French Campaign in Portugal, 1810–1811*. Trans. and ed. by Donald D. Horward. Minneapolis, 1973.
Pouzerewsky, Col. *La Charge de la cavalerie [polonaise] de Somo Sierra (Espagne), le 30 novembre 1808*. Paris, 1900.
Priego Lopez, Juan. *La guerra de la independencia, 1808–1814*. Madrid, 1947.
Read, Jan. *The War in the Peninsula, 1807–1814*. London, 1977.
Roux, Georges. *Napoléon et le guêpier espagnol*. Paris, 1970.
Toreno, José M. *Histoire du soulèvement de la guerre et de la révolution d'Espagne*. 4 vols. Paris, 1838.

Weller, Jac. *Wellington in the Peninsula, 1808–1814.* London, 1962.
Young, Peter, and J. P. Lawford. *Wellington's Masterpiece: The Battle and Campaign of Salamanca.* London, 1973.


## Campaign of 1809 (Wagram)


Bond, Gordon C. *The Grand Expedition: The British Invasion of Holland in 1809.* Athens, GA, 1979.
Bonnal, Henri C. *Le Manoeuvre de Landshut.* Paris, 1905.
Comeau, Baron S. J. de. *Souvenirs des guerres d'Allemagne.* Paris, 1900.
Fleishmann, Theo. *Expédition anglaise . . . en 1809: Conquête de l'ile de Walcheren et menace sur Anvers.* Reprint. Brussels, 1973.
Loy, L. *La Campagne de Styrie en 1809.* Paris, 1908.
Pelet, J. J. *Mémoires sur la guerre de 1809.* Paris, 1825.
Petre, F. L. *Napoleon and the Archduke Charles.* London, 1909.
Rauchensteiner, Manfried. *Die Schlacht bei Deutsch Wagram am 5 und 6 Juli 1809.* Vienna, 1977.
Saski, G. G. L. *La Campagne de 1809.* 3 vols. Paris, 1899–1900.
Thiry, Jean. *Napoléon Bonaparte: Wagram.* Paris, 1966.
Tranie, J., and J. C. Carmigniani. *Napoléon et l'Autriche: La campagne de 1809.* Paris, 1984.
Wohlfeil, R. *Spanien und die deutsche Erhebung, 1808–1814.* Wiesbaden, 1965.


## Russian Campaign, 1812


Belis, Roger. *La Campagne de Russie, 1812.* Cannes, 1966.
Brett-James, Antony. *1812: Eyewitness Accounts of Napoleon's Defeat in Russia.* New York, 1966.
Burton, R. G. *Napoleon's Invasion of Russia, 1812.* London, 1914.
Cate, Curtis. *The War of the Two Emperors: The Duel between Napoleon and Alexander: Russia, 1812.* New York, 1985.
Clausewitz, Carl von. *The Campaign of 1812.* London, 1843.
Duffy, Christopher. *Borodino.* London and New York, 1972.
Faber du Four, C. W. von. *La Campagne de Russie.* Paris, 1895.
Fabre, M. A. *Jérôme Bonaparte, roi de Westphalie.* Paris, 1952.
Jackson, W. G. H. *Seven Roads to Moscow.* London, 1958.
Josselson, Michael and Diana. *The Commander: Barclay de Tolly.* New York, 1980.
Mansuy, Abel. *Jérôme Bonaparte et la Pologne en 1812.* Paris, 1931.
Melchior-Bonnet, B. *Jérôme Bonaparte.* Paris, 1979.
———. *La Conspiration de Général Malet.* Paris, 1963.
Nicolson, Nigel. *Napoleon, 1812.* New York, 1985.

Olivier, Daria. *The Burning of Moscow, 1812*. New York, 1966.
Palmer, Alan W. *Napoleon in Russia*. New York, 1967.
Parkinson, Roger. *Fox of the North: The Life of Kutuzov*. New York, 1976.
Tarlé, E. V. *Napoleon's Invasion of Russia*. Trans. from the Russian by N. Guterman and R. Manheim. New York, 1942.
Turner, A. E. *The Retreat from Moscow and the Crossing of the Berezina*. Woolwich, 1898.

## Campaigns of 1813–14, First Abdication

Brett-James, A. *Europe Against Napoleon: The Leipzig Campaign, 1813, from Eyewitness Accounts*. London, 1970.
Dupont, Marcel. *Napoléon et la trahison des maréchaux, 1814*. Paris, 1970.
Foucart, Paul J. *Bautzen . . . 20–21 mai 1813*. Paris, 1897.
Friedrich, R. *Geschichte der Herbstfeldzuges 1813*. 3 vols. Berlin, 1903–1906.
———. *Die Befreiungskreig 1813–1815*. 4 vols. Berlin, 1911–1913.
Houssaye, Henri. *1814*. Paris, 1888.
Janson, R. von. *Geschichte der Feldzuges 1814 in Frankreich*. Berlin, 1903.
Lachouque, H. *Napoléon en 1814*. Paris, 1959.
Lanrezac, C. L. M. *Mémoires: Lützen*. Paris, 1904.
Lawford, J. P. *Napoleon: The Last Campaigns, 1813–1815*. London, 1977.
Maude, F. N. *The Leipzig Campaign, 1813*. London, 1908.
Mauduit, H. de. *Les Derniers jours de la Grande Armée*. Paris, 1847.
Odeleben, E. d'. *Relation de la campagne de 1813*. Paris, 1817.
Petre, F. L. *Napoleon's Last Campaign in Germany, 1813*. London, 1912.
———. *Napoleon at Bay, 1814*. London, 1914.
Thiry, Jean. *Leipzig . . . 1813*. Paris, 1972.
Tournes, R. *La Campagne de printemps en 1813: Lützen*. Paris, 1931.
Veltze, A. *Osterreich in den Befriedenskriegen*. 10 vols. Vienna, 1911–1914.

## The Hundred Days, Waterloo, Second Abdication

Beitzke, Heinrich. *Geschichte des Jahre 1815*. 2 vols. Berlin, 1865.
Blond, Georges. *Les Cent-Jours: Napoléon seul contre tous*. Paris, 1983.
Blücher von Wahlstatt, Prince G. L. *Blüchers Briefe*. Ed. by W. von Unger. Stuttgart and Berlin, 1913.
Brett-James, Antony. *The Hundred Days*. New York, 1963.
Chalfont, Lord, ed. *Waterloo: Battle of Three Armies*. London, 1980.
Chandler, David. *Waterloo: The Hundred Days*. London, 1980.
Cubberly, R. E. *The Role of Fouché during the Hundred Days*. Madison, WI, 1969.
Duforcq, A. *Murat et la question de l'unité italienne en 1815*. Paris, 1898.

Fiore, Enzo. *Un re al bivio: Il tradimento di Murat.* Rome, 1972.

Godlewski, G. *Trois cents jours d'exil: Napoléon à l'ile d'Elbe.* Paris, 1961.

Griffith, Paddy, ed. *Wellington, Commander: The Iron Duke's Generalship.* London, 1985.

Herold, J. C. *The Battle of Waterloo.* London, 1967.

Hibbert, Christopher. *Waterloo: Napoleon's Last Campaign.* New York, 1967.

Houssaye, Henri. *1815.* 3 vols. Paris, 1889–1902.

Howarth, David. *Waterloo: Day of Battle.* New York, 1968.

Keegan, John. "Waterloo," in *Face of Battle.* New York, 1976.

Kennedy, Gen. Sir John. *Notes on the Battle of Waterloo.* London, 1865.

Lachouque, H. *Waterloo, 1815.* Introduction by David Chandler. London, 1975.

———. *Waterloo: Fin d'un monde.* Paris, 1958.

———. *The Last Days of Napoleon's Empire: From Waterloo to St. Helena.* London, 1966.

Longford, Elizabeth. *Wellington: The Years of the Sword.* London, 1969.

MacKenzie, Norman. *The Escape from Elba: The Fall and Flight of Napoleon, 1814–1815.* New York, 1985.

Naylor, John. *Waterloo.* London, 1960.

Sutherland, John P. *Men of Waterloo.* London, 1965.

Thiry, Jean. *La Chute de Napoléon.* 7 vols. Paris, 1941–1945.

Weller, Jac. *Wellington at Waterloo.* New York, 1964.

# INDEX